Governance of Projects and Project Contractual Relations

Governance of Projects and Project Contractual Relations

By

Przemysław Lech

BRILL

This project was supported by the University of Gdańsk. This book was evaluated through a double-anonymous peer review process by two independent reviewers.

ISBN 978-90-04-75853-7
ISBN 978-90-04-75854-4 (PDF)
DOI https://doi.org/10.1163/9789004758544

Library of Congress Control Number: 2026904030

Brill and Koninklijke Brill BV are part of De Gruyter Brill.
www.degruyterbrill.com

Questions about General Product Safety Regulation: productsafety@degruyterbrill.com

Cover illustration: Project Management © geralt, 2022, via Pixabay.

Contents

Tables

Introduction

Projects play a crucial role in modern economies and the daily operations of organizations worldwide. Some authors even suggest the growing trend of the "projectification" of business and work life (Lundin et al., 2015; Midler, 1995), and the emergence of a "project society" or "project economy" (Lundin et al., 2015; Locatelli et al., 2023; Nieto-Rodriguez, 2021). Turner et al. (2013) estimate that 20% of the global economy operates through projects, and Nieto-Rodriguez (2021) cites Germany as an example, where projects accounted for 41% of GDP in 2019.

Projects are becoming a daily routine not only in traditionally project-based sectors such as construction, consulting, media, or information systems, but also in operations-driven businesses (Lundin et al., 2015). While daily operations keep these organizations running, projects are the primary drivers of change and innovation (Locatelli et al., 2023).

The body of knowledge on project management and its related literature is vast and continuously expanding. This growth is primarily driven by professional project management organizations, resulting in a practice-oriented focus. The literature often adopts the perspective of a project manager, emphasizing the skills and capabilities required to execute a project on behalf of, and in collaboration with, the project owner. This approach is particularly well-suited to scenarios where an organization manages a project internally, under the governance of an experienced project manager, utilizing a combination of internal and external resources. This perspective is both valuable and justified, as these organizations aim to educate and equip professional project managers.

However, the reality of project execution encompasses a broader range of potential setups. For example, an operations-based organization undertaking a one-time project may lack the necessary knowledge and capabilities to manage it internally. In such cases, they might hire external project managers to run the project, which can introduce agency problems. Alternatively, they may contract the entire project to an external entity, transferring responsibility for both management and delivery. This arrangement, however, raises issues such as conflicts of interest, incentive misalignment, and challenges in exerting control over a more knowledgeable agent. On the other hand, a project-oriented organization hired to execute such a project for its client may encounter problems in contractual relations related to the definition of a project goal, division of responsibility, and opportunistic behavior by the client.

 | HTTPS://DOI.ORG/10.1163/9789004758544-002

While some scholarly literature addresses these issues to a certain extent, it is often fragmented and tends to explain specific phenomena using selected theories. What is lacking is a comprehensive approach to project theory, especially in terms of the governance of project contractual relations through the lens of organizational science, management, and economics theories.

Therefore, this book complements existing textbooks and scholarly works on projects, project management, and project governance. Firstly, it emphasizes the contractual relationships between project participants in various settings, ranging from internal, hierarchy-based employment relationships to complex interfirm arrangements governed by legal contracts. Most importantly, it examines these aspects through the lens of dominant theories in economics, organizational science, and management, aiming to formulate a metatheory of projects and project governance. Secondly, it provides the perspective of the project owners, those accountable for the project's business objectives and requirements, but not necessarily equipped with the expertise to manage its delivery.

The aim of this book is twofold:

1. To develop a metatheory of governance for project contractual relations.
2. To propose a project governance framework for various contractual setups from the perspective of a project owner.

The book consists of four chapters.

In the first chapter, theories used to explain various aspects of projects and project contractual relationships are outlined, based on the existing literature. The chapter begins by discussing the classic set of theories from Organizational Economics, which are most commonly applied to explain project contractual relations. These include Transaction Cost Economics, Agency Theory, Information Asymmetry, and Contract Theory.

Next, a perspective on the rationale for establishing and executing projects is presented through theories from Strategic Management, including the Resource-Based View, Knowledge-Based View, and Dynamic Capabilities. Since these two prominent theoretical streams are considered complementary rather than contradictory, a connection between Transaction Cost Economics and the Resource-Based View is established.

Additionally, alternative or complementary theories, such as Stakeholder Theory, Stewardship Theory, Resource Dependence Theory and Social Theories, which help explain various aspects of projects and project behavior, are explored. The chapter concludes with an overview of recent developments in the formulation of project and project management theories. Generic project management theories, grounded in operations research and management theory, are discussed, leading to the formulation of definitions for both project and project management.

Chapter 2 introduces the concept of project governance, beginning with an examination of its nature. Two key perspectives on project governance are then distinguished and elaborated upon:

- Project governance, which primarily depends on specific project attributes such as the nature and stability of its outcomes, the definability of its methods, and its complexity.
- Governance of project contractual relations, which depends on the number of legal entities involved in the project and the nature of their interactions.

Both perspectives are explored in detail, with possible governance variants and selection criteria identified and described. In terms of project governance, the waterfall, agile, and hybrid methodologies are discussed, which align with the existing literature. A summary of the governance mechanisms typical for each methodology type is also provided.

This widely accepted view of project governance is further explored in the second part of Chapter 2, which focuses on the governance of project contractual relations. The discussion begins with identifying and describing various types of contractual setups among project participants. These setups address the number of legal entities involved in a project, as well as the allocation of risk and responsibility among the parties. They range from an internal setup, where the project is executed using the sponsoring organization's knowledge and resources, to various forms of intercompany cooperation. The analysis concludes that, according to Transaction Cost Economics, all contractual setups, except for the internal setup, represent examples of hybrid governance, as opposed to hierarchy or market governance. Consequently, the characteristics of hybrid governance in contractual relations, along with the applicable governance mechanisms, are examined in greater detail.

In Chapter 3, a metatheory of governance of project contractual relations is developed. The chapter begins with a summary of the current theoretical understanding of project contractual relations. This includes an overview of available contractual setups, contract types, project characteristics, potential governance mechanisms, and the lifecycle of a project contractual relationship. Each contractual setup is then examined in relation to projects with varying characteristics. Possible combinations of governance mechanisms are presented, along with theoretical implications for major project stakeholders. The advantages, disadvantages, and consequences of applying specific governance mechanisms are discussed from the perspectives of both the sponsoring organization (project owner) and the contractor(s).

The novelty of this metatheory lies in the deductive integration of established theories across a range of project types, contractual setups, and contract categories. It further offers a deductively reasoned evaluation of how various governance frameworks apply, highlighting their benefits and limitations in relation to specific project and contract configurations.

Chapter 4 introduces a framework for governing various types of projects from the project owner's perspective. A set of criteria for selecting an appropriate governance framework is presented. This is followed by an exploration of the combination of governance mechanisms associated with generic project management methodologies (waterfall, agile, hybrid) and governance mechanisms tailored to specific contractual setups.

The novelty of this approach stems from its comprehensive, deductive exploration of potential project governance models, tailored to specific project characteristics and the competencies of the sponsoring organization. It also offers a detailed analysis of the strengths and weaknesses associated with each proposed variant.

CHAPTER 1

Theories Related to Projects and Project Governance

In this chapter the theories used to explain the phenomena of projects, project management, project governance, and governance of project contractual relations will be presented, based on the existing literature.

Müller (2009, 2017), in his books on project governance, identifies agency theory, shareholder theory, stakeholder theory, stewardship theory, and Transaction Cost Economics as the most prominent frameworks in the field. In addition to these, general project management theories also influence project governance. However, a broader theory search conducted during the writing of this book uncovered a significantly wider range of theories used to explain various phenomena related to project governance. This search involved general queries in research databases such as Google Scholar, EBSCO, and Web of Science, using terms like "theory and project," "project theory," and "theory, project governance." It also employed the snowball technique, drawing from existing literature. The resulting collection of theories is presented in this chapter.

1.1 Organizational Economics Theories

Organizational Economics theories originate from the "theory of the firm" (Coase, 1937; Combs & Ketchen, 1999), which seeks to explain the existence, boundaries, and internal organization of companies (Foss, 1996). These theories also acknowledge the presence of hybrid governance structures that exist alongside traditional market and firm-based models.

In essence, Organizational Economics aims to understand the factors that drive individuals and organizations to structure their economic activities through different governance forms, and the mechanisms employed within these structures to safeguard stakeholder interests.

1.1.1 *Transaction Cost Economics*

Transaction Cost Economics (TCE) was initially developed to explain the existence of firms (Coase, 1937). The reasoning was following: if using the market was costless, there would be no need to create firms, as all transactions could

HTTPS://DOI.ORG/10.1163/9789004758544-003

be efficiently conducted within the market. However, TCE demonstrated that using the market involves costs that, under certain conditions, can be avoided by organizing activities within a firm. According to Coase (1988), these costs include: (a) search and information costs, (b) bargaining and decision costs, and (c) policing and enforcement costs. Williamson (1985) further distinguished between ex-ante and ex-post transaction costs. Ex-ante costs include drafting, negotiating, and safeguarding an agreement, while ex-post costs encompass maladaptation and haggling costs, the costs of operating governance structures, and the economic bonding costs required to ensure secure commitments. To provide a complete account, Coase's (1988) search and information costs, as well as bargaining and decision costs, should be added to the ex-ante costs, as these are incurred before the contract is drafted and signed.

Transaction Cost Economics also incorporates assumptions derived from behavioral theory, namely the bounded rationality of agents and the opportunism of at least some agents (Williamson, 1981). Opportunistic behavior is defined as self-interest seeking with guile (Dawson et al., 2010). Bounded rationality refers to the limited capacity of individuals to process information and to formulate and solve complex problems. Consequently, the assumption made by neoclassical economics, that every agent possesses full information about all possible choices, can rank those choices according to their preferences, and always selects the optimal solution (i.e., agents are fully rational), does not hold in the real world. Instead, agents attempt to act rationally but are constrained by their limited cognitive capabilities. As a result, they tend to seek a "satisficing" solution (the first option that meets acceptability criteria) rather than an optimal one, demonstrating bounded rationality.

Initially developed to explain the existence of firms, the transaction cost approach was later extended to address the existence of other governance structures (Williamson, 1979; Williamson, 1991) and the types of contracts associated with them.

Transaction Cost Economics posits that every governance structure incurs transaction costs, which depend on the following attributes of the transaction:

- Uncertainty,
- The frequency with which transactions occur, and
- The level of transaction-specific investments or asset specificity (Williamson, 1981).

The main proposition of Transaction Cost Economics is that agents should choose the governance structure that minimizes the sum of transaction costs and production costs.

Among these three attributes, transaction-specific investment (or asset specificity) requires further explanation. Transaction-specific investment occurs when specialized assets must be created to carry out a transaction. These assets cannot be easily redeployed to alternative uses without incurring significant losses in productive value (Williamson, 1991). Asset specificity is typically associated with the production and trade of highly idiosyncratic goods – that is, goods that cannot be easily traded in other markets. Once an investment in specific assets has been made, the buyer and seller effectively enter into a bilateral (or at least quasi-bilateral) exchange relationship that persists for a significant period of time.

The three main types of asset specificity are as follows (Williamson, 1981):
- Site specificity: This occurs when successive stages of the production process must be located near each other to optimize inventory and transportation costs (e.g., an electric plant and a coal mine).
- Physical asset specificity: This refers to situations where a specific piece of equipment is required to produce a good (e.g., specialized dies needed to produce a component in the molding process).
- Human asset specificity: This arises from skills developed through experience (e.g., learning by doing).

Investment in production-specific assets is typically attributed to the seller. In some cases, also the buyer may be required to make an additional transaction-specific investment in establishing and maintaining a governance structure (Williamson, 1979).

TCE predicts that, to minimize the sum of transaction costs and production costs, transactions differing in their attributes – i.e. asset specificity, uncertainty, and frequency – will be aligned with distinct governance structures. These governance structures vary in:
- their ability to adapt to disturbances,
- coordinating mechanisms,
- incentive levels,
- and control mechanisms (Williamson, 1991).

Each governance structure is further supported by a corresponding contract regime.

According to the criterion of asset specificity, Williamson (1979) classifies transactions as nonspecific, mixed, or idiosyncratic. Based on the criterion of transaction frequency, transactions are categorized as recurrent or occasional (with one-time transactions considered similar to occasional ones). According to the level of uncertainty accompanying a transaction, they are divided into those conducted under no uncertainty (certain) and those accompanied by medium to high levels of uncertainty.

The following mapping of governance structures to transaction types is proposed (Williamson, 1979, 1991):

1. **Market governance** is a governance structure ideally suited for trading non-specific goods with low transaction-specific investments. Its core attributes enable efficient operation in settings where parties act independently and goods can be readily substituted or traded elsewhere if a transaction fails to occur (Williamson, 1991). Below is an outline of its characteristics:
   - Autonomous adaptation to disturbances – buyers and sellers are not related to each other. Price is the only and sufficient statistics and it discounts all the changes in the market. Buyers and sellers adapt to the changes in the market autonomously, and spontaneously, without consulting each other, by either entering a transaction at a given price, or by omitting to do so.
   - High-powered incentives – the compensation is tightly linked to the result of work (or effort).
   - No coordination mechanisms, except for the price, to which the participants of the market react autonomously.
   - Limited administrative control – limited to courts which resolve disputes basing on the contractual agreements between the parties, and regulations on the specific markets.

As the traded good is non-specific, and the transaction costs of using the market are low, there is no dependency between buyers and sellers. The identity of the parties is unimportant, and if the contracts between the same parties are renewed, that is "only because current suppliers are continuously meeting bids in the spot market" (Williamson, 1991).

The level of uncertainty which accompanies the transaction does not alter the optimal governance structure for the trade of non-specific goods (Williamson, 1991). Increasing the degree of uncertainty does not change the fact, that continuity has little value and the new trading relations can be easily arranged. Market governance remains the optimal choice for trading of standard goods, no matter the level of uncertainty. **Market governance** is supported by the classical contracting, where all relevant future contingencies are described and discounted in the complete contract. Writing such a complete contract is relatively easy for such transaction, as most of the parameters of the transaction can be specified ex-ante and the characteristics of the good do not depend much (if at all) on the future contingencies. Williamson (1991) characterizes the classical contracting as "sharp in by clear agreement, sharp out by clear performance".

2. **Hierarchy** lies at the opposite extreme of governance structures and is optimal for recurrent transactions involving highly idiosyncratic goods. The greater the specialization of physical and human assets to a single use, making them non-transferable to alternative uses, the stronger the

need to incorporate them within a company (i.e., through vertical integration). Another factor that increases the attractiveness of hierarchy is its adaptiveness to uncertainty. In a hierarchical structure, adaptation to new and previously unknown circumstances can be achieved by fiat. The employment relationship is inherently an incomplete contract. By accepting such a relationship, employees agree that their superiors can direct their daily activities and closely monitor both their tasks and performance (Ouchi, 1980). This flexibility addresses the challenge of dealing with future contingencies without the need to resolve them all at once. Hierarchy also facilitates the coordinated realization of common objectives and coordinated adaptation to new situations. Adaptations can be made sequentially, without the need to consult, renegotiate, or revise interfirm agreements (Williamson, 1979). This is particularly valuable in environments characterized by high transaction uncertainty and frequent changes to transaction conditions. However, organizing transactions within a hierarchy comes with significant bureaucratic costs. These include the overhead associated with maintaining the hierarchical structure, administrative control and performance monitoring. Additionally, there are limits to the size of organizations, influenced by factors such as information processing capabilities.

Hierarchy has the following attributes (Williamson, 1991):

- Coordinated adaptation to disturbances – one of the most important characteristics of the hierarchy is that it induces the cooperative behavior – i.e. harmonizes to some extent the interests of the members of the organization, which otherwise would be in conflict with each other. If an unexpected event occurs, the members of the organization can therefore react to it jointly, in a coordinated manner. Frequent, sequential adaptations are relatively easy to perform, and they do not add much transactional cost.
- Low-powered incentives – i.e. compensation is not tightly linked to the result of work (or effort).
- Strong coordination mechanisms and administrative control – the desired behavior of the members of the organization can be achieved by fiat (authority relation) and controlled to much higher extent than it would be possible during any kind of interfirm relation. The members of the organization can therefore be made to act cooperatively in the name of a common objective.

As setting up a hierarchy, with all its administrative and bureaucratic mechanisms is the most costly option from the transaction cost perspective, it can be only considered if the other governance structures fail to work. This would be the case for:

- Highly idiosyncratic goods – where the asset specificity is high, with the asset specialized to a single use as an extreme example.

- Recurrent transactions – as one-time or occasional transactions would not justify the additional cost burden.
- High uncertainty and frequent disturbances – as reacting to disturbances and unforeseen contingences requires frequent, sequential adaptations of coordinated kind. Under market or hybrid governance this would require mutual agreement and change of contract every time an adaptation is needed. In hierarchy such adaptations can be induced by fiat.

Hierarchy is supported by the forbearance contract law (Williamson, 1991, p. 276): "The application of forbearance doctrine to internal organization means that parties to an internal exchange can work out their differences themselves or appeal unresolved disputes to the hierarchy for a decision. But this exhausts their alternatives".

3. **Hybrid** forms of governance lie in the middle between the two extremes: the market and the hierarchy. Hybrid is a governance structure, in which the autonomy of the parties is preserved, but there is bilateral dependency between the parties due to the transaction-specific investments. The parties are realizing their own, separate agendas, and have separate profit streams, as on the classical market. On the other hand, due to the non-trivial level of the transaction-specific investment, which will be lost if the transaction is terminated, they are interested to continue the relationship. The most frequently mentioned form of hybrid governance is long term contracting of different kind (Menard, 2004; Williamson, 2008), but it also includes reciprocal trading, franchising, public utility regulation (Williamson, 1991), networks of firms in the supply chain and distribution channels, collective trademarks, cooperatives, partnership, and alliances (Menard, 2004).

Hybrid governance is suitable for occasional transactions of mixed and highly idiosyncratic kind, and some recurrent transactions of mixed idiosyncratic kind. Trading of idiosyncratic goods involves transaction specific investments that are not easily transferrable to alternative uses. Such investments make the parties "locked into" the transaction and make the termination of a contract costly to both sides. Hybrid governance is accompanied by the neoclassical contracting. Neoclassical contracting means that the contract is still the main point of reference, but it cannot be complete due to the long-term relationship, and uncertainty, which means that the outcome of the transaction (characteristics of the good) is dependent on the future contingencies. The parties must supplement the contract with additional adaptive mechanisms, which will help to "work things out" when unexpected deviations from the contract occur (Williamson, 1979). Neoclassical contract differs from the classical one in that it "contemplates unanticipated disturbances for which adaptation is needed, provides a tolerance zone within which misalignments will be absorbed, requires information disclosure and substantiation if adaptation is proposed, and provides for arbitration in the event voluntary agreement fails" (Williamson, 1996; after Menard, 2022).

According to TCE, setting up a transaction-specific governance structure is justified for recurrent transactions. The deliberately incomplete contract is then supplemented with additional adaptive mechanisms that would work in case of disturbances. The nature of those adaptive mechanisms may range from elastic contractual clauses, putting the dispute solving procedures in the contract, putting contractual safeguards, to quasi authoritarian governance of the relationship through the private governments (Menard, 2004).

TCE claims that establishing a transaction-specific governance structure for occasional (or one-time) transactions is not economically justified. However, this claim does not hold true. Every one-time project involves some form of non-contractual, transaction-specific governance structure, which will be discussed further in this book.

The mode of governance depends on the level and nature of mutual dependency between the parties, and frequency and consequentiality of disturbances (uncertainty).

Mutual dependency is caused by the asset specificity and may cause opportunistic behaviors. It calls for control mechanisms that allow monitoring/metering and can prevent opportunism of the parties. Dealing with uncertainty requires coordination mechanisms which allow for cooperative adaptations (Menard, 2004). The more dependent are the parties, and the more frequent and consequential are disturbances, the more authoritarian mode of governance would be chosen (Menard, 2004).

In case of recurrent transactions of mixed idiosyncratic kind, hybrid governance can be also supported by relational contracting (Williamson, 1979). Relational contracts are informal agreements and unwritten codes of conduct sustained by the value of future relationships (Baker et al., 2002). They do not have to be specified ex ante and may include outcomes that are not verifiable by the third party. The formal contract stops to be the point of reference, and it is replaced by the judgment of the whole long-term relationship between the parties.

Hybrid governance supports both autonomous and coordinated/cooperative adaptations to disturbances. However, if coordinated/cooperative adaptations are needed, they have to be performed with mutual consent of the parties. As the parties are independent, and have separate profit streams, achieving such consent requires negotiations, which take time and effort. The cost of such adaptations may therefore be more than in case of hierarchy, where the cooperation can be achieved by fiat. Also the adaptive range of such governance structure is limited, as one party may at some point reject the proposals to adapt, made by the other party. Hybrid governance is therefore most suitable for such transactions, which need mixture of autonomous and coordinated adaptations.

Hybrid governance has the following attributes:

- Both mechanisms of adaptation to disturbances are possible – Hybrid supports autonomous adaptations through the price mechanism almost as good as the market governance, however at a greater cost. On the other hand it provides additional adaptive mechanisms, which allow for some level of coordinated/cooperative adaptations. Those adaptations are also costly, as they are performed across a market interface, by mutual, follow-on agreements (Williamson, 1979)
- Medium level incentives – compensation is linked to the result of work (or effort) but the incomplete contract allows for deviations from the planned values.
- Mixed coordination mechanisms and administrative control – depending on the adaptation mechanisms available, the parties have bigger possibility to coordinate and control than on the market, but smaller than through hierarchy.

The level of uncertainty also impacts the selection of the hybrid mode as the preferred governance structure for recurrent transactions. Uncertainty leads to disturbances, which can be characterized by their frequency and consequentiality, measured as the variance from the plan (Williamson, 1991). The more frequent and consequential the disturbances, the more costly it becomes to adapt to them cooperatively and in a coordinated way using hybrid governance, i.e., through follow-on agreements via the market interface. Transactions that require frequent, sequential, and coordinated adaptations are better governed through hierarchy.

Hybrid governance, on the other hand, is more suitable when disturbances are of low to moderate frequency and consequentiality. The hybrid mode of governance would also be more effective and incur lower transaction costs when mechanisms for adapting to disturbances can be defined a priori in the contract. This is possible if specific types of disturbances can be anticipated in advance, and the adaptations can be described in an elastic contract. The examples are adjustments for quantity or price changes tied to objective economic factors, such as the price of a raw material on a well-defined market. Therefore, hybrid governance may be chosen over vertical integration in case of recurrent transactions of mixed idiosyncratic kind, which are characterized by low to medium levels of uncertainty, both in terms of frequency and consequentiality.

Another factor that affects the selection between hybrid governance and hierarchy is the availability of resources and capabilities needed to deliver a good or service. In the short term, it may be impossible or too costly to develop the required combination of resources and capabilities within the company, especially for goods and services in the early stages of the product lifecycle (Menard, 2004; Williamson, 2008). Attempting to develop this combination of resources and capabilities internally can also reduce flexibility by creating irreversibility and weakening incentives (Menard, 2004). Under such circumstances, hybrid governance becomes the preferred choice. Long-term relationships can also result in transaction-specific savings "at the interface between supplier and buyer as contracts are successively adapted to unfolding events, and as periodic contract-renewal agreements are reached" due to communication economies and the development of institutional and personal trust (Williamson, 1979, p. 240).

The characteristics of the governance structures according to TCE are presented in the below table 1:

TABLE 1 Characteristics of governance structures, according to TCE

Characteristic	Market	Hybrid	Hierarchy
Adaptations to contingencies (reaction to uncertainty)	Autonomous, spontaneous, uncoordinated	Both types: autonomous and cooperative, but not best at any of the two; additional mechanisms to support incomplete contract, high cost of adaptation – agreement and change of contract needed each time	Cooperative, coordinated, sequential, imposed by fiat
Type of contract	Classical contract law, full contracts	Neoclassical contracting/ incomplete contracts or relational contracting	Forbearance doctrine
Level of incentives	High-powered	Medium	Low-powered
Coordination mechanisms and administrative control	Price as the only coordinating mechanism, Weak/no administrative control	Additional adaptive mechanisms are implemented to deal with disturbances in a coordinated way. However the parties remain autonomous, with separate goals. Therefore coordination has to be agreed via market mechanism, which has limitations and is costly.	Strong mechanisms through hierarchy/ administration. Hierarchy changes conflict system into cooperative ones. Many tools and incentives to impose the common goal

TABLE 1 Characteristics of governance structures, according to TCE (*cont.*)

Characteristic	**Market**	**Hybrid**	**Hierarchy**
Dispute solving	Courts	Relational contracting, arbitration, courts	Forbearance: internal parties work out their differences themselves or appeal unresolved disputes to the hierarchy for a decision

In summary, according to TCE, for every transaction, a governance form that minimizes the sum of transaction and production costs should be chosen (Williamson, 1985). The level of transaction costs for a specific governance form changes depending on the characteristics of the transaction: its asset specificity, frequency, and uncertainty.

Non-specific, generic goods are best traded on the market. The production of such goods does not require any asset specificity, so if the transaction is cancelled, the seller can trade them elsewhere with another business partner at little or no cost. Similarly, the buyer can easily find another supplier of the same good. The frequency and uncertainty of the transaction do not affect the choice of the market as the preferred governance structure for non-specific goods.

When asset specificity increases, i.e., when the seller must invest in assets that cannot be redeployed to alternative uses at little or no cost, market mechanisms become inefficient. The greater the asset specificity, the more challenging it is for the parties involved in the transaction to change business partners. Cooperation tends to become long-term, as both parties have interest in continuing the relationship due to the significant costs associated with switching partners. Consequently, the long duration of the transaction increases uncertainty and makes it more difficult and costly to account for all future contingencies in the contract. As a result, the contract becomes incomplete and must be supplemented by additional non-contractual governance mechanisms that enable the parties to adapt in a cooperative and coordinated manner when unexpected deviations occur. Thus, a hybrid form of governance becomes optimal for occasional transactions with a medium to high level of asset specificity. Under hybrid governance, the parties in the contractual relationship remain independent, but the contract is incomplete and supported by additional governance mechanisms that allow for adaptations in case of unforeseen contingencies. However, the range of possible adaptations is limited by the need to make them through the market interface. Each time a coordinated and cooperative adaptation is required, it must be agreed upon by the parties involved in the transaction. Since these parties are independent and have separate profit streams, reaching an agreement can be difficult, costly, and sometimes impossible.

As uncertainty increases – both in the frequency and consequentiality of disturbances – the cost of performing adaptations through the market interface may rise to the point where it exceeds the costs of establishing a hierarchical structure, making vertical integration the optimal solution. Also an increase in the frequency of transactions and the level of asset specificity incentivizes their inclusion within the company's hierarchy via vertical integration. However, because hierarchy is the most costly governance structure, due to its bureaucratic and administrative costs, it is justified primarily for recurrent transactions of a highly idiosyncratic nature.

In the context of projects, TCE has been used for years as a theoretical framework to determine the project contractual setup – whether the project should be done internally, or in cooperation with external companies (e.g. Aubert et al., 1996; Winch, 1989; Tan and Zhao, 2021), and to identify the transaction costs related to a specific contractual setup (e.g. Li et al., 2015; Abdel-Galil et al., 2022).

1.1.2 *Information Asymmetry*

In both market and hybrid governance scenarios, the parties involved in a contractual relationship may face information asymmetry. Information asymmetry arises when one party in a transaction possesses better information than the other party or parties, placing them in a potentially advantageous position (Clarkson et al., 2007). The party with superior information may behave opportunistically. Opportunistic behavior is defined as self-interest seeking with guile (Dawson et al., 2010).

Opportunistic behavior stemming from information asymmetry can occur either before a transaction or during a long-term transactional relationship. Prior to the transaction, parties may attempt to hide information that could negatively affect the terms of the agreement for them. Arrow (1984) refers to this issue as "hidden information." Examples include sellers of used cars concealing details about their actual condition, insurance buyers withholding information about high-risk exposure, or job seekers exaggerating their skills and qualifications when applying for a job. When one party benefits from hidden information known to them before the transaction, it can lead to adverse selection (Izquierdo & Izquierdo, 2007). A seminal example of this phenomenon is the used car market (Akerlof, 1970). If sellers hide the poor condition of some used cars, uninformed buyers will only be willing to pay a price that statistically accounts for the presence of low-quality vehicles. As a result, sellers with high-quality cars will be unable to secure an appropriate price, and, at least theoretically, only cars in poor condition will be traded in the market. This means the market leads to the adverse selection of items. As Arrow (1984) notes, adverse selection is just one specific outcome of the broader issue of hidden information.

Possible ways to reduce information asymmetry before a transaction include signaling (Spence, 1973; Connelly et al., 2011) and screening (Stiglitz, 1975). Signaling is an action performed by the better-informed party, in which this party communicates information about the quality of a good to be traded, usually in an indirect way. The less-informed party interprets the information as being positively correlated with the quality. For example, education can serve as a signal of a person's "ability to learn" (Spence, 1973).

Screening, on the other hand, is an action performed by the less-informed party to obtain the hidden information or to induce the other party to reveal it. As Stiglitz (1975) explains: "The identification of these qualities [of individuals, bonds, equities, brands of automobiles] we call screening, and devices that sort out commodities (individuals) according to their qualities we call screening devices". A specific type of screening involves screening games (Riley, 2001), in which the less-informed party designs offers in a way that the selection of a particular offer by the other party reveals their hidden information.

Opportunistic behavior arising from information asymmetry during a long-term transactional relationship is referred to as "hidden action" (Arrow, 1984). This occurs when one party in a long-term relationship hides information about their actions from the other party. Examples include a manager making decisions that serve their own interests rather than those of the company, employees shirking responsibilities because their salary is not tied to performance or because their individual contributions are difficult to observe, and a person exhibiting less cautious behavior after being insured against a particular risk.

A specific type of "hidden action," often used by some authors to describe the phenomenon as a whole, is moral hazard (Devos et al., 2008; Haines & Goodhue, 2003). Initially, moral hazard referred to the tendency of a better-informed party to take greater risks because the costs of those risks are borne by another party (Hölmstrom, 1979). As Arrow (1984) explains, "hidden action" and "hidden information" are frequently referred to as moral hazard and adverse selection, respectively. He adds that "these terms have been borrowed from the practice and theory of insurance and are really applicable only to special cases."

The ways to reduce hidden action include monitoring and metering (Dawson et al., 2010). Monitoring involves creating an information system that allows for the control of behavior, while metering focuses on controlling the output of that behavior.

In summary, the problem of information asymmetry arises when one party in a market transaction possesses better information than the other, leading to issues such as hidden information and hidden action (Arrow, 1984). Information is treated as a commodity that can be purchased or otherwise acquired at a certain cost, allowing the asymmetry to be reduced. Haines & Goodhue (2003) also note that in some cases, parties may choose to reveal hidden information at no cost.

The problem of information asymmetry affects both spot trades, such as car sales, and long-term relationships, such as projects. However, it is most commonly discussed in the context of long-term principal-agent (agency) relationships.

Information asymmetry is identified as a factor contributing to opportunistic behavior, particularly in projects with intangible outcomes such as software development or consulting (Dawson et al., 2010; Gallouj, 1997; Haines and Goodhue, 2003).

1.1.3 *Agency Theory*

An agency relationship is defined as "a contract under which one or more persons, the principal(s), engage another person, the agent, to perform some service on their behalf that involves delegating some decision-making authority to the agent. If both parties to the relationship are utility maximizers, there is good reason to believe that the agent will not always act in the best interests of the principal" (Jensen & Meckling, 1976).

This occurs due to two main problems identified by Eisenhardt (1989): goal conflict and differences in attitude toward risk. The goal conflict arises when "(a) the desires or goals of the principal and agent conflict and (b) it is difficult or expensive for the principal to verify what the agent is actually doing" (Eisenhardt, 1989). The problem with differences in attitude toward risk "is that the principal and the agent may prefer different actions because of the different risk preferences" (Eisenhardt, 1989).

The agency relationship is subject to hidden action because the principal typically lacks full information about the agent's behavior and goals. Consequently, much of agency theory focuses on designing appropriate control strategies to minimize information asymmetry and, therefore, hidden action (commonly referred to as moral hazard).

Two basic control strategies are identified: behavior-based (monitoring) and outcome-based (metering) (Haines & Goodhue, 2003). A contract is considered the primary mechanism for implementing these strategies (Eisenhardt, 1989).

Monitoring involves systematically tracking the agent's behavior to collect relevant information about it (Mahaney & Lederer, 2010). The principal "invests in an information source (such as a supervisor or information system) to oversee the agent. Monitoring assumes that the principal can, at a reasonable cost, obtain sufficient information to reduce agent opportunism" (Dawson et al., 2010).

The monitoring strategy is closely associated with the behavior-based contract, which specifies the desired behaviors of the agent (Dawson et al., 2010). In this type of contract, the risk remains with the principal, as the agent is not held accountable for the outcome. The agent is only required to act in accordance with the principal's instructions. As this type of contract does not resolve goal conflict between the principal and the agent, additional mechanisms, such as information systems (e.g., budgeting systems and reporting procedures) or governance structures (e.g., boards of directors, supervisors, or additional layers of management), must be implemented. These mechanisms provide the principal with information about the agent's behavior, reducing or eliminating information asymmetry. When the principal has complete information about the agent's actions, the agent is unlikely to act opportunistically, as they recognize that deception is not possible (Eisenhardt, 1989).

The ability to monitor an agent's behavior is limited not only by the cost of the monitoring system but also by the programmability of the task. Programmability is defined as "the degree to which appropriate behavior by the agent can be specified in advance" (Eisenhardt, 1989). If the principal cannot determine how the agent should behave, a behavior-based contract becomes less feasible.

An implicit assumption in this context is that the principal possesses the knowledge necessary to evaluate the appropriateness of the agent's behavior once it is disclosed.

Metering involves evaluating the outcome of the agent's activities and comparing the actual outcome with the one expected by the principal. As Dawson et al. (2010) explain: "Metering creates and enforces an outcome-based contract that precisely specifies the agent's desired work product. While an outcome-based contract does not reduce the agent's information advantage, it shifts the burden to the agent to perform consistently within the principal's goals."

While the outcome-based contract does not reduce information asymmetry, it does reduce the goal conflict between the principal and the agent, as the agent is rewarded only after achieving the outcome desired by the principal. However, it also shifts all the risks to the agent, who is now solely responsible for delivering the desired outcome. An additional issue is that the outcome usually depends on factors beyond the agent's control.

The ability to create an outcome-based contract is tied to the measurability of the outcome (Eisenhardt, 1989). If the outcome is difficult to measure or if it takes an impractically long time to assess, the outcome-based contract becomes less feasible.

As previously stated, agency theory assumes goal conflict between the principal and the agent, information asymmetry favoring the agent, and differences in attitudes toward risk between the principal and the agent.

If the assumption of goal conflict is relaxed, agency theory predicts that the agent will behave as the principal desires, regardless of whether their behavior is monitored (Eisenhardt, 1989; Haines & Goodhue, 2003). Under the assumption that the agent is risk-averse, a behavior-based contract should be implemented. The same applies in situations where there is no information asymmetry, i.e. the agent's behavior is transparent to the principal or easily observable. In such cases, the agent is unlikely to act opportunistically, making a behavior-based contract appropriate.

If the assumption about the agent's risk aversion is relaxed, an outcome-based contract becomes more attractive, as it transfers risk to the agent and eliminates the need for the principal to gather information on the agent's behavior. As Eisenhardt (1989) concludes: "The heart of principal-agent theory is the trade-off between (a) the cost of measuring behavior and (b) the cost of measuring outcomes and transferring risk to the agent."

The above discussion addresses the situation where the agent has already been selected, which is the focus of most agency theory literature. However, information asymmetry between the principal and potential agents may also exist before the agent's selection (Dahlstrom & Ingram, 2003). In such cases, the selection process is subject to issues related to ex-ante information asymmetry, such as hidden information (also known as adverse selection), and the mechanisms to mitigate it, namely signaling and screening.

Another issue, less commonly addressed in the mainstream agency theory literature, is the opportunistic behavior of the principal (Haines & Goodhue, 2003; Dawson et al., 2010). The principal may withhold information from the agent during the tendering process and contract negotiation. Additionally, the principal may exploit the agent by transferring risks to them, including risks that are beyond the agent's control.

Agency theory has been widely used to explain the interrelations between the project sponsor, as the principal, and the project manager or contractor, as the agent (e.g., Mahaney and Lederer, 2003, 2010; Müller and Turner, 2005; Turner and Müller, 2004).

1.1.4 *Contract Theory*

Both Transaction Cost Economics and Agency Theory regard the contract as the primary (though not the sole) tool for governing transactional relationships. Contract Theory adds to this perspective by explicitly addressing the characteristics of contracts.

First, Contract Theory distinguishes between complete and incomplete contracts. A complete contract is one that "describes the actions to be taken by each party in every possible contingency. The contract is complete if it can be designed in such a way that the prescribed actions can be freely adjusted to the contingencies that arise" (Al-Najjar, 1995). Additionally, the actions and/or outcomes specified in the contract must be verifiable by an external third party, such as a court (Baker et al., 2002). As Al-Najjar et al. (1995) observe: "A complete contract perfectly accomplishes two conflicting goals: it eliminates the freedom of the contracting parties to behave opportunistically, while at the same time leaving them with the maximum degree of flexibility to respond efficiently to the finer details of the contingencies that arise in the course of the transaction."

However, drafting a complete contract requires the parties to anticipate all possible contingencies, including future states of nature, actions resulting from these states, and corresponding outcomes, described in a way that is observable ex post by external parties, such as a court. This process may be too complex or costly, making incomplete contracts the best practical option (Hart & Moore, 1988).

Contractual incompleteness differs from information asymmetry. As Hart & Moore (1988) explain, in situations of information asymmetry, "certain contingent statements are infeasible because the state of the world is not observed by all parties to the contract." In contrast, contractual incompleteness arises even when all parties share the same information but face prohibitive costs in processing and implementing it to create a complete contract.

Incomplete contracts do not specify actions for every possible contingency but include clauses prescribing actions that are efficient on average across a range of scenarios (Al-Najjar, 1995). Consequently, there may be situations where the contract either provides no guidance or prescribes inefficient actions. To address this, incomplete contracts should be supplemented with non-contractual governance mechanisms that allow parties to adapt to actual contingencies, as discussed in the context of transaction cost economics.

If the parties encounter a contingency not foreseen in the contract, they may also choose to renegotiate once the state of nature becomes known (Hart & Moore, 1999; Schmitz, 2001). However, the possibility of renegotiation can undermine the value of drafting a near-complete contract. If the parties cannot commit to avoiding renegotiation, they might rely on a "null contract," described as "the quintessentially incomplete contract" (Hart & Moore, 1999).

Schmitz (2001) suggests that the possibility of renegotiation may explain why real-world contracts tend to be simpler than theoretically optimal ones. Renegotiation introduces additional challenges, particularly when transaction-specific investments are required. Such investments by one party shift bargaining power to the other party, as the investing party risks losing their entire investment if the trade fails. A fully rational second party may exploit this by extracting all potential surplus, up to the value of the investment. Anticipating this, the first party may forgo the investment altogether, knowing the returns would be captured by the other party. This situation is known as the "hold-up problem" (Schmitz, 2001).

Some authors claim that the problem of contract incompleteness can be addressed by appropriately allocating residual rights (Grossman & Hart, 1986). Residual rights are those not specified in the contract and therefore remain with the owner of the asset(s) used to produce the good involved in the transaction. This means the owner of the asset(s) has the right to any income remaining after fulfilling all contractual obligations.

Another approach to managing long-term relationships is relational contracting. Relational contracts are informal agreements and unwritten codes of conduct, upheld by the value of future relationships (Baker et al., 2002). These contracts can occur both within firms, as relational employment, and between independent companies, as relational outsourcing (Baker et al., 2002). Unlike formal contracts, relational contracts do not require the ex-ante definition of outcomes or behavior in a way that is verifiable by external third parties, such as courts. This flexibility makes them suitable for situations where specifying outcomes in advance is prohibitively costly and allows for easy adaptation to unforeseen contingencies. However, because they cannot be enforced by third parties, relational contracts must be self-enforcing, that is, "the value of the future relationship must be sufficiently large that neither party wishes to renege" (Baker et al., 2002). Relational contracts between firms often supplement incomplete formal contracts. However, a shock to the relationship may lead one party to renege on the relational contract and revert to enforcing the explicit terms of the formal contract (Baker et al., 2002).

In summary: Contract Theory and Transaction Cost Economics jointly provide insights into the role of contracts across different types of governance.

Market governance relies on classical contracting, which involves complete contracts. This governance is suited for trading non-specific goods, where the parameters are known ex-ante to market participants. The limited number of future contingencies allows for relatively straightforward specification of all contractual terms in a complete contract.

Hierarchy is supported by the forbearance law (Williamson, 1991). Employment contracts, typically highly incomplete, require employees to perform tasks as instructed by supervisors, within the broad scope of their job description. This flexibility enables organizations to adapt employee activities to changing contingencies. Internal disputes are generally resolved within the organization, without court involvement. Furthermore, employees are not held liable for mistakes unless made intentionally or in bad faith.

Hybrid governance employs neoclassical contracting, which uses incomplete contracts supplemented with additional governance mechanisms. These mechanisms, such as renegotiation, arbitration, transaction-specific governance structures, or relational contracting, allow parties to adapt to future contingencies. While the contract serves as the primary reference point, its inherent incompleteness due to the uncertainty of long-term relationships necessitates supplementary mechanisms to address unforeseen events as they arise.

Contract theory has been applied to determine the appropriate type of contract based on project attributes and to predict the impact of contractual provisions on project performance (e.g., Argyres et al., 2007; Turner & Simister, 2001; Turner, 2004).

1.1.5 *Shareholder and Stakeholder Theories*

Shareholder and stakeholder theories are normative corporate governance theories that determine whom a company should serve and, consequently, what goals its governance mechanisms should aim to accomplish. Shareholder theory (Friedman, 1970) assumes that a corporation exists to maximize the wealth of its owners – the shareholders. In the context of a project, this would typically refer to the project sponsor. In contrast, stakeholder theory posits that a firm should manage its relationships with all stakeholders, not just shareholders (Laplume et al., 2008). Stakeholders are defined as "any group or individual who can affect or is affected by the achievement of the organization's objectives" (Freeman, 1984). Freeman (1994) identifies the main groups of stakeholders as suppliers, customers, employees, stockholders, and the local community. In the context of projects, a stakeholder is an individual who is influenced by a project, has the ability to influence it, and/or has an interest in its outcome (Littau et al., 2010). Some stakeholders may be cooperative, while others might pose challenges to the project. Eskerod et al. (2015) summarize that stakeholders interact with the project in the following ways:

- "the project needs contributions (financial and nonfinancial resources) from the stakeholders,
- stakeholders often establish criteria for assessing the success of a project,
- stakeholders' (potential) resistance may cause various risks and negatively affect the success of the project,
- the project may affect stakeholders in both negative and positive ways".

It is therefore one of the responsibilities of the project management to properly identify and manage all the prominent stakeholders of a project. The processes, tools and techniques of identifying, and dealing with the stakeholders, including those outside of the project team, should be the part of the project governance framework.

A summary of the application of stakeholder theory in project management is provided by Derakhshan et al. (2019) and Littau et al. (2010).

1.2 Strategic Management Theories

The theories discussed in the previous chapter form part of organizational economics (Combs and Ketchen, 1999) or the "theory of the firm," which aims to explain the existence, boundaries, and internal organization of companies (Foss, 1996). As a side effect, these theories recognized the existence of a hybrid governance structures alongside the market and the firm. Another influential stream of theories explaining the firm's existence originates from strategic management, and includes the Resource-Based View (RBV), dynamic capabilities and the Knowledge-Based View (KBV). Similar to how transaction cost economics began with Coase (1937), the Resource- and Knowledge-Based Views trace their roots to Penrose (1959). Penrose conceptualized the firm as a collection of productive resources, both human and non-human, that produce goods and services for profit. Resource coordination and their allocation over time are guided by administrative decisions (Penrose, 1959).

1.2.1 *Resource-Based View and Dynamic Capabilities*

According to the Resource-Based View (RBV) organizations exist because they can organize resources to achieve sustainable competitive advantage

(Eisenhardt and Martin, 2000). These resources include human, physical, organizational and knowledge assets that can be used to implement value-creating strategies (Conner and Prahalad, 1996; Wernerfelt, 1984; Wernerfelt, 2007). For resources to deliver a competitive advantage, they must meet the VRIN criteria: being valuable, rare, inimitable, and non-substitutable.

The ability to acquire, integrate, configure, and deploy resources, using organizational processes, to achieve organizational goals is referred to as capability (Cragg, Caldeira, and Ward, 2011; Eisenhardt and Martin, 2000; Makadok, 2001). The literature distinguishes between two categories of capabilities:

- Operational capabilities: The ability to acquire, integrate, configure, and deploy resources effectively to achieve current operational goals.
- Dynamic (strategic) capabilities: The ability to acquire, integrate, adapt, reconfigure, and deploy resources to respond to or drive market changes (Cepeda and Vera, 2007; Dyduch et al., 2021; Krzakiewicz and Cyfert; Teece et al., 1997; Eisenhardt and Martin, 2000).

In simple terms, operational capabilities involve organizing resources to meet current operational objectives, while dynamic capabilities involve re-organizing resources to achieve new, strategic goals.

The Resource-Based View focuses primarily on the determinants of the firm's performance, in contrast to transaction cost economics (TCE), which seeks to explain why firms and other governance structures exist (Lockett et al., 2009). Consequently, RBV does not extensively discuss why firms are better than markets or hybrid governance forms at achieving VRIN resource combinations.

Teece (1997) highlights transaction and transfer costs in this context, as well as the inclusion of tacit knowledge in firm-specific assets. Moreover, the ongoing processes of acquiring, integrating, reconfiguring, and deploying resources to meet the demands of a changing environment are often more effectively coordinated within hierarchies than through market mechanisms because firms (hierarchies) excel at sequential, coordinated adaptations, as discussed in the TCE literature. A deeper examination of how different governance structures manage resource configuration could better connect RBV with TCE.

Additionally, RBV recognizes that capabilities, including dynamic capabilities, depend on the administration, management, and organizational efforts of firm managers (Lockett et al., 2009). Organizations are essential for absorbing, integrating, configuring and applying resources effectively (Kraaijenbrink et al., 2010).

The administration, management, and organizational work includes activities such as searching for novel uses of existing resources, reconfiguring resources to seize new market opportunities, and creating new resources (Lockett et al., 2009). However, RBV pays little attention to the costs associated with these activities or to the comparison of these costs across different governance structures.

Foss and Foss (2004) observe that RBV devotes "little or no attention to the managerial task or to organizational matters." While RBV recognizes the importance of dynamic capabilities – namely, the ability to acquire, integrate, adapt, reconfigure, and deploy resources – in achieving and sustaining competitive advantage, it largely overlooks the fact that these complex organizational activities are costly.

Although RBV, as a theory focused on exploring the sources of competitive advantage, does not necessarily need to address these costs (Kraaijenbrink et al., 2010), investigating the administrative, managerial, and organizational costs associated with acquiring, configuring, maintaining, and deploying resources could provide a valuable link between RBV and transaction cost economics (TCE).

The foundational literature on the Resource-Based View has largely focused on the characteristics and capabilities of firms (hierarchies), paying relatively little attention to hybrid forms of governance. Combs and Ketchen (1999) argue that inter-firm collaboration is primarily driven by the need to combine resources and capabilities (RBV) rather than by concerns about governance costs, as emphasized in transaction cost economics (TCE). Inter-firm collaboration enables activities that individual firms cannot perform alone due to a lack of requisite combinations of resources.

In the context of project management, Resource-Based View (RBV) and dynamic capabilities theories have been employed to identify the capabilities and resource combinations necessary for successful project execution, particularly within project-based organizations, as well as identification of project management skills as a strategic asset (Haas & Hansen, 2005; Jugdev, 2004; Killen et al., 2012).

In my view, the real strength of RBV and dynamic capabilities theories in explaining project-related phenomena does not lie in their core theoretical constructs, but rather in their peripheral implications – specifically, the recognition that each project demands a uniquely tailored combination of resources and the entities responsible for execution must possess the capability to acquire, configure, maintain, and deploy these resources in a structured and effective manner. Further research is needed to explore what these resource combinations are, as well as to assess the strengths and limitations of various contractual and governance structures in organizing and managing them.

1.2.2 *Knowledge-Based View*

The Knowledge-Based View asserts that a firm's primary resource is knowledge, and that "the primary role of a firm is integrating the specialist knowledge resident in individuals into goods and services" (Grant, 1996). Such integration is more effectively achieved within a hierarchical structure than through market mechanisms because "production requires coordinated efforts of individual specialists who possess many different types of knowledge" (Grant, 1996). Markets, on the other hand, "are unable to undertake this coordinating role because of their failure in the face of the immobility of tacit knowledge and the risk of expropriation of explicit knowledge by the potential buyer" (Grant, 1996). Markets are effective for exchanging knowledge only when that knowledge is fully "packaged within a product, and the buyers of the product can effectively utilize it without needing access to the knowledge embodied within the product" (Grant and Baden-Fuller, 1995).

However, producing goods or services typically requires combining specialized knowledge from various experts. Efficient integration of different types of knowledge is best achieved within firms through direction, where specialists establish rules and guidelines for others, or by creating organizational routines (Grant and Baden-Fuller, 1995; Conner and Prahalad, 1996). Kogut and Zandler (1992) similarly argue that "what firms do better than markets is the sharing and transfer of the knowledge of individuals and groups." Grant and Baden-Fuller (1995) also suggest that firms excel at integrating knowledge, whereas markets are more effective at exchanging perfectly product-embedded knowledge. They also identify specific circumstances where inter-firm collaboration (i.e., hybrid governance forms) outperforms both market and hierarchical structures:

1. **Exchanging and integrating explicit knowledge**: For instance, biotechnology companies often engage in regular exchanges of explicit knowledge.
2. **Transferring knowledge imperfectly embedded in products**: In such cases, beyond the exchange of products, knowledge must also be transferred and integrated independently of the product itself.
3. **Utilizing underexploited, non-product-specific knowledge**: A firm possessing surplus knowledge that is not product-specific may find it more advantageous to sell this knowledge to another company.
4. **Acquiring underutilized, product-specific knowledge externally**: If a company requires specific knowledge for a product but anticipates underutilization if developed internally, it may prefer outsourcing to an external partner.
5. **Managing uncertainty in knowledge investment**: When returns on investment in knowledge are highly uncertain, collaborating with external partners may be more beneficial than internal development.

6. **Addressing the need for rapid knowledge acquisition:** When a firm requires new knowledge urgently, such as during short innovation cycles, it may lack the time to generate the knowledge internally, necessitating inter-firm collaboration.

Williamson (2008) addresses this issue in a broader context of capabilities, stating: "Capabilities that, in the fullness of time, could be homegrown (successively built up) may simply be unattainable (except by creating alliances, joint ventures, and the like) as the urgency of real-time responsiveness becomes great."

In summary, a company should consider obtaining knowledge through inter-firm collaboration in the following situations:

- When creating and sustaining the required knowledge internally is difficult or impossible within the necessary time frame.
- When the knowledge, if developed internally, would be underutilized.
- When the return on investment in developing the knowledge internally is highly uncertain.

Additionally, inter-company knowledge transfer may be necessary when the product being traded requires the supplementary transfer of associated knowledge.

The Knowledge-Based View has not been widely applied in project-related research. Nevertheless, issues surrounding knowledge integration present a promising avenue for understanding why companies establish long-term inter-organizational project networks. Moreover, the extent of required knowledge integration may influence both contractual and non-contractual governance structures within a project. Projects composed of clearly delineated sub-products could lean toward market-like governance, whereas those requiring intensive knowledge integration across multiple contractors would favor hierarchy-like governance models.

1.2.3 *Linking Transaction Cost Economics with Resource-Based View and Knowledge-Based View*

The RBV, KBV, and TCE literature does not appear to give sufficient attention to the fact that acquiring, configuring, maintaining, and deploying a combination of resources, as well as creating and sustaining knowledge within a firm, involves significant costs. Similarly, obtaining resources and knowledge through the market or hybrid governance also entails substantial costs. Grant and Baden-Fuller (1995) note that "inter-firm collaboration may be highly inefficient in transferring and integrating tacit knowledge [but] efficiency benefits from fuller utilization of specialized but non-product-specific knowledge may offset the knowledge transfer inefficiencies associated with inter-firm collaboration." However, this observation is treated more as a side note in their work and does not delve deeper into the inefficiencies involved in transferring and integrating knowledge within different governance structures. The following proposition addresses this gap:

> Managing resources and knowledge incurs costs across all governance types. These costs are related to acquiring, creating, configuring, integrating, maintaining, and deploying resources and knowledge within an organization, as well as the transaction costs associated with acquiring and utilizing resources and knowledge through the market or hybrid governance.

Therefore, when evaluating the transaction and production costs of various governance options, as prescribed by TCE, agents should also include into the comparison:

- The cost of acquiring, configuring, integrating, maintaining, and deploying the combination of resources and knowledge in-house (ACIMD costs),
- The cost of outsourcing this combination of resources and knowledge.

This evaluation should also consider the feasibility of obtaining the required combination of resources and knowledge within the desired time frame, as well as the opportunity cost of underutilized resources and knowledge.

This proposition establishes a connection between the Resource-Based View (RBV), Knowledge-Based View (KBV), and Transaction Cost Economics (TCE).

1.3 Other Theories

1.3.1 *Social Theories*

Despite the theories rooted in organizational economics and strategic management, social theories also provide valuable insights into phenomena related to projects and project governance. The central premise of social theory in this context is that people's behavior and institutions are strongly influenced and shaped by social relations (Granovetter, 1985). This phenomenon is referred to as *embeddedness*, defined as "the extent to which economic action is embedded in structures of social relations" (Granovetter, 1985). These social relations exist both between specific actors engaged in economic activity (*relational embeddedness*) and within broader networks (*structural embeddedness*) (Jones et al., 1997). Social relations give rise to informal governance mechanisms that operate alongside formal contracts between firms and within organizations (Jones et al., 1997).

First and foremost, social relations foster trust between business partners (Granovetter, 1985), significantly reducing the transactional costs of economic interactions. It has long been recognized that social relations lead to the formation of networks of trusted partners who conduct economic exchanges and resolve related issues informally, rather than relying on formal agreements (Macaulay, 1963). The presence of stable networks, grounded in trust and informal social relations, has also been acknowledged in the context of projects (Eccles, 1981, Pryke, 2005).

Informal social relations also exist within firms (Granovetter, 1985). These internal social relations give rise to an informal organization that coexists alongside the formal structure.

The fact that people engage in social relationships is deeply rooted in the human need to belong (Baumeister and Leary, 1995; Braun and Kramer, 2019). As cultural anthropologists Braun and Kramer (2019) put it: "People gravitate toward and thrive in groups. [...] The way we structure our relationships differs from culture to culture, from place to place, and over time. What we all have in common, however, is an innate human desire to belong." The human tendency to form groups stems from the reality that, since ancient times, it has been easier for a group to survive than for an individual. According to Braun and Kramer (2019), every group must answer two fundamental questions in order to survive:

- How do we, as a group, adapt to the environment to survive?
- How do we, as a group, organize internally to enable this adaptation?

In answering these questions, a group develops its own culture: language, customs and beliefs, symbols, habits, and a ranking system, which shapes the social relations among its members (Braun & Kramer, 2019).

The aforementioned need to belong, deeply rooted in human nature since ancient times, drives people to develop informal social relationships regardless of other factors. This means that, with regard to the organization of economic activity, people tend to develop informal social relations under any formal form of governance, be it the market, a company, or any type of hybrid governance. Naturally, the formal governance structure influences the nature of informal social relations, and vice versa.

Granovetter (1985) argues that social relations within a company may be denser and more enduring than in other forms of governance, due to a stronger identification of the parties with the organization's common goals. He also hypothesizes that the absence of a personal network in the market, or the presence of relationships marked by conflict, disorder, opportunism, or fraud, can increase the pressure for vertical integration within firms.

Conversely, strong informal social relations among participants in market or hybrid governance arrangements can reduce the costs of drafting and safeguarding formal contracts, and facilitate dispute resolution without resorting to formal governance mechanisms (Macaulay, 1963; Jones et al., 1997).

In the case of projects requiring long-term contracting, the formation of a network of trusted contractors – a "quasifirm" – enables the combination of company-like coordination with market-like flexibility (Eccles, 1981). Structural embeddedness also "allows parties to use implicit and open-ended contracts for customized, complex exchanges under conditions of demand uncertainty" (Jones et al., 1997).

Informal governance, rooted in social relationships, naturally arises alongside formal structures. These mechanisms can complement, compensate for, or conflict with formal governance (Granovetter, 1985; Gulati & Puranam, 2009; Soda & Zaheer, 2012). Ideally, formal and informal systems reinforce each other (Soda & Zaheer, 2012). However, informal ties are often used to address issues that formal governance cannot resolve effectively (Gulati & Puranam, 2009). When informal structures undermine formal ones, it signals a serious problem requiring immediate attention. In summary, when analyzing any governance structure one must take into account that it is embedded in the social relations, which influence how governance actually works.

In the context of projects, social theories have been applied both to examine relational contracting between project parties (Cao and Lumineau, 2015; Nwajei, 2021) and to explore social relations within the temporary project organization (Pryke, 2005; Pryke et al., 2018).

1.3.2 *Stewardship Theory*

Stewardship theory, like agency theory, focuses on the separation of ownership and authority, specifically, a situation where "one or more persons, the principal(s), engage another person, the agent, to perform some service on their behalf that involves delegating some decision-making authority to the agent" (Jensen & Meckling, 1976). In both agency and stewardship theories, the most commonly discussed example of such a situation is the relationship between the shareholders and the management of a corporation.

The key difference between the two theories lies in their underlying assumptions about human nature. As previously mentioned, agency theory assumes that individuals are self-interested and focused on maximizing their own utility or profit. Under these circumstances, if the goals of the principal and the agent are not aligned, the agent is likely to prioritize their own utility over that of the principal. Consequently, agency theory emphasizes governance mechanisms designed either to control the agent's actions (monitoring) or to align the agent's goals with those of the principal by providing incentives tied to achieving the principal's objectives (metering).

Stewardship theory challenges the assumptions about human nature by asserting that, in certain situations, some individuals may maximize their utility through means other than profit maximization. Stewardship theory suggests that people can be motivated by "a need to achieve, to gain intrinsic satisfaction through successfully performing inherently challenging work, to exercise responsibility and authority, and thereby to gain recognition from peers and bosses" (Donaldson and Davis, 1991).

Additionally, "identification by managers with the corporation, especially if they have served there with long tenure and have shaped its form and directions, promotes a merging of individual ego and the corporation, thus melding individual self-esteem with corporate prestige" (Donaldson and Davis, 1991). In other words, some managers may choose to "do a good job, to be a good steward of the corporate assets" even when their interests are not perfectly aligned with those of the principal, driven by "a sense of duty, that is, normatively induced compliance" (Davis et al., 1997).

Consequently, stewardship theory supports governance structures that empower the agent, deliberately extending a steward's autonomy (Davis et al., 1997). According to stewardship theory, an agent (steward) should be granted authority and empowerment to perform their role, as they can be trusted (Donaldson and Davis, 1991). Control mechanisms may even be counterproductive, as they can undermine the steward's pro-organizational behavior by reducing their motivation (Davis et al., 1997).

Stewardship theory is not an alternative to agency theory but rather a complement to it. Different individuals and interpersonal situations may be better described by one theory or the other (Davis et al., 1997). Whether a governance structure should follow the prescriptions of agency theory, stewardship theory, or a combination of the two is subject to debate and requires further research. In the context of projects, stewardship theory suggests treating project managers as stewards who are motivated to act in the best interests of project sponsors or owners (Derakshan et al., 2019). It emphasizes trust as a key governance mechanism (Müller et al., 2013). Establishing a trust-based relationship between the project manager and the project sponsor can reduce transaction costs associated with constructing and maintaining control mechanisms. Evidence in the literature indicates that excessive control and overly rigid governance mechanisms can erode trust, encourage opportunistic behaviors, and negatively impact project performance (Müller et al., 2013; Toivonen and Toivonen, 2014). On the other hand, relying solely on trust poses risks, such as opportunistic behavior or fraud, if the agent acts unethically (Müller et al.,

2013). Therefore, a well-balanced mix of trust and control should be applied in project governance, making agency theory and stewardship theory complementary rather than conflicting.

1.3.3 *Resource Dependence Theory*

Resource Dependence Theory (RDT) was formulated by Pfeffer and Salancik (1978) and focuses on the interrelations between a company and its external environment. The core idea of this theory is that "all organizations critically depend on other organizations for the provision of vital resources, and that this dependence is often reciprocal" (Drees and Heugens, 2013). To manage these dependencies, companies establish various forms of interorganizational arrangements (Drees and Heugens, 2013).

These arrangements include mergers and vertical integration, joint ventures and other interorganizational relationships, boards of directors, political action, and executive succession (Hillman et al., 2009). Resource Dependence Theory complements other theories by addressing the processes involved in acquiring resources, whereas "most theories concentrated on internal processes of resource use instead of considering processes about gaining resources" (Nienhüser, 2008).

In this way, RDT is complementary to RBV (Resource-Based View) and KBV (Knowledge-Based View). The application of RDT in the project context pertains to the allocation of resources across different projects, portfolios, and programs (Derakhshan et al., 2019; Biesenthal and Wilden, 2014).

1.3.4 *System, Complexity and Contingency Theories*

While systems theory, complexity theory, and contingency theory constitute the foundational framework of contemporary project management theory and practice, the propositions they offer can be distilled into relatively concise and straightforward terms.

Projects, as other organizations, can be conceptualized as systems composed of interrelated and interacting components, including individuals, resources, technologies, and processes (Kast and Rosenzweig, 1981). A holistic perspective is essential for understanding such systems; however, as the number of constituent elements and the complexity of their interrelationships increase, the system's behavior becomes less linear and more difficult to model, control, and manage through centralized approaches.

Complexity theory further enriches this perspective by emphasizing that complex systems exhibit non-linear behavior and are inherently subject to variability and uncertainty. Moreover, minor and seemingly insignificant changes in one part of the system can trigger disproportionate and unpredictable effects in other areas, often amplified through feedback mechanisms (Cicmil et al., 2017; Curlee and Gordon, 2010).

This makes the traditional project life cycle model – where projects are planned and executed through a series of linear phases – too simplistic and inadequate for managing complex projects. Instead of trying to plan and control every detail, project management should focus on governance approaches that emphasize responsiveness to unexpected challenges, along with agility and resilience (Cicmil et al., 2017; Curlee and Gordon, 2010).

Contingency theory states that "if the effect of one variable V on the effectiveness E of an organization is moderated by a contingency C, the dependency can only be described by the causal statement of the trivariate relationship, including the contingency C" (Hanisch and Wald, 2012). Therefore, "a change in contingencies should lead a rational manager to adapt the organization to those changes to maintain an optimal level of effectiveness" (Hanisch and Wald, 2012). In terms of managing projects it means that "the best approach to managing a project depends on context: different conditions require different project organizational characteristics, and the effectiveness of the project is related to how well organization and conditions fit each other" (Howell et al., 2010).

In summary: projects are complex systems, subject to variability and uncertainty, and thus difficult to manage using linear, deterministic approaches. The optimal approach to managing a given project depends on its attributes and the environment in which it takes place.

1.4 Theory of Project and Project Management

The theory of projects and project management is still evolving, but several authors have significantly contributed to its development. Turner (1993, 1999) defined a project as: "A temporary endeavor in which human, material, and financial resources are organized in a novel way to undertake a unique scope of work, of given specification, within constraints of cost and time, so as to achieve beneficial change defined by quantitative and qualitative objectives" (in: Turner and Müller, 2003).

The PMBOK (2021) provides a widely cited definition: "A project is a temporary endeavor undertaken to create a unique product, service, or result". Both definitions emphasize a project's **temporariness**, described in PMBOK (2021) as: "The temporary nature of projects indicates a beginning and an end to the project work or phase of the project work." This temporary nature distinguishes projects from ongoing operations, which are designed to continue indefinitely

(Turner, 2006a). Thus, most authors characterize a project as a temporary organization (Lundin, 1995; Lundin and Söderholm, 1995; Turner and Müller, 2003; Söderlund, 2004a; Turner, 2006a; Shenhar and Dvir, 2007; Hanisch and Wald, 2011). Shenhar and Dvir (2007) define a project as "a temporary organization and process set up to achieve a specified goal under the constraints of time, budget, and other resources."

A key distinction is intentional temporariness: projects are intended to conclude at a specific point, unlike companies, which aim to sustain operations indefinitely, even though companies may eventually cease to exist, and some projects may last far longer than anticipated (Lundin and Söderholm, 1995; Turner, 2006a).

The second characteristic of a project is the uniqueness of its output (scope of work, product, service, or result). There is debate within the project management community about what "unique" means in this context. For example, the 15th vessel of a given class, built using the same design as the previous 14, may not seem "unique," yet its construction would still be considered a project due to its singular output, delivered within a specific timeline, using dedicated resources in a temporary organization.

Uniqueness varies among projects, and terms like "singular," "unitary," or "individual" may sometimes better describe the output. This consideration also applies to the uniqueness of methods used to develop the output. In some projects, such as the first Moon mission, methods are truly unique. In others, like constructing similar vessels, methods are largely standardized, requiring only minor adjustments to specific conditions.

In fact, "uniqueness bias" is one of key behavioral challenges in project delivery (Flyvbjerg, 2021). To improve outcomes, it is critical to standardize project delivery methods wherever possible (Flyvbjerg and Gardner, 2023). Since many projects are repetitive in nature, standardization is both achievable and desirable.

Therefore, it seems sufficient and practical to define a project based on its temporariness as a temporary organization established to achieve a specified goal or output within the constraints of time, budget, and other resources. However, the extent to which the output and methods are unique remains an important dimension of a project, influencing how it should and could be managed.

In addition to the predominant view of a project as a temporary organization, there is another perspective that regards the project as a nexus of contracts (Turner, 2006). This perspective is not an alternative but a complementary one, as project stakeholders are bound to one another through various types of contracts. These range from assignments within the organizational hierarchy to various forms of business-to-business agreements.

In summary, a project can be viewed as a temporary organization that operates as a nexus of contracts (of different types), established to achieve a specified goal or output within the constraints of time, budget, and other resources.

Like any other type of organization, a project requires clear goals and objectives, as well as the following essential elements:
- Organizational structure and culture,
- Knowledge, both explicit (codified in designs, processes, and procedures) and tacit (embedded in people),
- Processes and procedures that operationalize this knowledge, providing structured methods for applying it to daily operations,
- People with the appropriate knowledge and skills,
- Resources (material, financial, and informational).

These elements are subject to Fayol's functions of management: planning, organizing, commanding, coordinating, controlling and motivating (Andersen, 2006) to acquire, configure, integrate, maintain and deploy them in a way that guarantees the accomplishment of the goals and objectives in a coordinated way.

The temporary nature of a project, combined with the (relative) uniqueness of its output and methods, has significant implications. Unlike permanent organizations, where established organizational structures, processes, and resource allocations exist, projects require planning, organizing, and coordinating from scratch with each new endeavor.

In a permanent, operations-based company, human, material, and financial resources are allocated within the established framework. Employees are familiar with their roles, tasks, and hierarchy. Products and production technologies are defined, allowing managers to focus on monitoring deviations and resolving issues within a predefined plan.

In contrast, project management must initiate all planning, organizing, and coordinating activities from the ground up. The extent of effort required depends on the uniqueness of the project's output and methods. For repetitive projects, predefined frameworks often assist project managers in planning and organizing. However, project goals and objectives must still be clearly defined and aligned with controllable activities based on established technological processes and procedures.

Activities must be scheduled, resources identified, planned, and allocated to tasks. A project's organizational structure must be established, roles and responsibilities documented, and individuals with the required skills and knowledge assigned and informed of their duties. Governance mechanisms must also be defined, communicated, and implemented for every new project. The key distinction between unique and repetitive projects lies in the availability of reusable frameworks for the latter, which simplify some initial setup tasks.

The second consequence of a project's temporariness, the (relative) uniqueness of its output, and the (relative) uniqueness of its methods is project uncertainty (Turner and Müller, 2003) and, in some cases, ambiguity (Lech, 2022), which are significantly greater than in routine company operations.

Uncertainty arises when "the set of possible future outcomes is identified, but the related probability distributions are unknown or only subjectively understood" (Schrader, Riggs, and Smith, 1993). Risk is a specific type of uncertainty where both the set of possible future outcomes and their objective probability distributions are known. Ambiguity, on the other hand, refers to situations where "possible future outcomes are not identified or well-defined, and there may be conflicts regarding what they should be" (Schrader, Riggs, and Smith, 1993).

Every project involves some level of uncertainty due to future events that may affect its execution. For projects in well-defined disciplines with established histories, such as construction, planners can rely on historical data to identify potential events and their likelihood. They can assign probabilities to these events using a frequentist approach. In this context, planners can predict what might happen and with what probability, though the actual outcome remains unknown. This type of uncertainty, called risk, can be modeled using mathematical methods. Risk is managed through contingency planning, where action plans are developed for high-probability or high-impact events and executed if these events occur.

However, most projects are also subject to events for which probabilities cannot be assigned due to insufficient historical data. These events are known as "unknowable unknowns", and the associated uncertainty is referred to as Knightian uncertainty (Knight, 1921; Dibiasi and Iselin, 2021). This may occur when similar projects are rare or nonexistent, leaving no historical precedent for events affecting such projects. It can also apply to "black swan" events, which are rare and extreme occurrences with very low probabilities (Aven, 2017; Taleb, 2007). In some cases, the events may be unprecedented in recorded history.

Generating contingency plans for Knightian uncertainties is often impractical or impossible. The most reasonable approach is to include buffers in planned values to account for unexpected events. More importantly, project teams should prioritize flexibility and adaptability, enabling them to quickly identify, understand, and respond to unforeseen events (Pich et al., 2002; Collyer and Warren, 2009; Hagen and Park, 2013). The more unique the project's outcome, methods, and/or environment, the greater the uncertainties encountered during execution.

Uncertainty can also stem from poorly defined project goals and methods (Turner and Müller, 2003; Lech, 2021). Strategies to address such uncertainties include experimenting, selectionism, iterative work, and learning during the project (Collyer and Warren, 2009; Pich et al., 2002; Sommer and Loch, 2004).

Apart from risk and uncertainty, some projects are also subject to ambiguity. Ambiguity refers to situations where "goals are vague, problematic, inconsistent, or unstable" (March, 1978). It represents a state of multiple and conflicting interpretations, particularly concerning project goals (Lech, 2022). Unlike uncertainty, ambiguity cannot be reduced simply by sharing more information (Atkinson et al., 2006; Thiry, 2002). According to Walker et al. (2017), "ambiguity is a state where our assumptions, as the receiver of a communication message, are at odds with those of the intended communicator of the message." Ambiguity typically arises in projects with intangible outcomes, especially when there is knowledge asymmetry among project stakeholders (Lech, 2022).

Ambiguity should be gradually reduced throughout the project to achieve a shared understanding of the project's goals and methods among stakeholders. This process involves problem definition and structuring, sense-making, negotiation and debate, learning, selectionism, enhancing the project team's capabilities, and building trust between stakeholders (Atkinson et al., 2006; Collyer and Warren, 2009; Lech, 2021; Pich et al., 2002; Turner and Cochrane, 1993).

Another consequence of the temporary nature of a project is the challenge of maintaining sufficient motivation among team members, particularly in operations-based organizations where individuals may be simultaneously assigned to both a line of business and a project. Achieving high levels of teamwork and coordination can also be difficult, as team members may not have enough time to fully integrate with one another. Additionally, many projects require the transdisciplinary integration of internal and external experts, resources, and the project itself with the operating business (Hanisch and Wald, 2011; Turner and Müller, 2003).

In summary, the temporary nature of a project, combined with the uniqueness of its goals and methods (which vary by project type), necessitates the use of specific project management methods that differ, at least in part, from those used in traditional organizational management.

As Hanisch and Wald (2011) note: "In many cases, projects are carried out beyond the hierarchical lines of authority and, therefore, also require specific leadership skills, coordination mechanisms, and incentive schemes. As a consequence, a comprehensive set of tools, standards, and procedures for the management of single projects, as well as project portfolios and programs, has been developed in project management practice."

Following the exploration of the nature of a project, it is crucial to examine the concept of project management as well. The PMBOK (2021) defines project management as "the application of knowledge, skills, tools, and techniques to project activities to meet project requirements. Project management refers to guiding the project work to deliver the intended outcomes." According to Turner (2006b) "project management is the means by which the work of the resources assigned to the temporary organization is managed and controlled to deliver the beneficial change desired by the owner." Similarly, Shenhar and Dvir (2007) define project management as "managerial activities needed to lead a project" so that a "temporary organization achieves a specified goal under the constraints of time, budget, and other resources." The latter two definitions highlight the importance of "managerial activities" and "managed and controlled" as central aspects of project management. To avoid circular reasoning, where the term being defined is reiterated in the definition, it is helpful to decompose the term "management" using the Resource-Based View and Fayol's functions of management. This approach allows for a more precise and comprehensive understanding of the term.

Based on this perspective, the following definition of project management is proposed: Project management is the process of acquiring, configuring, integrating, maintaining, and deploying people, knowledge, and other resources (tangible, intangible, and financial) through planning, organizing, commanding, coordinating, controlling, and motivating to achieve a project goal in a coordinated manner, within the constraints of time, budget, and other resources.

A project, both as a temporary organization and as a nexus of contracts, requires governance so that standards, rules, structures and processes which project management should follow are set, and mechanisms for safeguarding, coordinating, and adapting the exchanges that take place between the project stakeholders are defined (Ahola et al. 2014).

CHAPTER 2

The Nature and Mechanisms of Project Governance

In this chapter the nature and tools of project governance will be presented.

2.1 The Nature of Project Governance

Samset and Volden (2016) define project governance as "processes, systems, and regulations that the financing party must have in place to ensure that projects are successful. This would typically include a regulatory framework to ensure adequate quality at entry, compliance with agreed objectives, management and resolution of issues that may arise during the project, and standards for quality review of key appraisal documents". Pitsis et al. (2014) characterize project governance as: "organizational structures, roles and responsibilities of boards and management, control systems, auditing and reporting mechanisms, and lines of communication, and the complexity of contractual design and execution". Müller (2017, p. 14) defines project governance as "the means by which individual projects, groups of projects (such as programs or portfolios), and the totality of projects in an organization are directed and controlled and managers are held accountable for the conduct and performance of them. Governance provides the value system, structures, processes and policies […] to allow projects to achieve organizational objectives and foster implementation".

Project governance is different from project management as project management "refers to the processes established to organize and manage resources required to complete a project within defined scope, quality, time, and cost constraints" (Samset and Volden, 2016). In other words project management "is mainly concerned with the operational control and execution of daily work" in a project (Biesenthal and Wilden, 2014, Turner 1999) while project governance is supposed to set the standards, rules, structures and processes which project management should follow.

When analysing the nature of project governance Ahola et al. (2014) identified two distinct streams of literature. According to the first stream project governance is an activity imposed by the project-oriented firm on a given project. The purpose of project governance in this view is to "define standards or rules that individual projects are expected to comply with, and to monitor the fulfilment of these rules" (Ahola et al. 2014). Project governance is a set

© 2026 THE AUTHOR(S) | HTTPS://DOI.ORG/10.1163/9789004758544-004

of principles, structures, and processes for undertaking the management of projects with the purpose of defining and regulating roles, accountabilities, decision-making, planning and controlling procedures for the projects in a centrally coordinated way (Crawford and Cooke-Davies, 2009, in: Ahola et al. 2014). Although the above-mentioned definitions differ in the level of generality and detailed list of project governance elements, they all acknowledge that project governance aims at setting standards and rules, and providing mechanisms for managing a project. After integrating all the above-mentioned views, the following definition of project governance is achieved:

Project governance is an activity aiming at:

- setting project standards and regulations regarding:
  - definition of objectives and scope,
  - quality of the outcome,
  - planning,
  - communication,
  - management and resolution of tasks, risks and issues,
  - decision making,
  - roles, responsibilities and accountability,
  - coordination and cooperation,
  - controlling and reporting of the progress;
  - identification and management of project stakeholders;
- defining of project structures, processes, procedures and tools which assure the work is done in compliance with the above standards and regulations in any individual project;
- controlling of the compliance of any individual project with the above standards and regulations.

Thus, the aim of project governance is to provide the standards, mechanisms, and tools allowing for structured management of a project.

This layer of project governance stems from the fact that every project is a temporary organization (Turner & Müller, 2003; Turner, 2006), which requires standards, regulations, structures, and processes to plan, coordinate, and control the efforts of participants, ensuring the optimal achievement of the planned goal. Such governance is essential for every project, whether performed by several independent firms or internally within a single firm using its own resources. All participants, regardless of their legal status or interrelations, must act, to some extent, as if they were internal to this temporary organization and adhere to its governance rules. This governance layer will be further referred to as project governance, as it applies universally to projects, regardless of their size, contractual arrangements, or legal structures.

For every project, a project governance authority must define standards and regulations concerning project objectives and scope, quality of outcomes, task planning and management, risk and issue resolution, decision-making, roles, accountability, and control. These standards and regulations are implemented in each project through organizational structures, processes, and procedures. Participants must familiarize themselves with project governance and adhere to it throughout the project lifecycle. Compliance with governance mechanisms must be monitored and ensured during all phases. In this way, project governance provides a structured framework for managing projects, ensuring they are executed in a consistent and organized manner.

Project governance offers a set of rules and tools for daily use by all participants, facilitating the structured execution of tasks and contributing to project success. Such definition of project governance is in line with the responsibilities of the Project Management Offices (PMOs) in organizations worldwide (see, e.g. Darling and Whitty, 2016; Monteiro et al., 2016; Spałek, 2012; Spałek, 2013). One of the roles of the PMO is to set unified standards regarding project management methodology and impose those standards on all the projects under the control of the PMO.

The second stream of literature views project governance as "arrangements that define shared practices for safeguarding, coordinating, and adapting the numerous exchanges that take place between project-based firms and (non-project-based) firms participating in the project" (Ahola et al., 2014). According to this perspective, project governance establishes "a shared set of rules and procedures that all firms participating in the project are expected to follow." Every contractual arrangement requires governance mechanisms to regulate relationships between project participants. As Ahola et al. (2014) explain, "when any two actors engage in an economic transaction, often under conditions of high uncertainty, asset specificity, and bounded rationality, they face the problem of how to safeguard, monitor, and adapt the focal transaction in the most efficient way (Williamson, 1975)", i.e. they require a governance structure. This layer of project governance stems from the view of a project as a nexus of contracts. It aligns with the Transaction Cost Economics perspective (Derakhshan et al., 2019) and will be referred to as governance of project contractual relations. The specific shape and scope of this governance layer depend on the contractual setup of the project. For internal projects, which are executed exclusively using the financing organization's internal resources, coordination and adaptation to unforeseen contingencies can be achieved through fiat (authority). However, employee participation must still be regulated, either within or outside their employment contracts. Employees should be made aware of their roles and responsibilities within the project's temporary organization, and their acceptance of these roles must be secured. Their involvement should also be evaluated, with appropriate consequences, positive or negative, applied.

For projects involving multiple legal entities, governance mechanisms are essential to ensure project success despite potentially conflicting participant goals, agency issues, and information asymmetry. This view assumes that projects are executed by multiple legally independent firms which "temporarily pool their resources, capabilities, and knowledge to achieve the shared goal specified by the project" (Ahola et al., 2014). Since the goals of participating firms may conflict with each other and the project's objectives, a governance structure is necessary to coordinate efforts, maintain control, and resolve conflicts so that all entities work toward the project's goals. The foundational governance mechanism in such cases is a contract. However, as already discussed, drafting a complete contract that specifies all potential outcomes and accounts for every future contingency is often impractical or prohibitively expensive. In such cases, incomplete contracts must be supplemented with additional governance mechanisms to facilitate smooth decision-making, coordination, conflict resolution, and control when unforeseen contingencies arise.

To summarize, a project's governance framework consists of two complementary and mutually interdependent layers:

1. **Project governance** – defining ways of working within a project as a temporary organization;
2. **Governance of project contractual relations** – determining contractual relations between the project participants.

In a recent synthesis of research (Sankaran et al., 2025), project governance is categorized into two types: contractual and relational (Lv et al., 2023; Nwajej, 2021). Contractual governance relies on explicit, formal, written agreements, whereas relational governance is grounded in trust and social norms (Cao & Lumineau, 2015; Roehrich et al., 2020).

While the notion that projects are governed through both formal and informal mechanisms (Roehrich et al., 2020) is well-established and remains valid, it is useful to integrate this perspective with the previously discussed distinction between two foundational aspects of project governance: one arising from the temporary organizational nature of projects, and the other from their characterization as a nexus of contracts.

Indeed, both the organizational dimension of project governance and the governance of contractual relations can be implemented through formal and informal mechanisms. Thus, rather than presenting a binary opposition, the following matrix offers a more nuanced classification of project governance mechanisms:

	Formal	Informal
Project governance	Formal organization: standards, regulations, structure, processes, procedures and formal tools	Informal organization
Governance of project contractual relations	Legal contract	Relational contracting

These mechanisms interact and influence one another in various ways. To begin with, every project functions as a temporary organization and simultaneously serves as a nexus of diverse contractual relationships. As such, each project requires a formal organizational framework, comprising structure, processes, and procedures, as well as formal contracts among its members. When a project is carried out within a company using internal resources, these contracts typically take the form of employment agreements. In other cases, they are commercial contracts between independent legal entities that agree to collaborate on a shared project. The type of legal contract can significantly influence the nature of interactions within the temporary organization. For instance, an outcome-based, fixed-price contract imposes minimal control over a party's day-to-day activities and entails less integration into the project's formal organization than an open-ended, resource-based time and materials agreement.

Informal social relationships among project participants also shape the formal aspects of a project. These interpersonal dynamics affect daily work, communication, information exchange, and problem-solving. Positive social relations can reinforce formal structures or compensate for their shortcomings, while poor social relations may hinder cooperation and coordination. In cases involving legally independent parties, strong social bonds may lead to relational contracting, resulting in more flexible, open legal agreements and collaboration that extends beyond the formal contractual provisions.

So far, the governance layers discussed above relate to a single project, which falls within the scope of this book. Naturally, the external environment surrounding such a project plays a crucial role in shaping and influencing its governance mechanisms.

For instance, governance standards established by a company's Project Management Office are designed to apply across all projects within the organization, not just one. As a result, the characteristics of other project types undertaken by the company influence the standards and procedures applied to each individual project. Moreover, project governance must align with the broader corporate governance framework and is therefore shaped by it.

Whether an inter-company project is executed as a one-time collaboration or within a stable alliance of regularly cooperating firms significantly impacts the level of trust, relational capital, and, most likely, the structure of the inter-company contracts.

It is worthwhile to briefly explore the levels of analysis presented in the project governance literature within this context. Söderlund (2004b) identifies four distinct lines of research related to projects:

- Project management – focusing on the planning, organization, and success factors of individual projects
- Inter-firm projects – addressing transaction costs, contractual arrangements, and client relationships in projects involving multiple contractors
- Multi-project firms – examining the coordination of work and resource allocation across multiple projects within an organization, including portfolio and program management
- Project ecologies – exploring the sociological and economic geographical dimensions of projects

In their recent summary of research on project governance, Sankaran et al. (2025) distinguish between the governance of single projects, groups of projects, and organizational project governance, which concerns "all project-related activities within a firm." A similar stance is taken by Müller (2017), who identifies the following governance levels:

- Governance of a single project (project governance) – "executed by a steering group, which directs and controls the project manager. This group often appoints the project manager, defines the scope, means (e.g., the methodology), and ends (e.g., objectives) of the project, and provides the resources to accomplish the objectives. It also defines the scope and frequency of reporting, reviews, audits, and so forth" (Müller, 2017, p. 18).
- Governance of groups of projects (governance of projects) – involving the standardization of governance mechanisms across all projects within an organization (including the selection of relevant project management methodologies), as well as cross-project strategic and operational decisions, such as project prioritization and resource sharing.
- Board-level governance of projects – encompassing strategic decisions regarding projects within the organization, "such as the extent to which the organization uses projects as building blocks for its business, the establishment of project management offices (PMOs), or the balance in hiring permanent versus temporary project managers" (Müller, 2017, p. 18).

It is evident that "single project" governance and management are considered here in a relatively narrow sense – focused on defining scope, imposing objectives and methodology, providing resources, and establishing reporting and control routines. Aspects related to the establishment of a broader governance framework are positioned at the "governance of groups of projects" level, alongside issues concerning the day-to-day management of project portfolios and programs. Moreover, neither Müller (2017) nor Sankaran et al. (2025) emphasize inter-firm project considerations, which Söderlund (2004b) does address. Sankaran et al. (2025) refer to research on interorganizational project networks (e.g. Müller et al., 2022; Roehrich et al. 2020; Wang et al., 2025), a specific, quasi-permanent form of intercompany project collaboration.

Within the typologies of project governance and management research outlined above, several distinct dimensions can be identified:

- Level of observation:
  - single project,
  - group of projects,
  - organization executing the projects (whether project-based, project-oriented or operations oriented),
  - project ecology – the broader environment, such as an economy or social group.
- Phenomenon under observation:
  - governance framework(s) for the project as a temporary organization(s),
  - contractual (formal and informal) and social relations,
  - strategic decision-making,
  - social and economic impact.

Some of these phenomena can be observed across multiple levels of analysis. Accordingly, the following matrix can be formulated:

	Single project	**Group of projects**	**Company**	**Ecology**
Governance framework(s)	X	X	X	
Contractual and social relations	X	X	X	
Strategic decisions		X	X	
Social and economic impact				X

In most cases, the project governance framework is established at the company level to encompass all projects undertaken within the organization. It reflects the company's strategic orientation toward projects and incorporates mechanisms to align project outcomes with corporate strategy and governance, along with metrics to monitor this alignment. Consequently, organizational project governance can be examined both at the company level and across groups of projects.

However, for large-scale and/or unique projects, the governance framework may be idiosyncratic – specifically tailored to the needs of the individual project. Moreover, the effectiveness of particular governance mechanisms depends on various project attributes, such as the definability and stability of outcomes or the contractual landscape. Thus, even when a governance framework is designed at the company level, its effectiveness may vary depending on the characteristics of each project and may require project-specific adaptations.

These considerations underscore the importance of investigating governance at the individual project level, extending beyond the conventional assessment of project performance within predefined constraints.

Similarly, contractual and social relationships can be studied at the organizational level, particularly within entities that form semi-permanent inter-company alliances to execute successive projects. These relationships can also be analyzed at the program or portfolio level. However, inter-organizational contractual and social dynamics established at higher levels manifest within individual projects, influencing their performance. Additionally, while contractual relationships sometimes originate at the project level, social relationships almost always do, giving each project its own distinct economic and relational context.

Accordingly, the unit of analysis in this book is the governance of a single project, examined in its broadest scope. This includes:

- The project governance framework, encompassing structure, roles, processes, procedures, and performance metrics
- Factors influencing the selection and effectiveness of specific governance mechanisms within a given project context
- Informal relationships within the temporary organization shaped by the governance framework
- The contractual setup, including types of contracts employed
- Factors influencing the choice and effectiveness of particular contractual arrangements in specific project settings
- Informal relationships developed within the contractual environment

While some of these variables may be determined at the project level, others may be established at higher organizational levels, such as within a project group or across the company, depending on the specific context. Crucially, however, all are examined from the perspective of the individual project.

2.2 Project Governance

2.2.1 *Selection Criteria for a Project Governance Framework*

As outlined in the previous sections, every project must have a project governance framework that aims to:
- Establish standards and regulations regarding project scope, quality, decision-making, structure, roles and responsibilities, processes and procedures, communication, coordination and cooperation mechanisms, project control, and reporting;
- Define project structures, processes, and tools to ensure compliance with these standards and regulations in individual projects;
- Monitor and enforce compliance with these standards and regulations in individual projects.

The contents of a governance framework depend on the project management approach adopted:
- A plan-driven, sequential, waterfall approach;
- A test-driven, iterative, agile approach (Spałek, 2016);
- Hybrid methods that combine a plan-driven approach for project initiation and finalization with an agile approach during delivery.

Each of these approaches is supported by multiple methodologies.

According to the subject-matter literature, the selection of the project management approach for a particular project depends on the following variables:
- definability of the project methods (Turner and Cochrane, 1993);
- definability of the project goal/outcome (Turner and Cochrane, 1993);
- physical characteristics of the outcome imposing sequential technological and organizational processes;
- criticality of the project outcome (Thesing et al., 2021);
- level of the project uncertainty;
- company's attitude towards uncertainty, company's culture, habits and beliefs regarding project management (Thesing et al., 2021);
- project structural complexity (Williams, 1999);

The first two variables affecting the selection of the project management methodology, and the two most prominent, are the definability of project methods and project goals/outcomes.

Projects in which both the outcome and methods are well-defined before initiation can be managed using traditional, plan-based, waterfall project management techniques. These techniques, rooted in operations research, rely on planning, monitoring, and control to achieve defined goals in the most efficient way (Koskela and Howell, 2001; Crawford and Pollack, 2004; Spałek,

2016). Governance mechanisms for such projects are well-documented in project management handbooks such as PMBOK, PRINCE2 and others. These approaches adopt a sequential (waterfall) stage-gate methodology, where the output of each phase serves as the input for the next. The phases: project initiation, planning, realization, and closure, are executed in sequential order. During initiation and planning, the project scope, budget, and schedule are carefully defined in detail. In the realization phase, the focus shifts to eliminating or minimizing deviations from the plan.

Projects that are natural candidates for the waterfall approach include most repetitive engineering projects, such as construction, shipbuilding, and infrastructure development. In such projects, the goal (e.g., constructing a specific building at a given location) is clear and tangible, the construction methodology is well-established, and potential issues can be anticipated based on extensive historical data.

Moreover, for certain types of construction projects, the plan-based waterfall approach is the only feasible option due to the physical characteristics of the outcome, which require sequential technological and organizational processes. For instance, many construction projects must be executed in phases that follow a logical order. When building a house, for example, the foundation must be laid first, followed by the walls, and then the roof. The sequential nature of these physical processes means the project must adhere to a waterfall approach, leaving little room for agile prototyping.

The second group of projects consists of those with ill-defined goals but well-defined methods. This group includes information systems/technology projects, where the exact scope is difficult to define, but the methods for developing or configuring software are well-established (Turner and Cochrane, 1993). Agile methods were designed specifically for such projects, enabling outcomes to be gradually achieved through time-boxed iterations (sprints) with active engagement from key stakeholders. Agile approaches assume fixed project duration and budget/resources while maintaining flexibility in the scope (Maranda et al., 2021). By doing so, agile methods address the uncertainty caused by poorly defined scope. This uncertainty is reduced progressively as project outcomes are iteratively developed during sprints, which are immediately reviewed and approved by product owners.

However, it remains questionable whether organizations fully accept the lack of a predefined scope, as the final outcome is often unclear until the project concludes (West, 2011). Whether the project is conducted internally or contracted, the financing party typically expects the scope, budget, and schedule to be defined before kickoff. In such scenario hybrid methods become a viable option. Hybrid methods, such as water-Scrum-fall (West, 2011), offer a compromise between plan-based and agile governance approaches (Jamous et al., 2021). In hybrid methods, the project initiation and planning phases follow waterfall principles, fixing the project's boundary conditions. The realization phase, however, is executed in agile mode, with fixed-duration sprints, each delivering a usable product increment. Finally, project closure reverts to waterfall principles, ensuring comprehensive testing, documentation, and release to production of the final product, rather than handling each sprint outcome separately.

In the above reasoning the fact that an outcome is well-defined (or not well-defined) is treated as an independent variable, based on which the project governance approach is built. At this stage, it is worthwhile to reflect more deeply on the factors that influence the definability of the outcome. These factors can be categorized as intrinsic or extrinsic.

Intrinsic factors are immanently related to the physical nature of the outcome and answer the questions:
- considering its physical nature, can a project outcome be at all defined in detail?
- how much effort and time is needed to define a project outcome in detail considering its physical nature?

For all tangible outcomes the answer to the first question is "yes". Also some intangible outcomes, including software programmes and systems can be defined in detail, providing that there exist a notation which allows for the unambiguous representation of the product features. The answer to the second question depends on the tangibility and complexity of the outcome. It is easier to define a tangible product (than an intangible one) due to the fact that some of its characteristics are constrained by Newtonian physics and due to the fact that in most cases similar objects already exist and are known to the stakeholders. In addition, engineering provides an unambiguous and commonly understood notation for representing technical features of virtually any physical artifact. For both tangible and intangible outcomes, the more complex is the object, the more effort is needed to exactly describe it. For intangible outcomes, besides their level of complexity, also the features of the notation used to represent the outcome and the means of visualization of the outcome contribute to the effort and time needed to define it. For a given outcome, the intrinsic factors determining the level of its definability would be the same.

Extrinsic factors are shaped by the internal and external environment of the project, which implies that these factors may vary between two projects with the same desired outcome. Extrinsic factors answer the following questions:
- does the project outcome have to be described in detail?
- does it make sense to describe the outcome in detail?

– are the project stakeholders capable of describing the project outcome in detail?

The obligation to define the project outcome in detail may result from legal regulations, internal regulations and/or the criticality of the outcome. Criticality of a project outcome refers to the consequences of a breakdown of a project product after it is released to operation. Highest criticality means people's life or health would be in danger in case of a breakdown. Nuclear power plant and its operating systems, operating system of an airplane, a bridge, electronic control unit of the brake system in a car are the examples of critical products. Multimedia system in your car, a video game or your favourite social media system are not. One would expect rigid forecasting, planning, and contingency planning as well more frequent control and revision of the forecasts and plans for the projects with critical outcomes. In many cases external regulatory bodies would also require a certain standard of the project outcome documentation before they issue the release to service.

For projects with outcomes that are non-critical but can be clearly defined, it is reasonable to perform a cost-benefit analysis for the process of defining the detailed project scope. The estimates of effort and time needed to describe the outcome and prepare the detailed project plan should be confronted with the projected benefits of detailed planning.

The two remaining categories of projects are characterized by ill-defined methods, leaving trial-and-error as the only viable approach. Projects with well-defined goals but ill-defined methods aim to achieve specific objectives for the first time. Examples include missions to the Moon or Mars, designing a new class of drugs, or developing a revolutionary medical procedure. These projects rely on trial-and-error and lessons-learned processes, where alternative methods are designed, tested, evaluated, and abandoned until an optimal approach to achieving a desired sub-goal is discovered. Governance mechanisms are required to enable rapid and frequent evaluation of alternative solutions, prioritize those worth pursuing, and discontinue others to minimize wasted resources, budget, and time. However, some degree of resource "waste" is inevitable due to the exploratory nature of such projects and must be accounted for within the governance framework.

In these projects, uncertainty is accepted, and the loss of money, time, and resources on dead ends is considered part of the process. Governance mechanisms should facilitate knowledge exchange, evaluation, accumulation, and codification, ensuring that methods for achieving the desired goal are developed, documented, and formalized as outcomes of the project. Exploratory projects of this kind may also incorporate agile practices to guide the development of tangible results.

Turner and Cochrane (1993) also describe projects with both ill-defined goals and methods, suggesting that such projects often include research and organizational change initiatives. They argue that defining the project goal as early as possible is essential to transform the project into one with well-defined goals and ill-defined methods, enabling appropriate governance. This approach is particularly relevant for organizational change projects.

However, there are at least some projects in which neither goals nor methods are deliberately defined: namely, exploratory research projects. While most research projects fall into one of the three previously mentioned categories (achieving something new with known methods, discovering better methods to achieve a known goal, or testing hypotheses with known methods), some research aims to explore entirely new, uncharted areas.

The governance of such exploratory research projects is relatively simple: allocate a specified amount of money and time to a team of talented individuals and allow them the freedom to work on a broadly defined topic. At the end of the allocated time and budget, the project either delivers a tangible result for further development or is discontinued to avoid further resource expenditure.

The **secondary variable** influencing project governance mechanisms and tools is uncertainty and the company's attitude toward it. Some uncertainty arises from unclear goals and/or methods before the project begins (Williams, 1999), as discussed earlier. Another source of uncertainty is volatility, or the likelihood that well-defined goals may change during the project (Szpitter and Sadkowska, 2016). Additionally, uncertainty stems from unknown future contingencies, both within the project and in its external environment.

In general, uncertainty can be understood as a lack of information about the current and future states of the system's elements, their interactions, and their relationship with the environment (Geraldi et al., 2011). While information about current states and interactions can be obtained (at a cost), future states can only be anticipated, also at a cost. The effort required to predict future states, the methods and tools used to make such predictions, and the approaches to managing contingencies vary across project management approaches. Simply put, managing uncertainty comes with a cost, and this cost differs depending on the chosen approach.

The **waterfall approach** emphasizes detailed planning in the initial stages of the project. If the project scope is well-defined and stable, the methods of achieving outcomes are well-known, and the environment is predictable, planning can be completed upfront with minimal adjustments required later. Even in stable environments, future contingencies, both internal and external, remain unknown, but they are often limited, making it feasible to anticipate and plan for them.

However, when project scope is subject to change or new methods for achieving goals emerge, the number of potential future scenarios can grow exponentially, whether due to internal decisions or external factors. This requires greater effort to anticipate and plan for every possible contingency. Without frequent reviews and adjustments to the initial plan, the project risks delivering outcomes that may no longer be relevant. Despite these challenges, it is still possible to execute volatile projects in turbulent environments using waterfall methods, provided significant resources, effort, and time are allocated to continually revisiting and updating plans. In essence, managing uncertainty using the waterfall approach is feasible but costly.

Agile approaches were developed specifically to address uncertainty and change by reducing upfront planning and enabling rapid adaptation through iterative delivery of partial solutions. Agile methods rely on short-term planning, iterative development, and intensive collaboration among stakeholders in time-boxed iterations (sprints). Agile approaches offer significantly lower costs for managing uncertainty compared to waterfall. However, this cost reduction comes with reduced predictability in the final project outcome, as project scope is not fixed upfront and can change frequently during execution. Controlling such scope changes can be challenging, especially in larger projects.

Some projects, particularly those with intangible goals, multiple solution options, high stakeholder participation, and conflicting stakeholder expectations, face not only uncertainty but also ambiguity. Ambiguity involves multiple and conflicting interpretations, especially regarding project goals (Lech, 2022). Unlike uncertainty, ambiguity cannot be reduced by sharing more information (Atkinson et al., 2006; Thiry, 2002). In the presence of ambiguity, detailed upfront planning becomes unfeasible. The only viable approach is the iterative, gradual development of partial solutions with immediate feedback – an essential feature of agile methods.

The final variable, which may influence the choice of project governance mechanisms and tools to a lesser extent, is project structural complexity. Structural complexity refers to the number of elements in a project and the interdependencies between them (Baccarini, 1996; Williams, 1999). Higher structural complexity increases uncertainty, as well as the cost and effort required to reduce that uncertainty and perform contingency planning. The effort to obtain information about the current and future states of all project elements, as well as the interactions between them, grows with the number of elements and interdependencies.

In some projects, such as critical ones, these costs must be borne. In such cases, project governance frameworks should account for the structural complexity by incorporating mechanisms to model the complexity and perform cycles of planning, controlling, and adjusting.

However, for other projects, such as non-critical ones with intangible outcomes, it may be more advantageous to adopt scaled agile or decentralized project management approaches instead, which can better accommodate complexity while reducing costs.

To summarize, the selection procedure for a governance approach follows this pattern:

1. **Sequential Processes:** If the nature of the outcome necessitates a technological and/or organizational process that is inherently sequential, the waterfall approach is the appropriate choice. Construction projects, for example, are inherently sequential by definition.
2. **Non-Sequential Processes:** If the process does not inherently require a waterfall approach, additional criteria should be considered:
    a. Well-Defined Outcome and Methods: If both the project outcome and methods can be well-defined prior to the project, the choice should be made between waterfall, hybrid, or agile approaches based on the following factors:
        i. If the project or outcome must be defined in detail due to legal or internal regulations and/or is critical, there is a stronger inclination toward waterfall.
        ii. If the project is subject to high levels of uncertainty, the inclination is toward agile or hybrid approaches.
    c. Ill-Defined Outcome: If the project outcome cannot be well-defined prior to the project, the natural choice is agile or hybrid.
    d. Ill-Defined Methods: If the methods for achieving the project outcome are unknown, a trial-and-error, agile-like approach should be adopted. This enables rapid and frequent evaluation of alternative solutions, prioritization of those worth pursuing, and discontinuation of others to minimize wasted resources, budget, and time.

The underlying assumptions and characteristics of each type of governance framework are detailed in the following sections.

2.2.2 *Waterfall Methods*

Waterfall methods is the family of traditional, plan-based, sequential approaches grounded in operations research (Spałek, 2016). These methods assume that the project plan is created upfront, covering the scope, schedule, budget, resources, and risks. Contingency planning is conducted to address anticipated risks. Simultaneously, a project management plan is developed, which includes the governance framework for the project. Project execution is then carried out and monitored against the plan. In the event of deviations, corrective actions are designed and implemented to bring the project back on track.

The advantages of waterfall methods lie in their stability, predictability, and rigor. Since a detailed plan is created before the start of the delivery phase, it is relatively straightforward to determine at any point whether the project is on track or if there are deviations that need to be corrected or addressed. However, this approach requires that both the project outcome and the methods for achieving it are well-defined and remain stable throughout the project execution.

The disadvantages of waterfall methods also stem from their inherent stability, predictability, and rigor. If the project outcome is not clearly defined, cannot be decomposed into detailed components, or changes frequently and/or significantly during execution, waterfall methods become ineffective. In the best-case scenario, adapting plans to accommodate these changes requires substantial effort and expense.

The examples of waterfall management frameworks are Project Management Body of Knowledge (PMBOK 2013, 2017, 2021), PRINCE2 (2009) and PM^2 (2023). Waterfall approach assumes the project is done sequentially, i.e. the phases follow each other. PMBOK (2013, 2017) distinguishes the following project phases:

- Pre-project work;
- Starting the project;
- Organizing and Preparing;
- Carrying out the Work;
- Ending the project.

In addition there are monitoring and controlling processes, which take place in every of the above phases. PRINCE2 (2009) uses stages instead of phases and names them slightly different, i.e.:

- Pre-project
- Initiation stage
- Subsequent delivery stages
- Final delivery stage.

PRINCE2 emphasizes that the project is done in stages and every stage is subject to approval and is followed by go/no-go decision, which means a project may be cancelled after any stage.

The European Union PM^2 Project Management Methodology Guide (PM^2, 2023) uses the following naming convention for the subsequent phases in the project lifecycle:

- Initiating
- Planning
- Executing
- Closing.

An attempt to map the phases/stages is depicted in table 2.

Regardless of the differences in naming conventions, the activities and outcomes of the subsequent phases are largely similar. For simplicity, the PM^2 naming of the phases will be used going forward.

The **Initiation Phase** focuses on establishing a high-level view of the project's benefits, scope, schedule, budget, and risks, as well as identifying the project stakeholders. The key outputs of this phase are the business case and project charter, which include the aforementioned elements. The final outcome of this phase is the authorization (or lack thereof) to start the project.

If the project is authorized, it proceeds to the **Planning Phase**, during which a detailed plan is created, addressing both product-related and project management aspects. The product-related plan (project plan) must specify in detail:

- What the project is supposed to deliver (the scope)
- How the defined scope will be delivered (the activities which constitute the schedule)
- By whom (resources), and
- How much it will cost (the budget).

TABLE 2 Project phases in waterfall methodologies

PMBOK	PRINCE	PM^2	**Basic outcome**
Pre-project Work	Pre-project	Initiating	High level project business case and project charter including expected benefits, scope, schedule, budget, risks and identification of stakeholders
Starting the project Organizing and preparing	Initiation stage	Planning	Project charter/handbook, detailed project plan and project management plan
Carrying out the Work	Subsequent delivery phases	Executing	Delivery of project outcomes according to the schedule
Completing the project	Final delivery stage	Closing	Delivery of the project final outcome

Therefore, at minimum, the following planning activities must be performed and documented:

- The project scope is detailed and described in the form of the work breakdown structure (WBS) – i.e. the "a hierarchical decomposition of the total scope of work" (PMBOK, 2017, p. 157). At the lowest level of WBS there are work packages – the smallest observable semi-products or outcomes for which a state of done/not-done can be established;
- The project schedule is decomposed into activities – i.e. "specific actions to be performed to produce the project deliverables" (PMBOK, 2017, p. 173). Activities are assigned to work packages on the n:1 basis – a work package can have one or more activities assigned to it, an activity should be assigned to one work package. The duration of the activities is estimated and resource demand is determined. Activities are then sequenced, i.e. connected to each other with the technological and resource constraints in mind; and represented on a timeline so that a detailed schedule is created;
- The resource plan is created so that human and non-human resources are identified and assigned to each of the activities on the timeline;
- A procurement plan is made so that purchase of resources and materials for every activity in every work package is planned on a timeline, and a supplier is identified;
- Budget and cash flow plan is prepared to secure the financials for the above.

The specifics of the plans mentioned above largely depend on the type of project outcome and the technology involved in creating that outcome. Certain domains have established their own standards and procedures for representing scope, activities, and other relevant aspects (e.g., construction, shipbuilding, and software engineering have domain-specific methods for defining requirements). Project management frameworks such as PMBOK and PRINCE2 are designed to be generic. They do not address these domain-specific processes but instead provide general guidance on the areas that a project manager should address. Additionally, a project management plan must be developed, which includes procedures for managing all aspects of the project (PMBOK, 2017; PRINCE2, 2009):

- benefits,
- scope;
- change (change of the scope/requirements during the project and organizational change needed to accomplish the project);
- schedule;
- costs/budget;
- quality;
- resources;
- communications;

- risk;
- issues;
- procurement;
- stakeholder relations/engagement;
- integration – i.e. assuring that the above aspects are aligned with each other and form a consistent framework.

A project management plan serves as a detailed exemplification of the project governance in a specific project. Project management frameworks provide only a general overview of the areas that should be addressed and how they might be handled. The specific processes, methods, procedures, and tools must either be adapted from the organization's existing project governance framework or developed specifically for the project at hand.

Once the project plan and the project management plan are approved, the project moves into the **Execution** phase. In this phase, the actual work is performed to achieve the project outcome. The project manager's role during execution is to organize and direct the work, monitor progress, and manage risks and issues to ensure that any deviations from the plan are addressed promptly with corrective actions to realign the project.

Key project management activities during the execution phase include:

- Acquiring and developing the project team,
- Conducting procurement activities,
- Monitoring and controlling project status,
- Identifying and managing changes in project scope,
- Recognizing and addressing issues and risks,
- Designing and implementing corrective actions to mitigate risks and resolve issues,
- Managing and controlling project communications, and
- Overseeing and facilitating stakeholder engagement (PMBOK, 2017; PRINCE2, 2009; PM^2, 2023).

The **Project Closing** phase involves pre go-live activities, such as testing and preparation for productive start, go-live activities, leading to the productive launch of the project outcome, as well as activities related to project formal closure: formal sign-off procedure, transfer and sign-off of related project documentation, settlement of all due payments, gathering of lessons learned.

In summary, all waterfall methods follow the same principle: first plan, then execute according to that plan. Project management focuses on preparing the plan, monitoring progress against it, and implementing corrective actions for deviations (issues) or anticipated risks. The strength of waterfall methods lies in their structured, controllable environment for delivering a predefined outcome. However, this requires the outcome to be well-defined before the project starts, allowing for detailed scope decomposition, activity sequencing, resource allocation, and budgeting.

While waterfall methods excel in projects with well-established, stable scopes and minimal changes, such as construction projects, where sequential workflows and detailed blueprints are essential, they are less suited for projects with undefined or frequently changing outcomes. The high effort required for upfront planning and costly re-planning makes them impractical for many projects, particularly those with intangible or evolving deliverables.

2.2.3 *Agile Methods*

For projects with intangible outcomes, it is more difficult to visualize and describe the expected scope in detail, which can lead to ambiguities during execution. Another often-overlooked aspect of such projects is that they lack physical barriers to scope changes later on, which makes such changes mentally more acceptable for the decision-makers. For example, once a building or road is constructed, nobody would argue that moving it to a new location is costly and difficult. This is not always the case with software development, where changes to existing code can also be challenging and expensive.

Because intangible outcomes are difficult to visualize, describe in detail, and fix, many projects aiming to deliver such outcomes have been (and still are) subject to scope changes during the later stages, such as during the delivery phase or even at project closure. For projects using waterfall methodologies, this has caused significant problems, as there is often a long gap between the planning phase, when requirements are defined and documented, and the execution phase, when the requirements are realized in the form of a product (typically in the late execution or early closure phases). This means that if there is ambiguity in understanding the requirements, it may only be clarified very late, after most of the effort has already been expended. Additionally, during this lengthy period, requirements may change due to shifts in the project environment or other factors. In any of these situations, adjusting the outcome to meet the new requirements requires considerable effort. Furthermore, processing changes within the rigid waterfall governance framework demands significant effort from project managers.

A highly represented group of projects with intangible outcomes includes software development and information systems projects. It is no surprise that an alternative family of project management methods originated in this context. These are agile methods, which aim to address the problems mentioned above by incrementally and collaboratively producing project outcomes in time-boxed iterations.

Unlike waterfall approaches, where the scope is planned in detail and fixed before project delivery begins, agile methods fix time and resources, while the scope is only estimated and may change during the project if needed to deliver value to the customer (AgilePM, 2014, p.17). This point is often not emphasized enough: in agile methods, the scope is expressed in general terms, not specified in detail before the project, and may change during execution. Time and resources, however, are fixed. This means the project may not deliver all the requirements outlined in the general scope statement, and that is perfectly acceptable. Quotes from well-established agile sources that support this statement are presented in table 3.

TABLE 3 Quotes on the definition of scope in agile

Source	Source organization	Link	Quote
Agile Manifesto	Agilemanifesto.org	http://agilemanifesto.org/principles.html	Welcome changing requirements, even late in development. Agile processes harness change for the customer's competitive advantage.
Aljaber T. (2023)	Atlassian	https://www.atlassian.com/agile/agile-at-scale/agile-iron-triangle	Unlike waterfall development, agile projects have a fixed schedule and resources while the scope varies. While the scope of a project might change in agile development, teams commit to fixed iterations of work: sprints if you're using a scrum framework and WIP limits if you're using a kanban framework. However, agile focuses on high-level requirements rather than trying to come with deep and detailed requirements upfront. The scope of a project gets regularly managed and groomed (prioritized) by the product manager ...

TABLE 3 Quotes on the definition of scope in agile (*cont.*)

Source	Source organization	Link	Quote
Sliger (2010)	Project Management Institute (PMI)	https://www.pmi.org/learning/library/project-scope-creep-agile-methodologies-6552	In the traditional method of defining scope, a bottom-up approach was used that defined scope in a very granular detail, at the very beginning of the project, before any development work was started. The resulting definition of the detailed requirements was then set or "fixed," and project managers estimated resources and time based on the collection of fixed requirements. Agile flipped the triangle on its head. **Instead of fixing the requirements, they chose, instead, to fix things that were more well-known and less likely to change: resources and time. Features that would make it into production were then estimated based on these constraints. Because it is possible for either time or money to run out before all features are completed, agilists had to focus on completing the most important features first.** Thus, rather than being plan-driven, agile is a value-driven approach to product development.
Schwaber & Sutherland (2020)	Scrum Guide™	https://scrumguides.org/scrum-guide.html	The Product Backlog is **an emergent**, ordered list of what is needed to improve the product.

TABLE 3 Quotes on the definition of scope in agile (*cont.*)

Source	Source organization	Link	Quote
DSDM Agile Project Framework Handbook (2014)	Agile Business Consortium	https://www.agilebusiness.org/dsdm-project-framework/philosophy-fundamentals.html	DSDM's approach to managing the project fixes time, cost and quality at the end of the Foundations phase while contingency is managed by varying the features (the requirements) to be delivered.

Although various agile methods differ in their details, they all operate according to the same fundamental rules, which are derived from the principles outlined in the Agile Manifesto (2001):

- The scope is expressed in general terms, is not fixed, and may change during the project.
- Delivery is executed in fixed time-boxes, which last from one to four weeks.
- Agile teams are small (up to ten people), cross-functional (including all members necessary to deliver the outcome), and self-organizing.
- Project work relies on constant, synchronous cooperation and personal communication among members of the agile team. The client representative is part of the agile team and must participate in the project work on a daily basis.
- Items to be developed during a given time-box are selected by the project team and must be finalized within that time-box.
- Every time-box includes the complete development life cycle, which involves detailed analysis of the requirements, design, development, testing, sign-off, and release to production (optional in some frameworks).
- Every time-box concludes with the delivery of working functionality.

The most popular agile method, often equated with agile as a whole, is Scrum. It is described comprehensively and in simple terms by its authors in Schwaber and Sutherland (2020). The best approach to familiarize oneself with Scrum, is to consult this source. However, it may be beneficial to review how the agile principles are exemplified in Scrum.

The scope of a project in Scrum is defined at a high level in the form of the product goal and the product backlog. The product goal is a general statement describing the desired outcome of the project. The product backlog is a list of features that need to be developed to fulfill the product goal.

Work in Scrum is carried out in fixed-length events called sprints. Every sprint must deliver one or more increments, i.e., a usable set of features that meet the definition of done. The definition of done is a "formal description of the state of the increment when it meets the quality measures required for the product" (Schwaber and Sutherland, 2020).

Before each sprint, the project team conducts sprint planning. During sprint planning, the team selects features from the product backlog to be delivered in the current sprint. These items form the sprint backlog, which is a subset of the product backlog specifically targeted for delivery in the sprint. Once planning is complete, the team begins working on delivering the features from the sprint backlog. The requirements for the features are detailed and refined as needed, and the product backlog may be updated with new information.

During the sprint, progress is monitored, and team coordination is ensured through daily Scrum. The daily Scrum is a 15-minute event held every day, whose purpose is "to inspect progress toward the sprint goal and adapt the sprint backlog as necessary, adjusting the upcoming planned work" (Schwaber and Sutherland, 2020).

Each sprint concludes with a sprint review, which is a meeting of the Scrum team and project stakeholders to inspect the results of the sprint, sign them off, update and adjust the product backlog, and outline the plan for the future. Every sprint must deliver at least one increment – a working piece of a solution that meets the definition of done.

Another meeting at the end of each sprint is the sprint retrospective, during which the Scrum team discusses potential improvements in the organization of work based on the experiences of the previous sprint. Sprints are repeated until the planned time and/or budget is exhausted.

The Scrum team consists of only three roles: the product owner, developers, and the Scrum master. The product owner is responsible for defining the product requirements, creating the product backlog, communicating requirements to the rest of the team, testing, and signing off on delivered functionality. (S)he acts as the client representative within the Scrum team. Scrum explicitly states that the product owner must be a single person, not several people or a committee (Schwaber and Sutherland, 2020). The relationship between the product owner and other client company representatives is described as follows: "The product owner may represent the needs of many stakeholders in the product backlog. Those wanting to change the product backlog can do so by trying to convince the product owner" (Schwaber and Sutherland, 2020).

Developers are the individuals responsible for delivering functionality that fulfills the requirements specified by the product owner in the product backlog. Scrum assumes that developers self-organize their work. They select items from the product backlog to include in the sprint backlog and distribute the work among themselves.

The final role is the Scrum master, who is not equivalent to a project manager. According to Scrum, the team is self-managing. As such, the Scrum master does not assign work to developers or issue commands regarding their tasks. Instead, the Scrum master's role is to:

- Coach the team members in self-management and cross-functionality
- Remove obstacles and challenges faced by the team
- Assist the product owner in managing the product backlog
- Facilitate the team's work (Schwaber and Sutherland, 2020).

To function effectively, a Scrum team must be small, typically ten people or fewer, to enable self-organization and coordination using only the sprint backlog and daily scrums (Schwaber and Sutherland, 2020). As the Scrum Guide states: "Scrum is simple." This simplicity is both an advantage, likely contributing to its popularity, as it is easy to understand and implement, and a disadvantage, as it may not always accommodate the complexity of certain projects, environments, or corporate ecosystems.

Not every team is capable of self-organizing, even with the guidance of a mentoring Scrum master. Additionally, it is not always feasible to designate a single person as the product owner who possesses all the knowledge required to formulate the product backlog (although the Scrum Guide acknowledges that the product owner may involve other people). It can also be challenging to meet the condition that "for product owners to succeed, the entire organization must respect their decisions" (Schwaber and Sutherland, 2020).

In more complex situations, it may be necessary to modify some of the Scrum's assumptions to adapt its simple governance framework to the specific circumstances. Nevertheless, Scrum remains an attractive and valuable agile methodology. Many concepts derived from Scrum, such as daily meetings, sprints, and backlogs, are widely adopted by organizations worldwide, even when they do not strictly adhere to the core Scrum principles.

Another popular agile methodology, which accounts for some of the complexities missing in Scrum is DSDM Agile Project Framework (DSDM, 2014; AgilePM, 2014). In general, DSDM just like Scrum follows a set of basic principles derived from the Agile Manifesto:

- time, cost and quality are fixed while the scope may change during the project,
- the scope is defined only at a high-level at the beginning of the project,
- the work is done iteratively in fixed time-boxes, lasting from two to four weeks,

- each of the time-boxes ends with a completion of a verifiable deliverable,
- the work involves continuous cooperation and communication between the team members,
- during the time-box the work is coordinated and progress is inspected with the use of the daily stand-up.

The difference is that DSDM provides more structure and complexity in comparison to Scrum. The project has phases: Pre-project, Feasibility, Foundations, Evolutionary Development, Deployment and Post-Project. The scope is defined at a high-level at the end of the Foundations phase and although a change to the scope after this phase is not strictly forbidden, it "needs to be formally controlled in order to ensure ongoing alignment with the business vision for the project and to keep control of the scope" (DSDM, 2014). There is more emphasis on planning, as besides the Timebox Plan, which covers the activities of one time-box, a Delivery Plan is also prepared to cover the high-level activities for the whole duration of a project. The project is led by the project manager, who "coordinates all aspects of management of the project at a high level but, in line with the DSDM concept of empowerment, the Project Manager is expected to leave the detailed planning of the actual delivery of the product(s) to the members of the Solution Development Team" (AgilePM, 2014). There are more roles in the team, some with slightly pompous names, like "business visionary" or "business ambassador". However, what makes a difference is not a number of roles but the fact DSDM acknowledges that:

- there are business, technical and management roles on the project level, which coordinate the work of development team(s);
- although the team members are empowered, there exists a project manager role with the responsibility to coordinate and control work;
- there is a business analyst role, responsible for filling the culture gap between the business and technical team members;
- except from the main business role in the development team (the business ambassador), there is a business advisor role, responsible for providing information on the requirements.

The spectrum of agile methods is not limited to Scrum and DSDM, but these two methods give a good insight into the span of this spectrum. In both cases the authors encourage the users of the methods to adjust them to their needs, so one can blend their own agile approach by adding or eliminating some of the artifacts, roles or activities, providing that the core principles are kept.

One of these principles is that agile teams are small (up to ten people) so that they can cooperate instantly and align their work without sophisticated, hierarchical coordination mechanisms. The issue arises when agile is to be used for a project which involves more people. The natural solution is to form

several agile teams, each of them consisting of up to ten people. However, if a project involves more than one agile team, the problem of coordination between the teams arises. Adjusting agile methodology so that it can be used in large and/or complex projects is called scaling agile. In particular, scaling agile takes place for projects which meet one or more of the following criteria:
- are too large or too complex for one agile team to accomplish,
- take place in complex organizational or legal environment,
- involve geographically dispersed or legally dispersed teams (Ambler and Lines, 2011).

While Scrum is by definition dedicated to one agile team, DSDM is scalable, as it foresees business, technical and management roles on the project level which may be used to coordinate the work of more than one agile team.

There are, however, methodologies that focus exclusively on scaling agile. The two examples are Scrum@Scale® (Sutherland, 2022) and Scaled Agile Framework (SAFe, 2023). Scrum@Scale® is a simple, linear propagation of Scrum methodology to more than one team. For up to five teams the idea is that the scrum masters and product owners of all these teams work together in the so-called Scrum of Scrums, using the same procedures and artifacts as a single team is using: product backlog, sprint backlog, daily scrum, sprint review and sprint retrospective, only on the aggregated level for all the teams involved. For more than five teams the same repeats one level up, so the Scrum of Scrums of Scrums is put in place. In addition, the higher-level equivalent of scrum master and product owner are introduced: scrum of scrums master, and chief product owner, whose role is to coordinate the work of the teams. The approach presented in Scrum@Scale® is tempting due to its simplicity, and it may work well for medium-sized projects: up to the five teams, as prescribed by Scrum@Scale® on the first level of scalability. However the efficacy of linear scaling of the method to much larger number of teams is dubious (Rolland et al., 2016; Joskowski and Marcinkowski, 2023).

Scaled Agile Framework (SAFe) is on the other side of the spectrum of the scaling agile frameworks, as it is considered to be relatively complex, yet well-documented (Kowalczyk et al., 2022). First of all, SAFe offers four options, tailored to different sizes of the agile undertaking (SAFe, 2023):
- essential – for delivery of a single product,
- large solution – for delivery of a larger solution, comprising of several interconnected products,
- portfolio – for several parallel projects managed as portfolio on a company level,
- and full – for several large solutions managed as portfolio on a company level.

As this book is about projects, the most suitable SAFe versions to be described here are essential and large solution versions.

The Essential version of SAFe consists of two layers: Agile Team and Agile Product Delivery. The Agile Team in SAFe primarily follows the Scrum approach, though Kanban is acknowledged as an alternative or complementary method. The team is small, self-organizing, and self-managing, consisting of a Product Owner, Scrum Master, and Developers. It is responsible for exploring, defining, building, testing, and deploying functionalities from the team backlog within fixed, two-week time boxes called iterations (instead of sprints in Scrum). Work is coordinated and controlled through daily team meetings, referred to as Team Sync (instead of the Daily Scrum). Each iteration concludes with two key events:

- Iteration Review, during which the results of the increment are reviewed and signed off.
- Iteration Retrospective, where suggestions for improvement are considered.

As all of the above aligns closely with Scrum (aside from naming conventions), the Agile Product Delivery layer and its interactions with the Agile Team layer are where SAFe introduces notable differences. The two central constructs of this layer are:

- Agile Release Train (ART)
- Planning Interval (PI) (in some sources, PI stands for Program Increment).

The Agile Release Train (ART) is described as “a long-lived team of Agile Teams that incrementally develops, delivers, and often operates one or more solutions” (SAFe, 2023). It is a cross-functional, virtual organization of 50 to 125 people, grouped into Agile Teams, that plans, commits, develops, and deploys together (SAFe, 2023).

The ART has its own backlog, which is decomposed into the teams’ backlogs. It operates in time-boxed cycles called Planning Intervals (PIs), which are typically 8–12 weeks long and consist of four development iterations. Each PI is preceded by PI Planning, a critical, face-to-face meeting of all ART members. During this event, the Agile Teams plan, coordinate, align, and refine their backlogs for the upcoming Planning Interval. As the SAFe official site states:

“PI planning is essential to SAFe: If you are not doing it, you are not doing SAFe” (SAFe, 2023). Thus, the Agile Release Train is a higher-level organizational construct that coordinates the work of multiple Agile Teams to achieve a common goal. It functions through Planning Intervals, which include four iterations (sprints), all planned during the PI Planning event.

The Agile Product Delivery layer also introduces the following additional roles:

- Business Owners,
- System Architect,
- Product Management (a higher-level Product Owner),
- Release Train Engineer (a higher-level Scrum Master).

In the SAFe version for Large Solutions, the Enterprise Solution Delivery layer is added. This layer integrates multiple Agile Release Trains into a Solution Train, with its own: Solution Train Backlog, Solution Management, Solution Architect and Solution Train Engineer. The full version of SAFe introduces two additional layers: Lean Portfolio Management and Organizational Agility.

In summary, SAFe is a formalized framework that introduces a significant number of roles, procedures, routines, and artifacts to structure Agile work across teams and organizational layers.

There are, of course, more agile scaling frameworks than the two mentioned above. A comprehensive summary of the most common frameworks can be found in Almeida and Espinheira (2021). In general, their role is to coordinate the work of multiple agile teams in such a way that they work towards the desired goal without killing agility in the process.

In summary, agile methods favour personal interaction and iterative, incremental delivery of partial solutions over up-front detailed planning. The scope in agile project is planned only in general terms and may change as the project proceeds. The strength of agile methods lies in the incremental delivery of partial solutions in fixed time-boxes, which allows for fast verification if the outcome meets the requirements and quick implementation of corrective actions if it does not. Agile methods reduce the planning effort, as they are based on "hands-on", short, complete: analyse – design – develop – test – approve – deploy cycles within a time-box. The weakness of agile methods comes from the fact that the scope is not determined in much detail a-priori, which makes it difficult to formulate a contract (internal or external) for an agile project as well as to formally assess if the project has met its goals. It could be a problem for many big, hierarchical and formalized companies which have governance rules for funding and signing-off the projects that require the exact definition of the project goal, determination of activities and resources necessary to achieve this goal, and budget estimation (West, 2011). Also, if the changes to the scope are not introduced in a thoughtful and disciplined way, the project may well go off-the rails and not deliver anything meaningful at the end of the planned time interval.

Agile methods are a fit for exploratory projects and for projects with ill-defined scope. The natural candidate for agile approach are software development projects, from which the idea of agile has actually started. Other types of projects with non-tangible outcome also could benefit from agile approach. The projects with tangible outcome would rather be delivered with the use of waterfall methods, with the exception of exploratory projects, which welcome the trial and error, agile-like, development.

2.2.4 *Hybrid Methods*

Several studies suggest that although agile methodologies have gained extreme popularity, they are rarely adopted in their book version (Gemino et al. 2021; Špundak, 2014, Serrador and Pinto, 2015; West, 2011). Gemino et al. (2021) identified 14,9% of the 477 projects they studied as purely agile, while Serrador and Pinto (2015) found only 6% of 1386 projects to be completely or nearly completely agile. At the same time, many of the projects in the above mentioned studies (65% in Serrador and Pinto, 2015; 50% in Gemino et al., 2021) were using some agile practices (e.g. working in time-boxes, using product and sprint back-logs, doing daily meetings).

The approach which combines agile and plan-driven practices is called hybrid or hybrid agile (Kuhrmann et al., 2017). Kuhrmann et al. (2017) define hybrid approach as "any combination of agile and traditional (plan driven or rich) approaches than an organizational unit adopts and customizes to its own context needs". Gemino et al. (2021) have a similar view as they state that "at its most general level, a hybrid project management approach combines methodologies and practices from more than one project management approach". Two questions arise:

1. Why do companies and project teams introduce hybrid project management instead or using pure agile or pure waterfall to managing their software (and the like) projects?
2. What "any combination of agile and plan-driven" means or, more specifically, what combination of plan-driven and agile approaches makes sense for managing projects?

First of all, software companies and teams attempt to move from pure waterfall to agile as agile has proven to deliver better results in terms of stakeholder satisfaction (Serrador and Pinto, 2015; Gemino et al. 2021). What is interesting, Gemino et al. (2021) did not find any difference between agile and waterfall approaches regarding scope, budget, and schedule project success measures. The only advantage of agile over waterfall regarded stakeholder satisfaction, meaning that the agile approach ensures better alignment of the project outcome with the stakeholders' requirements.

On the other hand, in many organizations, applying the 'book version' of agile, i.e. strictly adhering to all principles from the Agile Manifesto, is infeasible due to several factors. These include (Gemino et al. 2021; West, 2011):

- Companies have governance rules for making any investment, which require a plan including detailed scope, schedule, and budget prior to the investment decision.
- Governance rules for signing-off a project require the comparison of the final outcome and budget with the planned outcome and budget.
- Robust documentation is required due to governance and/or compliance requirements.
- People are accustomed to asynchronous work: for example, those who set the requirements do not want to participate in the design and development, and design is often done by a different team than development.
- Some teams are unable to self-manage themselves and require a manager to coordinate and streamline the work.
- Releases to production are infrequent due to the high complexity of the IT architecture and related risks.

The basic point here is that companies heavily rely on plans. As Winter (2011) states: "Governance rules require many organizations to define requirements and plans before starting work. In some companies, these plans form the basis of a contract between the business and IT that defines project direction, timeline, and budget." Regardless of whether it's an internal contract with their own IT department or a legal contract with an external supplier, managers signing a contract want the subject and terms clearly defined. Companies and their managers want to have the plan upfront so that they know what to expect and can track the project's progress against that plan.

Furthermore, in many companies releases to production are infrequent, often requiring extensive regression testing and a period of hypercare. These releases can also be quite risky. Hybrid methods emerged to address this conflict between the managers' need for a contract-based and plan-based, disciplined, and controlled approach, and the development teams' desire for flexibility, responsiveness to change, and speed (Kuhrmann et al., 2017).

Although the specific blend of waterfall and agile practices can vary, the general structure of hybrid methods often resembles the water-scrum-fall model (West, 2011; Schlauderer, 2015). As the name suggests, the initial and final phases of the project are managed using a waterfall approach, while the execution phase utilizes agile principles. The project commences with requirements analysis, specification, scheduling, and budget estimation. Once the scope, schedule, and budget are established, the agile team(s) is/are formed and they proceed with the agile approach during execution. They work in fixed time-boxes (sprints) during which they select items from the product backlog, analyze them, design, develop, test, and deliver an increment of the solution. Deployment to production, including final testing, regression testing, release, and hypercare, typically follows a more rigid, waterfall-like approach, often occurring infrequently.

In water-scrum-fall, the overall scope cannot be freely altered during the project (it is subject to waterfall change management procedures). However, since detailed requirements analysis occurs within the sprints, the initial scope definition can (and should) be relatively high-level. This prevents the team from harmful overplanning, which can lead to inflexibility and decreased responsiveness to changing needs. As Serrador and Pinto (2015) note: "Serrador and Turner (2013) found an "inverted U" relationship between planning and project success; in terms of the effort (time) taken to plan comprehensively. That is, they found that too much effort and time spent planning can have just as negative impact on project success just as can as too little."

In water-scrum-fall, teams do not have the authority to modify the high-level scope. However, they have the freedom to shape their work within the sprints, collaboratively detail requirements, design the appropriate solution, and implement it. In essence, the 'what' of the project remains largely fixed, while the 'how' – the specific approach and implementation details – is determined by the agile team within the defined scope.

In many cases, the specific set of practices is chosen ad hoc by the project team to best fit the particular situation in the project (Kuhrmann et al., 2017). Water-scrum-fall is not the only hybrid agile project management method. A brief description of other methods can be found in Jamous et al. (2021).

2.2.5 *Basic Non-Contractual Governance Mechanisms*

As mentioned earlier, the primary objective of project governance and project management, regardless of the contractual setup within the project, is to ensure a coordinated effort of all resources towards the project's goal. The governance framework should include mechanisms that project management can use operationally during the project to ensure this coordination. The range of governance mechanisms varies significantly depending on the project management approach (waterfall, agile, or hybrid), specific project management methodologies, and domain-specific standards and procedures. However, it makes sense to define at least a minimal common set of governance mechanisms for both waterfall and agile approaches, as hybrid projects will incorporate elements of both.

2.2.5.1 Governance Mechanisms in Waterfall Approaches

1. The Plan

The project plan serves as the central governance mechanism in waterfall methodologies. The project outcome is broken down through a work breakdown structure (WBS) into work packages. Activities necessary to achieve each work package are assigned accordingly. Resources capable of executing these activities are also allocated. The duration of activities and dependencies between them are identified to create a project schedule. Once communicated to project participants, this plan becomes a valuable coordination mechanism by defining roles, tasks, and timelines.

2. Project organization and roles

Behind every governance mechanism, there must be people who make it happen. Every project requires a structure and roles with appropriate personnel assigned to them. Different project management methodologies define various sets of governance and management roles, but common elements include:

- Steering Committee/Project Board: This is the highest-level organizational element in a project, comprising C-level executives from the sponsoring organization and the supplier(s). Its duties include approving stage gates of the project (i.e., authorizing the project to move from one phase to the next) and resolving critical issues that cannot be resolved at lower levels of the project hierarchy.
- Project Management: The role of Project Management is to manage the project on a daily basis, which involves planning, organizing, coordinating, directing, and controlling project resources and activities. Project Management is accountable for delivering the project outcomes of agreed quality within the constraints of time, budget, and resources. Depending on the contractual setup of the project, Project Management may comprise one or several people, which will be discussed further in the subsequent chapters.
- Delivery Management/Team Leads: These are domain experts responsible for delivering project outcomes in their specific fields. They lead field teams and report to Project Management on task status, risks, and issues. They collaborate with other delivery managers/team leads to coordinate activities across teams to achieve project goals.
- Delivery Teams: These are the people who actually get the job done. The structure of the Delivery Teams depends much on the project domain and its technical requirements.
- Project Management Office (PMO): The PMO is a specialized element of the organizational structure responsible for establishing project governance standards and ensuring compliance within projects. PMOs are typically found in companies that frequently execute projects: either project-oriented firms delivering outputs as projects to customers or large corporations where the volume of internal projects justifies the investment in an internal PMO.

3. Domain-specific processes, procedures and roles

A project also, or rather most of all, requires domain-specific processes, procedures, and roles. Processes and procedures dictate how the project's outcome will be delivered, while the structure determines who will deliver it, and roles map the processes to the elements of the project structure. Together, these elements constitute the domain-specific part of the project methodology. Although it is tautological, it's still worth emphasizing that domain-specific methodology is intricately linked to the project's domain and the technological specifics of the delivery process. For instance, the process of building a ship differs from constructing a highway, which in turn differs from bringing a new drug to market. The ability to deliver a specific output is a key reason why projects or their components are often outsourced rather than developed in-house, a topic that will be explored further in the subsequent chapters.

4. Information systems and communication mechanisms

To make progress toward the project goal in a coordinated manner, all participants must be informed about:

- The desired state of the outcomes, related activities, and interrelations between them at any given moment – known as the project plan.
- The current state of the outcomes, related activities, and interrelations at any given moment.

Firstly, project participants need to understand their expected responsibilities within a specific timeframe, so the project plan must be effectively communicated within the project organization. Secondly, the Project Management team requires up-to-date information about the project's current state to implement control and corrective measures in case of deviations from the plan. Additionally, delivery teams should be informed about the planned and actual outcomes and activities of other teams in real-time to enable them to plan and adjust their actions accordingly.

Therefore, a project information system is necessary, comprising at least:

- An up-to-date high-level status of the project plan's realization, including the current status of project scope, schedule, and resource consumption.
- Low-level project status information tools, such as a RAID log (Risk, Actions, Issues, Decisions), updated during and between status meetings. "RAID" can also stand for risks, assumptions, issues, and dependencies, though I personally prefer the former. Regardless of the naming convention, project management requires a tool that enables dynamic tracking of:
  - Actions/activities/tasks: tasks to be completed by specific deadlines, assigned resources, and responsible individuals. The core set of activities is derived directly from the project schedule, with additional tasks arising

from status checks that identify risks or issues needing mitigation. Decisions are considered a subtype of actions, so a separate category in the RAID log may not be necessary.
- Issues/problems: deviations from the project plan requiring corrective actions.
- Risks: potential future issues/problems that can be mitigated preemptively through appropriate corrective actions.

The RAID log (or equivalent) serves as the fundamental tool for continuous coordinating, directing, and controlling project work on a daily basis. It should be reviewed daily by project management and updated in real-time by the project team. There are numerous IT-supported project management information systems available on the market that can fulfill this purpose effectively.

Some methodologies recommend using separate logs for issues/problems and risks. As mentioned earlier, a problem refers to a situation that has already caused a deviation from the plan and requires correction (rather than changing the plan, although changing the plan may also be a valid reaction in certain situations), whereas a risk is a potential future problem.

It is common practice to assign impact rankings (ranging from 1 to 3, 1 to 5, or 1 to 7) to both problems and risks, indicating the severity of their impact on a project. Additionally, a subjective probability ranking is assigned to risks to assess the likelihood of their occurrence. The graphical representation of risks on a two-axis diagram, with impact on one axis and probability on the other, is known as a risk matrix.

Apart from this, the subsequent procedures for managing risks and problems are generally similar. Therefore, one should evaluate the advantages of consolidating all items requiring attention in one place versus maintaining separate logs.

A project also requires well-designed and executed communication mechanisms throughout its duration. These should include, at a minimum:
- Contact list: A comprehensive list detailing roles and responsibilities to ensure clarity on who to contact in specific situations.
- Communication procedures and tools: Defined protocols outlining reporting lines, methods, and circumstances for communication, as well as technical tools used to communicate.
- Status meetings: Regular gatherings of the project team (or its representatives) to discuss the current project status, issues, risks, mitigation efforts, and any topics requiring coordination or integration between multiple project teams.

The last component involves documentation procedures and standards, which specify how communication outcomes are documented and where these documents are stored and in what format. The standard approach is to use a project repository for storing the project documentation.

It is worth noting that communication breakdown among project stakeholders is considered one of the primary factors contributing to project failure, particularly in projects with ill-defined or changing scopes, such as IT projects (Kappelman et al., 2006; Karlsen, 2002; Lech, 2016). Therefore, identifying and addressing communication problems should be among the top priorities for project managers during both the planning and execution phases of a project.

5. Control mechanisms

There must be control mechanisms that facilitate comparison between the actual project state and the planned state to promptly identify any deviations and implement corrective actions. The range of control mechanisms varies depending on the project's nature and includes:

- Physical inspections of the project site for projects with tangible outcomes.
- Status meetings of the project team, during which members report on progress versus the plan, identify potential risks and issues, plan corrective actions, and verify current status.
- Asynchronous status reporting through status reports or updates to project information systems (including the RAID log) made asynchronously by project participants.
- Regular review of the RAID log, ideally conducted no less frequently than during every status meeting.
- Participant observation of project work: Participant observation is a valuable, albeit less frequently mentioned, control mechanism involving monitoring project progress through on-site presence. It offers several advantages. Firstly, it makes shirking and other forms of opportunistic behavior by project team members difficult to conceal. Additionally, it enables the project manager to identify risks and problems that might otherwise go unreported, either because team members did not notice them or because they intended to conceal them for various reasons.

6. Procedures for problem-solving and corrective actions

The information and control mechanisms, if well implemented, facilitate the prompt identification of problems (issues) and risks (potential future problems). This should be followed by appropriate procedures aimed at resolving identified issues and mitigating risks. In terms of issue/risk solving and change management, there are numerous problem-solving methods and procedures discussed in the literature. Personally, I favor the simplest ones, such as the

ideal problem solver (Bransford and Stein, 1984 as cited in Jonassen, 2000), which consists of the following steps:
- Identifying the problems;
- Defining and representing the problem;
- Exploring possible strategies for resolving a problem;
- Acting on a selected strategy;
- Looking back and evaluating the effects of the activities.

Similar approach is prescribed by the American Society for Quality (ASQ, 2024):
- Define the problem;
- Generate alternative solutions;
- Evaluate and select an alternative;
- Implement and follow up on the solution.

Of course, the governance procedure must detail on these steps. As it was already mentioned, a RAID log or its alternative could be a tool for managing the risk/issue solving process. As it was mentioned earlier, the procedure of mitigating risks and problems is basically the same.

The ultimate authority for problem-solving within the project organization is the Steering Committee. Issues that cannot be resolved through standard procedures are escalated to the Steering Committee. Typically, these are problems that necessitate decisions affecting one or more project parameters, such as scope, schedule, or budget. If the Steering Committee is unable to reach a consensus on a problem, resolution may require involvement of external authorities, such as legal courts.

2.2.5.2 "Governance" Mechanisms in Agile Approaches

Agile approaches to project delivery prioritize "individuals and interactions over processes and tools", "customer collaboration over contract negotiation", and "responding to change over following a plan" (Agile Manifesto, 2001). As a result, discussing governance mechanisms in an agile context might seem paradoxical. However, agile methodologies must (and indeed they do) provide ways to coordinate team efforts toward achieving the desired goals.

1. **Interpersonal cooperation and face-to-face communication**
   The primary method of coordination and communication in agile methodologies is through interpersonal cooperation. Agile teams are designed to be small enough to facilitate direct face-to-face communication among all members. Ideally, agile teams work together synchronously in the same physical location, enabling efficient information exchange, decision-making, coordination, and synchronization of activities through direct conversations among team members.

2. **Planning of work – product backlog, sprint planning and sprint backlog**
The scope of an agile project is generally defined in the product backlog, which contains high-level descriptions of the project's features or deliverables. Each time-boxed iteration (sprint) begins with a sprint planning session, during which the team selects items from the product backlog to be delivered within that sprint. These selected items form the sprint backlog.
3. **Controlling of progress – daily meetings, kanban board, sprint review and definition of done**
During a sprint, the agile team selects items from the sprint backlog, analyzes and elaborates on them, designs appropriate solutions, develops, tests, and approves them, aiming to deliver a working outcome – an increment – at the sprint's conclusion. Progress monitoring during the sprint is facilitated through daily meetings (scrums) and visualized using a kanban board. According to the Scrum Guide: "The daily scrum is a 15-minute event for the developers of the scrum team. To reduce complexity, it is held at the same time and place every working day of the sprint. [...] Developers can choose whatever structure and techniques they prefer, as long as the daily scrum focuses on progress toward the sprint goal and produces an actionable plan for the next day of work" (Schwaber and Sutherland, 2020). Typically, each team member reports on their activities from the previous day, any encountered issues or risks, and plans for the upcoming day's work.

Progress is visualized using a kanban board, where each item from the sprint backlog is represented by a card. The kanban board comprises columns representing different statuses, such as:
- To-Do: Items from the sprint backlog not yet started.
- Work-in-Progress: Items currently being worked on.
- Validate: Items ready for testing or undergoing testing.
- Done: Items that have successfully passed validation.

Cards are moved through these columns based on their reported status during daily scrums. To be considered 'done', an item must meet the predefined 'definition of done', which includes formal criteria for completion and usability.

At the end of each sprint, progress is assessed during a sprint review session where the team presents the sprint outcomes to stakeholders and develops plans for the subsequent sprint. "The product backlog may also be adjusted based on new opportunities" (Schwaber and Sutherland, 2020).

2.3 Governance of Project Contractual Relations

2.3.1 *Selection Criteria for Governance of Project Contractual Relations*

From the review of the theories performed in Chapter 1, it is evident that there are three possible governance structures for managing transactions: market, hierarchy (a company), and hybrid contractual governance. Market governance works best when trading non-specific goods, regardless of the frequency and uncertainty of transactions. For such goods, the level of transaction-specific investment is low. Non-specific goods can be easily traded elsewhere at a similar or the same value if the transaction does not occur, and therefore there is no dependency between buyers and sellers. Continuity of the relationship between the parties of the trade has little value, as new trading relationships can be easily arranged. As projects are, by definition, medium to long-lasting temporary undertakings, resulting in the development of a unitary (if not unique) outcome, market governance is not suitable for projects.

Therefore, while planning a project, a company may choose between performing it with its own internal resources (i.e., within a hierarchy) or executing it in cooperation with external entities (i.e., engaging in a long-term, hybrid contractual relationship). It should compare the transaction cost and project execution cost of these two governance frameworks.

Transaction Cost Economics states that hierarchy is the most expensive form of governance due to large administrative costs, so it makes sense to perform vertical integration (i.e., include the transaction within the company) only if the transaction is recurrent, the level of transaction-specific investments is high, and there is a need for a high level of coordination of people and resources to adapt to uncertain events and achieve a common goal.

In addition, while evaluating the option to execute the project internally within the organization, a company should take into account the cost of acquiring, configuring, integrating, maintaining, and deploying the combination of resources and knowledge needed to develop the capacity necessary to execute a project of a given type, and the expected utilization rate of this capacity over time. The development of project capacity internally would be too costly if it is supposed to be used only occasionally. Therefore, occasional (and one-time) transactions of highly idiosyncratic and mixed idiosyncratic types are candidates for hybrid governance, while for recurrent projects, the company may consider developing the relevant project capacity internally.

Another factor affecting the decision regarding the preferred governance structure is uncertainty. The more frequent and consequential unforeseen disturbances are, the greater the need for sequential, cooperative, and coordinated adaptations which is best achieved via hierarchy. In hybrid governance, each adaptation has to be done through the market interface, and the agreement of the independent parties has to be achieved, which is more time- and cost-consuming. Therefore, a high level of uncertainty would steer the transaction to be vertically integrated, while a low level of uncertainty might favour hybrid governance.

Summing up, theory predicts that the firm would choose a hybrid form of governance (i.e., involve in a long-term contractual relationship with another company) for occasional and one-time projects and consider it for those recurrent projects that involve a low to medium level of uncertainty. In the case of recurrent projects with high uncertainty, the company would incline towards executing the project in-house.

2.3.2 *Project Contractual Setups*

The particular mechanisms used for governing project contractual relations are related to the contractual setup of a project, as listed in Table 4. The contractual setup refers to the number of legal entities involved in a project and the division of risk and responsibility between the parties.

TABLE 4 Project contractual setups

Name	No of legal entities	Risk/responsibility ownership	Description
Internal (unilateral)	One	Project owner	Internal project within the financing organization. The project is managed and performed with the use of internal resources.
Prime-contractor (bilateral)	Two (can be more on the second level of dependency)	Mostly the prime-contractor	The financing organization outsources the project to the prime-contractor, who assumes the majority of responsibility and risk. The prime-contractor is responsible for setting up and performing the project under the conditions agreed upon with the financing party. The prime-contractor may execute the project with their own resources or contract parts of the work to other entities. In any case, the prime-contractor remains the single point of contact for the financing party (project owner)

TABLE 4 Project contractual setups (*cont.*)

Name	No of legal entities	Risk/responsibility ownership	Description
Multilateral centralized	Two or more	Project owner	The financing organization remains the active owner of the project, responsible for project planning, management, and execution. Some parts of the work are outsourced to specialized companies. These companies are responsible only for the delivery of their work, while the overall responsibility for the project remains with the financing organization
Alliance/ committee (multilateral decentralized)	Two or more	All the project parties (committee)	Two or more legal entities are performing joint project in which they play relatively equal role in terms of ownership and responsibility. The project is managed jointly by the participants, who share responsibility and risk.

SOURCE: OWN ELABORATION

Internal (unilateral) projects are executed exclusively by the personnel of the financing organization (the project owner). Therefore, the governance of contractual relations with the project members is achieved by authority/fiat, as the project participants are employees of the project owner. They may be assigned to a project as they would be to any other task within a hierarchy and should obey the authority of project management based on their employment contract. The governance of a project is performed according to the rules of a selected project management methodology and the related project governance framework. A temporary project organization is set up, consisting of the project structure, roles and responsibilities, processes and procedures, and individuals assigned to a project function within the project organization based on their employment contracts.

An additional aspect to consider is when a person is not assigned to a project full-time, meaning that they either share their time between several projects or between regular activities within a hierarchy and a project. In such situations, an employee becomes subordinate to two or more managers with possibly conflicting requirements regarding their involvement. Additional governance mechanisms should be put in place to resolve those conflicts.

In a **prime-contractor** (bilateral) setup, the project owner (the client) signs a contract with a single external entity – the prime-contractor – who assumes the majority, or all, of the responsibility and risk for achieving the project outcome. The contract should clearly define the relationship between the client and the prime-contractor, including the project outcome, schedule, financing, division of risk and responsibility, mechanisms for addressing unforeseen contingencies, information exchange processes, and conditions for imposing penalties.

This bilateral arrangement requires control mechanisms to ensure the prime-contractor fulfills their responsibilities as specified in the contract. The client must verify that project progress and outcomes align with the agreed plan and prevent any opportunistic behavior by the prime-contractor. Control measures may include metering the project outcomes, monitoring the prime-contractor's actions, or both. Additionally, unforeseen contingencies or ambiguities in the contract may necessitate decision-making during the project. This requires effective communication and coordination between the client and the prime-contractor. The volume and frequency of these interactions depend on the a-priori definability of the project outcome and uncertainty; more defined outcomes and lower uncertainty require less coordination and communication.

If the prime-contractor engages subcontractors, they must establish a governance structure similar to a multilateral centralized model (described below). It may also be necessary to integrate this structure with the client-prime-contractor communication framework to minimize biases and streamline information flow.

In a **multilateral centralized** setup, the project owner (the client) not only finances the project, provides information, and controls the progress, but also remains the active owner of the project, i.e., is responsible for project planning, management, and execution. The client signs separate contracts with multiple contractors to perform specific tasks or deliver specific parts of the project outcome. The contracts should specify the scope of work, acceptance conditions, delivery schedule, penalties, and other characteristics crucial to the transactions. In addition, the contract and/or other supplementary governance mechanisms should specify the coordination mechanisms between contractors, including responsibility distribution, contingent actions, and remuneration in case another contractor delays or does not deliver. As the work involves many legally independent entities whose work depends on each other, there must be non-contractual governance mechanisms enabling instant coordination, information sharing, and decision-making. There also must be a conflict resolution authority in case there is a problem between contractors. Such an authority would most likely use both contractual and non-contractual mechanisms to resolve conflicts between project participants.

An **alliance/committee** (multilateral decentralized) setup assumes that there are several legal entities with relatively equal rights and obligations. The contract should attempt to define the rights, roles, and obligations of each party, which can be challenging in a near-democratic setup. In addition, there must be a decision-making authority, possibly a committee, which acts in the face of contingencies not foreseen by the contract and supervises the progress of the project. There also must be a mechanism to coordinate the activities of each party on a daily basis, such as a project management team. The management team may consist of representatives from each party, involve one external project manager, or a project manager related to one of the parties.

Summing up, with regards to the governance of project contractual relations, internal projects are subject to governance mechanisms within a hierarchy, which are expanded and tailored to the specifics of each project. All other contractual setups require hybrid contractual governance, the exact nature of which depends on the project's contractual setup. Each project also requires non-contractual governance mechanisms to ensure proper coordination beyond the contract (Ruuska et al. 2011).

It should be noted that long-term projects have a characteristic that differentiates them from other forms of hybrid governance: a limited time-frame. Most forms of hybrid governance discussed in the literature do not have a predetermined termination date. Integrated supply chains, food suppliers' certificate of origin associations, and franchises, similar to fully integrated organizations, do not have a specified duration. They are of a recurrent type in terms of Williamson's typology of transaction frequency (recurrent, occasional, one-time). Projects have a fixed duration and therefore are one-time or occasional undertakings (if a certain project is followed by another one for the same client). The occasional or one-time character of a project has several implications:

- According to the TCE literature, the setup of sophisticated governance mechanisms for such transactions is not justified. However, empirical evidence from projects around the world does not support this view. Projects are commonly supported by non-contractual governance mechanisms, which will be discussed in subsequent chapters.
- The relational contracting incentive, i.e., the value of the future relationship, is not as strong as in other forms of hybrid governance. There may be future projects with the same customer, but these projects are uncertain

even if the current project is delivered successfully. In some cases, when a project is a "once in a lifetime" undertaking, the incentive for a future relationship is zero.

The nature of hybrid governance of project contractual relations and related governance mechanisms are described in the following sections.

The factors determining the choice of a given contractual setup and the conditions necessary for its application will be discussed in Chapter 3.

2.3.3 *Characteristics of Hybrid Governance of Contractual Relations*

Menard (2004) defines hybrid forms of contractual governance as "agreements among legally autonomous entities doing business together, mutually adjusting with little help from the price system, and sharing or exchanging technologies, capital, products, and services, but without a unified ownership". In other words "hybrid form is a specialized governance structure for dealing with bilateral dependence without going as far as integration" (Menard, 1996). Hybrids are "systematically oriented towards organizing activities through interfirm coordination and cooperation" (Menard, 2004) while maintaining strong, monetary incentives that pure integration lacks (Menard, 1996). As Menard (2004) concludes: "Hybrids exist because markets are perceived as unable to adequately bundle the relevant resources and capabilities, while integration in a hierarchy would reduce flexibility by creating irreversibility and weakening incentives."

It should be noted that there is another stream of research where the concept of hybrid organizations refers to entities that straddle the line between the public and private sectors, or between profit and non-profit organizations (Billis, 2010; Haigh and Hoffman, 2012). This interpretation of hybrid organizations is not within the scope of this book, which focuses on hybrid governance as a form of long-term cooperation between separate legal entities.

Under hybrid governance, the parties in the contractual relationship remain independent and maintain their own profit streams. The transaction requires an investment in transaction-specific assets from one or both parties. This investment, which cannot be re-used outside the transaction, makes the parties 'locked-in' and creates an incentive to continue the cooperation, as the investment would otherwise be lost. However, this situation leads to the hold-up problem – i.e., the party that invested less (or not at all) may behave opportunistically and drain the rents of the second party up to the level of the transaction-specific investment. If this second party anticipates opportunistic behavior from the prospective partner, they will not engage in the contractual relationship, which would otherwise be beneficial.

As the relationship between the parties is usually long-term, defining the scope of the transaction in a complete contract, including all possible future contingencies, is difficult, making the contract likely incomplete. Furthermore, a long-term relationship requires sequential, coordinated adaptations to unforeseen contingencies. The higher the uncertainty of the transaction, the greater this need becomes. However, the parties to the contract are independent, profit-maximizing entities with separate agendas, and their goals may conflict. They may be unwilling to adjust if the adjustment affects their profit margins. Since the contract is incomplete, it does not specify how the parties should act in the face of a given disturbance. Therefore, the parties must supplement the contract with additional adaptive mechanisms to 'work things out' when unexpected deviations from the contract occur.

Menard (2022) divides the hybrid forms of governance into the following categories:

1) Information-based networks – loose alliances which coordinate mainly through information sharing, "while keeping strategic control over their key assets, so that they basically remain distinct residual claimants" – the examples are the network in diamond industry and biotechnology firms exchanging experience;
2) Third party – "governance structures in which partners keep full control over the hard core of their assets, although they simultaneously develop some relationship-specific investments that require delegating significant decision rights". They rely on the independent third party to resolve issues and coordinate effort – the examples are food region/quality certification institutions in Europe;
3) Strategic centers – governance structures close to integrated firms in which "partners relying on tight coordination of their decisions as well as control over their pooled resources through the implementation of formal strategic centers empowered with statutory authority over strategic investments. However, they differ from a firm in that parties remain legally distinct entities with coordination capacity limited to pooled resources." The examples are joint ventures in R&D and strategic alliances in the airline industry.

Menard (2022) focuses his research on hybrid forms of governance that are predominantly multilateral and aim at pooling strategic resources to create value that would not be created otherwise. He intentionally omits long-term contracting between two (or more) firms, which, according to Williamson (2008), is the most popular form of hybrid governance. As mentioned earlier, long-term contracting is also a form of hybrid governance used in projects.

Two or more legal entities must shape their relationship for the duration of the project in such a way that they cooperate in a coordinated manner towards the project goal while protecting their interests at the same time. To achieve this, they use a combination of contractual and non-contractual governance mechanisms. The particular mix of these mechanisms depends on the attributes of the project and the contractual setup selected for its execution.

In summary, hybrid forms are created to enable the cooperation of two or more independent entities in a coordinated manner (similar to a hierarchy) while these entities remain independent in terms of decision-making, goals, profit streams, and property rights. Hybrid forms of governance exist because it would be too costly to develop and maintain a combination of resources and knowledge within a hierarchy, and the market is not capable of providing sufficient coordination. Incentives are stronger than in a hierarchy, but coordinated adjustments face challenges due to the independence of the hybrid governance partners.

2.3.4 *Mechanisms for Hybrid Governance of Project Contractual Relations*

The parties in a project contractual relationship must use a combination of contractual and non-contractual governance mechanisms to enable cooperation in a coordinated manner while protecting their interests at the same time.

The first mechanism used to govern a contractual relationship is the contract. As mentioned earlier, contract theory distinguishes between complete and incomplete contracts. Complete contracts aim to specify the desired outcome and the methods for achieving that outcome in detail. They anticipate all possible contingencies and define the relevant actions. Incomplete contracts lack these elements and, in their most extreme form, known as the null contract, include only the parties' intention to cooperate in good faith. The complete contract is a self-sufficient mechanism for governing contractual relations, as it encompasses all potential contingencies and the corresponding actions of the parties involved. However, in long-term project relationships, contracts are often incomplete (Müller and Turner, 2005).

With regards to the control mechanisms, the agency theory divides the contracts into outcome-based and behavior-based. In an outcome-based contract, the agent (typically the supplier) is expected to deliver a specific work product according to the principal's (the client's) specifications. Control is maintained through metering, where the actual outcome is compared to the expected one. A behavior-based contract specifies the desired behaviors of the agent (Dawson et al., 2010). Control is exercised through monitoring of the agent's behavior.

Project management literature provides a classification of contracts, depending on the payment terms (Turner, 2004) or, more precisely, depending on what the supplier is paid for. As Müller and Turner (2005) point out: "contracts can be seen on a continuum with fixed price contracts at one end, and cost-plus (or time and material) contracts on the other end". A fixed price (lump-sum) contract "is a contract where the contractor is paid a fixed amount for the whole scope of works defined in the contract" (Suprapto et al., 2016). Under a cost-plus contract "the contractor is repaid all their expenses, plus agreed profit margin", which can be calculated as a percentage of the cost, as a fixed amount or as an incentive fee related to achieving a defined success criteria (Turner and Simister, 2001).

A time and materials contract, commonly used by consulting and law firms (among others), is similar to the cost-plus contract. In a time and materials contract, the client pays an agreed unit price for the actual usage of resources (e.g., consulting hour), but unlike a cost-plus contract, they may not have visibility into the specific breakdown of costs and profit margins. The important common feature of both cost-plus and time and materials contracts is that the contractor is paid for the actual usage of resources.

There are also variations of time and materials and cost-plus contracts, known as time and materials to budget and target cost, respectively. Under these types of contracts, the buyer pays for the actual usage of resources, but up to a cap agreed upon upfront. According to Turner (2004), such agreements should be transformed into fixed-price contracts, as they impose additional transactional costs (of controlling the actual costs during the project) and provide no additional benefits for any of the parties. This is true for projects with an agreed scope; however, time and materials to budget/target cost contracts may be the solution for agile projects, in which the scope is not fixed, but the duration and resource engagement are (Eckfeldt et al. 2005).

As already stated, in long-term contractual relationships, such as projects, most contracts tend to be incomplete (Müller and Turner, 2005). An incomplete contract, in order to be executable, must be to some extent inexact, meaning it should "state a broad requirement in order to restrict a range of possible actions without restricting the parties to specific actions within that range" (Al-Najjar, 1995). In other words, such a contract should not "pretend" that it is complete. If the parties of a seemingly complete contract (i.e., appearing to describe every possible contingency and respective actions) find themselves in a situation not foreseen by this contract, they will either take a wrong action or will have to renegotiate the contract. Therefore, an incomplete contract should include elastic contractual clauses. It may also include additional governance mechanisms such as the definition of a tolerance zone within which misalignments will be absorbed or the definition of dispute-solving procedures (Menard, 2004).

Incomplete contracts also require non-contractual governance mechanisms, which, at minimum, allow the project owner and the manager of the project to:
- "Make mutually agreed adaptations in the contract to meet unforeseen variations.
- Communicate with each other to identify such variations, and agree the required adaptations to the contract" (Turner, 2001; Müller and Turner, 2005).

The non-contractual governance mechanisms mentioned in the literature include:
- control over residual rights (Al-Najjar, 1995),
- third party arbitration (Williamson, 1979),
- mediation (Goltsman et al., 2009),
- constant renegotiation of the contract, every time an unexpected disturbance occurs (Hart & Moore, 1988),
- transaction-specific governance structures (Ménard, 2022):
  - regular meetings to exchange information and coordinate actions,
  - dedicated committees,
  - formal strategic centers,
- relational contracting (Williamson, 1979).

Residual rights are "all the rights except those specifically mentioned in the contract" (Grossman and Hart, 1986). When one party is assigned the residual rights, it grants them a level of control similar to that of a company (Aghion and Holden, 2011). In most project situations, the primary issue arises rather from the division of risk and the subsequent allocation of additional duties and responsibilities when a contingency unforeseen in the contract arises during the project (Müller and Turner, 2005). There is not much of a use of this governance mechanism in project contracting, however time and materials projects are by default using the assignment of the residual property rights to the buyer.

Arbitration involves a third party assistance in resolving disputes (Williamson, 1979). "Under arbitration, a neutral third-party renders a decision after hearing proofs and arguments from each party. While both the agreement to arbitrate and the presentation of these arguments is voluntary, the arbitrator's decision is binding, in the sense that courts will enforce it against a reluctant party" (Goltsman et al. 2009). The arbitrator has more flexibility than the court in educating themselves regarding the matter of the dispute (Williamson, 1979). Additionally, the arbitrator may possess a higher level of domain knowledge on the matter of the dispute compared to the court. Mediation also involves a neutral third party, but s/he has no authority to impose a settlement (Goltsman et al. 2009) and can only suggest a solution which has to be accepted by the parties. Renegotiation or unfacilitated negotiation refers to the direct and voluntary exchange of information between the two parties until a resolution is reached. In this process, external assistance is not involved. If the negotiation fails to provide a resolution, the dispute must then be subjected to more robust governance mechanisms, such as arbitration or court intervention, or alternatively, the contract may be terminated.

The governance mechanisms described above apply when the situation goes off the rails. The transaction-specific governance structures, on the other hand, are introduced to support coordination and cooperation between the parties of a hybrid arrangement. They vary from the low-powered, i.e. meetings to exchange information and coordinate actions and committees overseeing the performance of a hybrid arrangement to the high-powered ones, i.e. formal strategic centers which have the authority similar to that in hierarchy (Menard, 2022). The examples of the use of the latter form are the union of French millers, owning the separate brand name and providing high-quality flour to the franchised bakers (Menard, 2013) or an entity monitoring a joint-venture (Menard, 2022). These examples are the hybrid forms of governance far from the project contractual relationship. The remaining two transaction-specific governance structures, i.e. meetings to exchange information and coordinate actions as well as committees overseeing the performance of a hybrid arrangement may complement the contract in a way that they facilitate smooth cooperation and coordination of activities between the parties within the tolerance zone of the contract.

As Menard (2022) summarizes: parties of a hybrid governance "have the motivation to develop a specific governance structure that relies on a mix of (incomplete) contractual agreements allowing mutual adjustments to unexpected events and of devices coordinating their joint activities". The balance of power between the contract and the other, non-contractual governance mechanisms may vary from a purely contract-based approach to the form closer to semi-integration depending on the characteristics of the hybrid arrangement (Menard, 2004, 2022).

Another mechanisms which supplements the formal contract in hybrid forms of governance is relational contracting. As it was already mentioned in Chapter 1, relational contracts are informal agreements and unwritten codes of conduct sustained by the value of future relationships (Baker et al. 2002). As Williamson (1983) concludes, contrary to what theory predicts, in practice not so many disputes between the parties are brought to court. Many agreements are self-enforcing, meaning that the only consequence of violating an agreement is its termination. The possible explanation is in transaction-specific investments which play a role of a 'hostage' in the contractual relationship. If the transaction is recurrent, this effect is amplified by the value of possible future contracts using the transaction-specific investments which were already made. While governing a hybrid transaction through relational contracting, the selection of proper partners is of great importance. According to Menard (2022) the selection of reliable contractual parties is based on the past experience from previous hybrid arrangements. If the parties have no previous experience, the selection is based on reputation on the market, frequently distributed through informal social networks. Formal bidding is used infrequently, mostly to test the market and discipline the partners (Menard, 2022). Also, relational contracting is often based on trust between the parties, gained during past hybrid arrangements. Trust helps the parties deal with the situation not foreseen by the incomplete contract (Czakon and Czernek, 2016; Czernek and Czakon, 2016; Doney and Cannon, 1997, Menard, 2022).

Below is the summary of what is known from the literature so far regarding the governance of project contractual relations.

The basis of a hybrid project relationship is a contract. According to the criterion of completeness, the contract may be:

- complete – i.e. determining exactly the scope of the contract, as well as any possible future contingency together with the relevant action;
- incomplete – i.e. determining the scope in (more or less) general terms, including elastic contractual clauses and tolerance zones within which misalignments will be absorbed,
- null – i.e. essentially incomplete contract, containing only general intentions of co-operation.

Since the complete contract already anticipates any possible future situations and specifies the appropriate actions for the contractual parties, there is no need for additional governance mechanisms. Incomplete (and null) contracts necessitate additional mechanisms to govern contractual relations. These mechanisms should facilitate the coordination of the joint activities, identification and communication of unforeseen variations, as well as enable mutually agreed adaptations in the event that such variations arise. The mechanisms can be divided into two main categories depending on their relation to the contract:

1. Operational with the contract – These mechanisms enable effective execution of the contract on a daily basis, provide tools for managing situations not foreseen in the incomplete contract as well as tools for managing deviations from the contract which are in the range of a tolerance zone. In other words – they are used to "oil" the project "machinery" in such a way that the parties are able to solve the issues in cooperation, rather than refer to the contract in a hard way. These mechanisms include:
   a. relational contracting,
   b. regular meetings to exchange information and coordinate actions,
   c. dedicated committees,
   d. and, to some extent – re-negotiations.
2. Complementary to the contract – These mechanisms are utilized when the parties encounter a situation that was not foreseen by the contract and falls outside the agreed-upon tolerance zone. Such situations can pose significant challenges to the project and necessitate formal reference to the contract. Since the contract does not specifically outline actions to be taken in these circumstances, the parties have several options available:
   a. They can choose to re-negotiate the contract amongst themselves,
   b. They may opt to submit the dispute to mediation,
   c. They can elect to submit the dispute to arbitration,
   d. If the above means fail to resolve the dispute, they may resort to litigation in court.

In any of the above cases the project governance structure and procedures are required to allow smooth project planning, coordination and control. The interlink between the project governance and governance of project contractual relations will be discussed in detail in Chapter 4.

Depending on the payment terms, the contracts are divided into two major categories: fixed price and time and materials (cost-plus). The selection of one of the two forms of contract has both prerequisites and consequences. In a fixed price contract the contractor is paid a fixed amount for the whole scope of works. This means that the scope must be defined in detail prior to the contract. Every significant change to the scope or other crucial parameters of the agreement must either be specified in the close-to-complete contract or the incomplete contract must be subject to re-negotiation. In addition, in a fixed-price contract majority of the risk is attributed to the contractor, which has prominent consequences in the light of agency theory and transaction cost economics. Under time and materials (cost-plus) contract the contractor is paid for actual usage of resources (plus a margin). Such agreement leaves more elasticity regarding the definition and subsequent changes to the scope, so the contract may be incomplete. However, the risk of opportunistic behavior of the contractor is significant, and majority of the risk is attributed to the buyer.

The metatheory of governance of project contractual relations will be further developed in Chapter 3, while the interlink between project governance and the governance of project contractual relations will be covered in Chapter 4.

CHAPTER 3

Metatheory of Governance of Project Contractual Relations

In this chapter, a metatheory of governance of project contractual relations is developed by combining propositions from the theories presented in Chapter 1 and adapting them to the specific nature of projects.

The novelty of this metatheory lies in its comprehensive, deductive application of existing theories to an as-exhaustive-as-possible combination of project types, contractual setups, and contract types. It also includes a deductively derived assessment of the applicability, advantages, and disadvantages of various governance frameworks for different project types and contractual scenarios.

3.1 Review of Existing Knowledge on Project Contractual Relations

To advance the discussion on the theory of project contractual relations, it is essential to summarize the key findings.

Project contractual setups

This book identifies the following types of contractual setups:

- Internal (unilateral) – The project is managed and performed with the use of internal resources of the sponsoring organization;
- Multilateral centralized – The sponsoring organization retains active ownership of the project, taking responsibility for project planning, management, and execution. Some parts of the work are outsourced to one or more specialized companies. Those companies are responsible only for delivery of their work, while the responsibility for the project as a whole remains with the financing organization. The financing organization plans the work, coordinates activities between project participants, and solves disputes between the sub-contractors.
- Prime-contractor (bilateral) – The financing organization outsources the project to the prime-contractor, who takes majority of responsibility and risk. Prime-contractor is responsible to set-up and perform a project under conditions agreed with the financing party. The prime-contractor may either execute the project with its own resources or subcontract parts of the work to other entities. In the latter case, the multilateral centralized contractual

relation emerges between the prime-contractor and their sub-contractors. The prime-contractor remains a single point of contact for the financing party.
- Alliance/committee (multilateral decentralized) – Two or more legal entities are performing joint project in which they play relatively equal role in terms of ownership and responsibility. The project is managed jointly by the participants, who share responsibility and risk. The planning, coordination, control of a progress and other management functions are performed by the committee of participants having equal rights and obligations.

Types of contracts

In contract theory, contracts are categorized into three main types based on their definition of outcomes:
- Complete contracts: A complete contract is one that fully specifies the desired outcome and outlines the parties' reactions to all possible future contingencies. In other words, it "describes the actions to be taken by each party in every possible contingency." (Al-Najjar, 1995);
- Incomplete contracts: An incomplete contract is characterized by its inability or impracticality to describe every possible contingency. Instead, it includes clauses that prescribe actions considered efficient on average across a range of contingencies (Al-Najjar, 1995 (Al-Najjar, 1995);
- Null contracts: The null contract represents an extreme form of an incomplete contract. In this case, the parties declare their intention to cooperate in good faith but do not specify specific outcomes or prescribed actions. Such contract is predominantly unenforceable in front of a court.

With regards to the control mechanisms, the agency theory divides the contracts into:
- Outcome-based contracts: In an outcome-based contract, the agent (typically the supplier) is expected to deliver a specific work product according to the principal's (the client's) precise specifications. Control is maintained through metering, where the actual outcome is compared to the expected one. This type of contract transfers the risk of achieving the desired outcome to the agent;
- Behavior-based contracts: A behavior-based contract specifies the desired behaviors and actions of the agent (Dawson et al., 2010). Control is exercised through systematic monitoring of the agent's conduct. In this case, the risk remains with the principal, as the agent is not responsible for the final outcome.

There is, however, another option, not so well explored in the literature, which can be called resource-based contract. Under such a contract resources of a given specification are put at the disposal of the principal for a given time, at a given price. The principal has the right and responsibility to direct the resources at their own will. The resources are treated as "internal" so the governance is executed as within hierarchy. The contract can be "null" with regards to the outcome and behavior. The attributes of the resources should be specified in as much detail as possible, which can be particularly challenging when contracting individuals with specific knowledge and skills.

Depending on the payment terms, contracts can be divided into two main types: cost plus/time and materials, and fixed price, each of which can have various sub-variants (Turner, 2004). In cost plus/time and materials contracts, the contractor is paid for the actual usage of resources plus a margin (which may or may not be transparent to the buyer, depending on the sub-type of the contract). In a fixed price contract, the contractor is paid a lump sum for delivering a project product or sub-product according to the agreed specification.

An attempt to combine the above-mentioned classifications of contracts results in the following conclusions:

1. A fixed price contract requires a detailed specification of the desired outcome. Therefore, a fixed price contract should aim to be complete at least in terms of the definition of the final outcome. Moreover, the more comprehensive the description of potential contingencies and the corresponding actions, the lower the risk for the vendor. In a fixed-price contract, the contractor is paid a lump sum for delivering a project product or sub-product, making the control mechanism naturally outcome-based. In summary: fixed price contracts are outcome-based and should be complete regarding the detailed definition of the outcome. In terms of the description of future contingencies they can be either complete or incomplete, depending on the level of risk acceptance by the vendor. The control of the vendor performance is done via metering – i.e. comparison of the actual outcome with the outcome described in the contract.
2. Time and materials contracts encompass a wide range of possible contractual arrangements. The common denominator of all time and materials contracts is that the supplier is compensated for the actual work and resources utilized, rather than for the outcome of this work. Consequently, the outcome does not need to be described in detail. This raises the question of how the buyer (the principal) controls the performance of the vendor (the agent). One method is through a behavior-based contract and monitoring, which involves systematically tracking the agent's behavior to gather information. The agent's behavior must be described in a behavior-based contract to allow comparison between the actual behavior and the behavior desired by the principal. Such a behavior-based contract should be comprehensive, prescribing

the desired behavior of the agent in any possible contingent situation, thereby enabling effective monitoring. Another method is by directing and monitoring the resources of the agent assigned to the project, based on a resource-based contract.

Characteristics of a project

The following characteristics of a project, which affect the way it should be managed, can be identified:

- definability of the project goal/outcome (Turner and Cochrane, 1993);
- definability of the project methods (Turner and Cochrane, 1993);
- criticality of the project outcome (Thesing et al., 2021);
- project structural complexity (Williams, 1999);
- level of the project uncertainty;
- level of the project ambiguity (Lech, 2022a);
- company's attitude towards uncertainty, company's culture, habits and beliefs (Thesing et al., 2021).

As mentioned during the discussion of project governance, the key attributes that determine the approach to project governance are the definability of the project goal/outcome and the definability of the methods. The same applies to the governance of project contractual relations, including viable contractual setups, types of contracts, and non-contractual governance mechanisms. The definability of the project goal or outcome, whether intrinsic (arising from the physical characteristics of the project goal) or extrinsic (influenced by the project's environment), determines the suitability of an outcome-based contract. A well-defined methodology, on the other hand, is a prerequisite for utilizing a behavior-based contract.

Criticality of the project outcome is an extrinsic factor imposing detailed definition of the project outcome while project structural complexity makes the exact definition of the outcome difficult and costly.

Uncertainty in projects can be related to:

- unclarity in the definition of the goals and/or methods,
- likelihood of the goals to change during the project (volatility of a project goal) due to the changes in stakeholders expectations or changes in the project environment;
- unknown future contingencies inside or outside the project which affect its execution.

Poor definition of goals makes the outcome-based contract unfeasible. Unclarity with regards to the methods precludes the behavior-based contract. Uncertainty related to the volatility of a project goal and unknown contingencies increase the cost of writing a complete contract as all of the changes should be foreseen and respective actions should be prescribed in the contract.

Alternatively, an incomplete contract should be put in place and supplemented with non-contractual mechanisms able to address the uncertainties.

Ambiguity is a state of multiple and conflicting interpretations, especially regarding the project goals (Lech, 2022a). In contrast to uncertainty, ambiguity cannot be reduced by sharing more information (Atkinson et al., 2006; Thiry, 2002). In the face of ambiguity of project goals the detailed up-front planning becomes unfeasible, so does the outcome-based contract. Either a behavior-based contract, or time-restricted resource-based contract are an option for ambiguous projects.

Company's culture, habits, beliefs and attitude towards uncertainty may significantly influence the way it manages it's project contractual relations. There are companies which impose detailed specifications of the outcomes in every possible situations, as well as "agile oriented" businesses which would apply agile principles and related contractual schemes whenever possible. In extreme cases, company's culture, habits, beliefs may even completely deviate the approach from the one prescribed by theories (and, sometimes, common sense). I personally faced the situations when companies' procurement departments applied one-size-fits-all approach to project contracting and governance, regardless if the project involved installing new machinery or implementing a new Information System. This led to situations in which the contract and related governance mechanisms were perfectly suited to some projects and completely out of reason for others. The latter had to be executed "in spite of the contract", and contractual agreements were mostly ignored both by the client and the supplier.

Governance structures

Transaction Cost Economics distinguishes three forms of governance of contractual relations: market, hierarchy and hybrid. Market is driven by the price mechanism, which is the only coordination mechanism between the autonomous parties, high-powered incentives (i.e. the compensation is tightly related to the result of work), autonomous adaptation to disturbances, and administrative control limited to the courts which resolve the disputes basing on the contracts. Market governance is supported by the classical contracting, where all relevant future contingencies are described and discounted in the complete contract. Hierarchy is supported by the forbearance contract law which means that "the parties to an internal exchange can work out their differences themselves or appeal unresolved disputes to the hierarchy for a decision" (Williamson, 1991, p. 276). In other words, in hierarchy, adaptation to new, previously unknown circumstances can be achieved by fiat. The employment relation is an incomplete contract and by accepting it an employee agrees that the superiors can direct his/her activities from day to day and closely monitor those activities, and performance. Hierarchy promotes the realization of common objectives and coordinated adaptation to the new situation as the adaptations can be made in a sequential way without the need to consult, complete or revise the interfirm agreements (Williamson, 1979). The disadvantage of hierarchy is high cost of setting up and maintaining it with all the necessary administrative and bureaucratic mechanisms.

Hybrid is a governance structure, in which the autonomy of the parties is preserved, but there is bilateral dependency between the parties due to the transaction-specific investments. On the one hand the parties are realizing their own, separate agendas, and have separate profit streams but on the other hand they are interested to adapt to unforeseen contingencies, cooperate in a coordinated way and continue the long-term relationship due to the non-trivial level of the transaction-specific investment, which will be lost if the transaction is terminated. The most frequently mentioned form of hybrid governance is long term contracting of different kind. Hybrid governance is accompanied by the neoclassical contracting in which the contract is the main point of reference, but as it is incomplete due to the long-term relationship and uncertainty, the parties must supplement the contract with additional, non-contractual governance mechanisms.

Lifecycle of a contractual relationship

The lifecycle of a contractual relationship can be decomposed into the pre-contracting, contract creation, contract execution and contract closure phases. The pre-contracting phase includes identification of a need, definition of the scope of work, development of a sourcing strategy and selecting of a partner (Macbeth, 2012). The contract creation phase involves drafting a contract template, negotiating the terms and conditions, contract approval and signing. The contract execution phase is when the contract work is done and the outcomes are delivered. The fulfillment of the contract provisions is monitored, corrective actions are undertaken in case of deviations, and possible disputes are being resolved. The contract closure phase involves final delivery of the contract outcome, acceptance procedure, final payments and contract termination.

How the lifecycle of a contractual relationship interrelates with the project lifecycle depends upon the project contractual setup. In the prime-contractor (bilateral) and alliance (multilateral decentralized) setups the pre-contracting and contract creation phases will be most likely performed during the project initiation (pre-project) phase. The detailed project planning would then be performed jointly by the contractual partners. In the multilateral centralized setup the project ownership is fully on the financing organization, so the search for the contractual partners may be performed during the detailed planning phase or late in the project initiation phase. The internal projects do not need formal contracts as the personnel is assigned to the project basing on the current employment contracts. Some form of internal agreement, determining the project parameters may thus be needed.

Additional aspects influencing the contractual relationship

There are additional aspects, not discussed so far, which affect the contractual relationship between the project parties. The first one is the level of **co-production** needed to achieve the project outcome. Co-production means that the clients' contribution to the project delivery process is indispensable to the project success, affecting both the quality of the outcome and the clients' satisfaction (Bettencourt et al., 2002; Lech, 2022b). Co-production may be restricted to continuous exchanging of information between the parties during the project delivery (Zięba and Kończyński, 2019; Lech, 2022b) or may also require the client to perform actual work on the project deliverables.

Speaking of the information exchange between the project contractual parties, it has two major attributes:
- concurrency (synchronous vs asynchronous communication),
- frequency (one-time/periodic vs continuous communication).

The choice of the communication mode is related to the definability of the outcome, both intrinsic and extrinsic, and the stability of the outcome over time. If the outcome is well-defined and can be described using methods understood by all project parties, leaving no room for ambiguity, asynchronous communication may be suitable. Additionally, if the outcome is stable and not prone to change during the project, communication may be either one-time or periodic. In an extreme case, the client provides the outcome definition before the project begins, the supplier accepts the requirements, and carries out the project without the client's continuous involvement. The client formally reviews and accepts the project outcome upon its completion. Such projects may be subject to outcome-based, complete contracts.

On the other extreme there are projects which require continuous, synchronous information exchange between the client and the supplier, due to the low definability of the outcome, change of the outcome during the project or sequential interdependencies between the project partial outcomes which cannot be specified up-front. In such cases, an outcome-based, complete contract is unfeasible. These projects can be managed using behavior-based or time-constrained, resource-based contracts. In this case, the behavior-based contract should describe the behavior of both parties.

In another scenario, the client may not only be required to supply the information to the supplier, but also to deliver additional activities and outcomes. When the delivery can be divided into discrete outcomes with a clear distinction of responsibilities between the parties, a two-sided outcome-based contract can be employed. However, if the parties must collaborate on the same set of outcomes, behavior-based or resource-based contracts become the preferred choice. It must be noted, that in a behavior-based contract the behavior of both sides of the contract should be described.

The second aspect, not discussed so far, which may affect the contractual relationship between the project parties is **knowledge asymmetry.** "Knowledge asymmetry between two contractual parties means that one party does not possess the knowledge to evaluate the effort invested or the outcome accomplished by the second party (Sharma, 1997). Knowledge asymmetry is different to information asymmetry, as information asymmetry can be reduced by obtaining information at a given cost (Dawson et al., 2010). To reduce knowledge asymmetry, a less knowledgeable party would have to invest significant time, effort and money to obtain the specialized knowledge, similar to the knowledge possessed by the more knowledgeable party" (Lech, 2022b). Knowledge asymmetry increases ambiguity in the definition of project outcomes and behaviors (Lech, 2022a). Consequently, both outcome-based and behavior-based contracts may give rise to disputes due to potential misinterpretations of contract definitions by the involved parties.

3.2 Foundations of a Metatheory of Governance of Project Contractual Relations

The basic relations between the contract and the theory of organization was outlined in Turner and Simister (2001) who state that:

1. "The purpose of project organization is to create a cooperative system between client and contractors based on shared objectives", instead of a conflict one;
2. "A conflict system is one in which individuals have objectives that are not jointly consistent. It organizes through exchanges and other interactions between strategic actors. A cooperative system is one in which individuals act rationally in the name of a common objective."
3. "A conflict system can arise either through bounded rationality (the participants would like to act rationally but through human frailty fail to) or opportunism (the participants try to optimize their position at the expense of others)";
4. Therefore, the contract should allow for goal alignment between the client and the contractors, as well as limit the chances of opportunistic behaviors;

5. The total cost of a project for the client is the out-turn (actual) cost of a project and a transaction cost of setting up and administering the contract;
6. The transaction costs of setting up and administering the contract vary depending on the contract type;
7. Under different contract types the out-turn (actual) cost of a project may also vary, as these "contract types incentivize the contractor in different ways" (Turner and Simister, 2001).
8. The client should thus select a contract type which minimizes the sum of project out-turn cost and transaction cost of setting up and administering the contract.
9. The contract type depends on the uncertainty in the definition of the product and the uncertainty in the process of delivering the product.

The above is a good starting point for developing a more comprehensive metatheory of governance of project contractual relations, which will combine the predictions from theories, presented in Chapter 1 with the characteristics of the projects and available contractual relationship governance mechanisms. It is important to notice, that the stance taken here is that the presented theories are complementary rather than contradictory. They explain various facets of organizational reality, different scenarios organizations may encounter, or offer different perspectives on organizations. Instead of favoring one theory over another it makes sense to combine them to highlight when each theory is most relevant in predicting organizational behavior. Therefore an integrative and comprehensive approach will be applied here by acknowledging the merits of multiple theories and recognizing their applicability in different contexts. This approach is novel in that it synthesizes existing theories into a comprehensive theoretical framework.

To begin with, the determinants of the available options for project contractual setup and governance should be identified. Contrary to what most literature claims, the primary determinant is the availability of project capacity: *the structured combination of people with relevant knowledge and skills, physical, financial, organizational, and knowledge resources necessary to execute a project of a given type*. Project capacity is a rival good, meaning that once it (or part of it) is allocated to a given project, it cannot be used elsewhere. Project capacity must either be developed and maintained within a company (which is time-consuming and costly) or outsourced from an external entity. To develop project capacity, an organization must possess project capability. According to the Resource-Based View, capability is the ability to acquire, integrate, configure, and release/deploy resources in a way that accomplishes a desired outcome (Cragg et al., 2011; Eisenhardt and Martin, 2000; Peppard and Ward, 2004;

Teece et al., 1997). In relation to the project, project capability refers to the ability to acquire, integrate, configure, and release/deploy people with relevant knowledge and skills, physical, financial, organizational, and knowledge resources in such a way that the project accomplishes its goals in a coordinated manner. In other words, project capability is the organizational ability to plan, prepare, and execute a project of a given type. As the nature of the required resources and the ways they need to be integrated, configured, and deployed vary drastically between various project domains, project capability is, in most cases, domain-specific.

In addition to project capability, the following types of knowledge and skills (and related resources) are necessary to form project capacity for every project:

- Domain-specific knowledge and skills: This refers to the expertise directly related to the specifics of the delivery process for a given type of project outcome and the characteristics of the outcome itself. Every project requires individuals with expertise in delivering a specific project outcome, as well as related processes and procedures. For instance, a construction project necessitates architects, engineers, builders, electricians, painters, etc., while an Information System project requires analysts, solution architects, UI designers, programmers, and testers. These individuals must adhere to processes and procedures specific to the project domain throughout the project work.
- Domain-specific project management knowledge: A company planning a project needs to establish relevant structures, roles and responsibilities, planning and control mechanisms, processes, and procedures to ensure that people with relevant knowledge and skills, machinery, and other resources are coordinated in a manner that guarantees the achievement of project goals. These mechanisms are, to some extent, dependent on the specifics of the project outcome and the process of delivering this outcome, requiring domain-specific project management knowledge.
- Domain-agnostic project management knowledge: In addition to the above, knowledge is required on how to manage any kind of project, as provided by professional project management associations.

Their accessibility within the organization determines the available contractual setups for the project. Attributes of the project, such as the definability of the outcome and methods, determine the particulars of the governance mechanisms within the selected contractual setup.

The following propositions can thus be formulated:

> **Proposition 1:** *Available options for project contractual setup and related governance depend on the accessibility of project capacity, consisting of the structured combination of people with relevant knowledge and skills,*

physical, financial, organizational, and knowledge resources for the sponsoring company within a desired time frame.

Proposition 2: *To develop project capacity, an organization requires project capability, i.e., the ability to acquire, integrate, configure, and release/deploy people with relevant knowledge and skills, physical, financial, organizational, and knowledge resources in such a way that the project accomplishes its goals in a coordinated manner.*

Proposition 3: *The attributes of the project, including the definability of the outcome and methods, are the secondary factors determining the particular mechanisms of project contractual governance.*

The focus is on the first and second proposition for now.

If the sponsoring company possesses the project capacity in-house, it can choose to perform a project by itself, i.e. use unilateral (internal) contractual setup. However, if any of the above resources or capabilities is missing, the company needs first to obtain them.

At the two ends of the spectrum, deficiencies can be either point-specific or holistic, with various intermediate options in between. Point-specific deficiencies occur when a company has the project capability and most of the resources with other types of knowledge, but either lacks specific resources in some points or lacks a knowledge in areas which can be fairly easy isolated from the rest of the project. The examples would be a company which knows how to run the Information System projects but lacks several programmers or a company familiar with construction projects which does not have expertise in electrical engineering. Programmers can be hired on the market and integrated into the existing project structure, and electrical subsystem in a building can be fairly easily separated as a sub-project with a well-defined outcome, and therefore sub-contracted. Also project management knowledge, both domain-specific and domain-agnostic can be fairly easily acquired by hiring experienced project managers. All of these come at cost, but this cost is easily measurable and comparable to the cost of maintaining the same kind of resources in-house. Integrating of such point-specific resources into the project structure is also relatively easy and does not carry significant transaction costs or risks of opportunism. In such cases a multilateral centralized contractual setup can be applied, in which the sponsoring organization retains active ownership of the project, taking responsibility for project planning, management, and execution but some parts of the work are outsourced to one or more specialized companies.

The other side of the spectrum is holistic deficiency, when the sponsoring company lacks project capability, domain-specific knowledge and skills, or both. As it was outlined in Chapter 1, where the link between Resource-Based View and Transaction Cost Economics was presented, acquiring, configuring, integrating and maintaining the combination of resources and knowledge which guarantees the accomplishment of a project goal is difficult, time-consuming, costly and not always viable in a desired time-frame. Therefore, the cost of acquiring, configuring, integrating, maintaining and deploying the combination of resources and knowledge – ACIMD cost – must be taken into account while deciding whether to do a project in-house or outsource it. In addition, achievability of a required combination of resources and knowledge in a desired time-frame, and opportunity cost of the resource and knowledge combination being underutilized should also be considered. The alternative would be to involve a prime-contractor who possesses the required knowledge, capabilities and resources, and engage in a bilateral (prime-contractor) contractual setup. This, of course, is related with the premium for the prime-contractor and transactional costs of setting-up and maintaining the contractual relationship.

The scarcity of structured combinations of knowledge, skills, competences, and related resources capable of delivering specific outcomes is one of the core motivations for establishing alliance (multilateral decentralized) contractual setups. In these setups, the diverse competences of the parties are joined together in a unique way to deliver an outcome that would be otherwise inaccessible to each party separately.

Summing up, the following proposition can be formulated:

> ***Proposition 4:*** *A company planning a project should compare:*
> - the cost of acquiring, configuring, integrating, maintaining and deploying the combination of resources and knowledge (the ACIMD cost) in-house,
> - and the cost of developing a project capability, i.e. the ability to perform the above
>
> with
> - the transaction cost of contracting the appropriate, structured combination of resources, knowledge, skills and capabilities from external entities.

Following the logic of Transaction Cost Economics, and extending it to projects, the notion of Total Cost of Project (TCP) will be introduced here. The Total Cost of Project includes all costs incurred during the full project lifecycle, from pre-project (initiation) to closure. The first component of TCP is the cost of provision of the structured combination of resources, knowledge, skills and capabilities necessary to accomplish a project goal in a coordinated way as mentioned above.

Summing up, a company planning a project can choose from the following contractual setups:

- it may run a project internally,
- it may outsource some works to contractors in a multilateral centralized setup,
- it may form an alliance with the contractors,
- or it may outsource a project to a prime-contractor.

The first parameter to be considered in decision-making is the cost of acquiring the structured combination of resources, knowledge, skills, and capabilities. A company that possesses all the necessary knowledge, skills, and capabilities for conducting a project in-house does not need to assess the cost of their acquisition, as this cost has already been incurred in the past and is irrecoverable (and thus irrelevant to the current decision). Instead, it should take into account the opportunity cost of using this bundle of resources elsewhere. The greater the deficiencies in knowledge, skills, and capabilities, the higher the cost of acquiring, configuring, integrating, and maintaining the combination of resources and knowledge in-house, providing a stronger incentive to outsource the project.

Nevertheless, there are also other attributes associated with each of the contractual setups that may influence the decision on which one to choose.

3.3 Internal Project Governance Setup

In an **internal** (unilateral) setup the sponsoring company performs the project with the use of its own resources. The attributes of this setup would thus be similar to those of a hierarchy. There are, however, also differences. First of all, every project is a temporary, one-time endeavor, so a project governance structure always has to be set up from scratch, regardless whether a project is done internally or in any type of a cross company cooperation. Definition of the project standards, structures, processes, procedures and tools, roles and responsibilities has to be established for a project. The cost of setting up a project governance structure is the second element of the Total Cost of Project (TCP). Secondly, while hierarchy is perceived as the most costly governance structure due to high bureaucratic cost, the same does not apply to internal project setup. The cost of setting up and running a project governance structure would be present in every type of contractual setup and there is no reason to believe that it would be higher in the unilateral (internal) setup, providing that the sponsoring organization has the necessary project management knowledge and capabilities. This leads to the following propositions:

Proposition 5: *The cost of setting up and running a project governance structure is present in every project regardless its contractual setup.*

Proposition 6: *The cost of setting up and running a project governance structure is independent from the project contractual setup.*

In addition, the unilateral (internal) setup would have lowest costs of maintaining the governance of contractual relations, as the coordinated adaptations to the unexpected changes in the project may be achieved by fiat. The attributes of the unilateral (internal) setup in terms of governing contractual relations are similar to those of a hierarchy:

- Strong coordination mechanisms: As project team members are employees of the sponsoring organization, their desired behavior can be enforced through authority relations (by fiat), facilitating cooperative actions in pursuit of a common objective.
- Low-powered incentives: This implies that compensation is not tightly linked to the results of work or effort.
- Coordinated adaptation to disturbances: Due to the aforementioned factors, frequent sequential adaptations in response to unexpected events are relatively easy to perform and do not incur significant transactional costs. The combination of low-powered incentives and strong coordination mechanisms fosters cooperative behavior, harmonizing the interests of project team members that might otherwise be in conflict. In the face of an unexpected event in the project, there is no need for haggling or renegotiation of contracts; instead, the project team can react jointly and in a coordinated manner. Potential issues and disputes can be addressed through the authority of the hierarchical structure of the company.
- Strong administrative control: Transaction Cost Economics states that within a company, members of a hierarchy can be controlled to a much higher extent than would be possible in any kind of interfirm relation. This holds true for internal projects as well. If project members are employees of the financing organization, they can be controlled by fiat. There is no difference in the level of administrative control in a hierarchy compared to a project executed within a hierarchy.

Executing a project using the company's internal employees also brings about specific consequences that may not necessarily arise in day-to-day operations. While low-powered incentives facilitate coordinated adaptations to unforeseen disturbances, they can simultaneously undermine motivation to achieve a planned project goal within the given schedule and budget constraints. In other words, an individual under an employment contract may not be greatly concerned if their responsibilities change, unless the alterations align with the typically broad terms and conditions of the employment relationship. On the other hand, they may not prioritize whether the project goal is attained, as their compensation is not directly tied to the accomplishment of this objective.

Another potential problem arises when employees are not dedicated full-time to a project but instead divide their efforts among multiple projects or between a project and day-to-day operations. In the latter scenario, employees are more likely to prioritize their day-to-day duties over the project since these duties are considered 'permanent,' and failing to fulfill them could result in lasting harm to their position and reputation within the company. A project is temporary, and therefore neglecting one's duties may have a smaller impact, as the relationship with its participants (including superiors) tends to fade after its completion. While allocating their time across multiple projects, employees may prioritize those projects whose managers are more 'assertive' or 'demanding' in ensuring task completion. The issue of conflict of authority, prioritizing concurrent tasks, along with the related problem of potentially overscheduling company employees, should be addressed through appropriate governance mechanisms within the company's hierarchy.

The following propositions may be formulated in relation to the internal (unilateral) project setup:

Proposition 7: *Internal (unilateral) project contractual setup, similar to hierarchy, is characterized by strong coordination mechanisms, low-powered incentives, coordinated adaptations to disturbances, and strong administrative control.*

Proposition 8. *The combination of low-powered incentives and strong coordination mechanisms promotes cooperative behavior aligning the interests of project team members that might otherwise be in conflict and facilitating dispute resolution through authority.*

Proposition 9: *Low-powered incentives in an internal (unilateral) project contractual setup undermine participants' motivation to achieve a planned project goal within the given schedule and budget constraints.*

Proposition 10: *The assignment of an employee to multiple projects or to both projects and day-to-day operations causes overscheduling and conflicts of authority.*

As a project under a unilateral contractual setup is conducted entirely within the company and utilizes its internal resources, the following proposition can be formulated:

Proposition 11: *In an internal (unilateral) project contractual setup, accountability for the project outcome, responsibility for delivering the project outcome, responsibility for project management functions and tasks, as well as project risk, are solely attributed to the sponsoring organization.*

The company must establish the project governance structure and mechanisms, plan the project concerning the definition of the project outcome, schedule, and budget. It needs to define and allocate an appropriate mix of resources, perform the project activities according to the schedule, oversee and manage the project on a daily basis, monitor progress, identify and address risks and issues, and perform all other activities as outlined in general project management methodologies so that a project steers towards the desired outcome.

3.4 Hybrid Project Governance Setups

All subsequent types of contractual relationships involve two or more legally separate entities with separate value streams, who involve in a long-term relationship. Therefore they fall into the hybrid form of contractual relationships.

As it was discussed in Chapter 1, Transaction Cost Economics (TCE) posits that hybrid governance possesses the following attributes (Williamson, 1981, 1991).

- Both mechanisms of adaptation to disturbances are possible – Hybrid governance supports autonomous adaptations through the price mechanism almost as effectively as market governance, albeit at a higher cost. On the other hand, it provides additional adaptive mechanisms that allow for some level of coordinated/cooperative adaptations. These adaptations are also costly, as they are carried out across a market interface through mutual follow-on agreements.
- Medium-level incentives – Compensation is linked to the results of work (or effort), but the incomplete contract allows for deviations from the planned values.
- Mixed coordination mechanisms and administrative control – Depending on the available adaptation mechanisms, the parties have a greater possibility to coordinate and control than in the market but less than through a hierarchy.

I suggest that specific types of hybrid contractual governance in projects vary significantly depending on the project attributes. These variations appear in the types of contracts considered suitable and the balance between contractual and non-contractual governance mechanisms. When considering the potential variants of governing hybrid contractual relations, it is essential to remember that the primary objective of a project, functioning as a temporary organization, is to achieve a desired outcome in a coordinated manner. Therefore, all project participants must collaborate within the designated organizational structures, regardless of the type of contractual relationship. The contract and other non-contractual governance mechanisms should facilitate such cooperation or, at the very least, not hinder the parties from collaborating in a coordinated fashion.

While the attributes of hybrid contractual governance derived from Transaction Cost Economics (TCE) are correct, they are specified too generally for projects. In terms of incentives, some hybrid contractual relations may be more similar to the market, while others may resemble hierarchy. The same applies to administrative control: in some hybrid governance situations, it may be limited to contractual agreements (with disputes possibly resolved in courts), resembling market transactions. Conversely, in other scenarios, contractors may opt for a cooperative approach similar to a quasi-hierarchy. The required level of coordinated adaptations to disturbances can also differ significantly and may be realized through various means, including contract re-negotiation, flexible contract clauses, non-contractual coordination mechanisms, or, in some cases, the intentional disregard of specific contractual clauses. The aspects mentioned above will be addressed below, with emphasis on the following:

- Feasible types of contracts, along with their respective pros and cons.
- Power of incentives.
- Required level of coordinated adaptation to disturbances and available coordination mechanisms.
- Level of administrative control and the available control tools.
- Equilibrium between contractual and non-contractual governance mechanisms.

3.5 Multilateral Centralized Hybrid Governance Setup

The first type of hybrid project contractual setup is a multilateral centralized one in which the sponsoring organization remains the primary and active owner of a project but contracts specific tasks or particular parts of the project outcome to other legal entities. To apply this kind of project contractual governance, the sponsoring company must possess domain-specific and domain-agnostic project management knowledge and project capability. The motivation behind implementing a multilateral centralized setup is the lower cost of contracting the appropriate, structured combination of resources, knowledge and skills from external entities compared to acquiring, configuring, integrating, and maintaining this combination of resources and knowledge in-house in certain areas. In this setup, the sponsoring organization retains accountability for the project outcome, overall responsibility for delivering the project outcome, responsibility for project management functions and tasks, and project risk. Specific tasks or particular parts of the project outcome are contracted to other legal entities, and the type of contractual relationship between the sponsoring company (the principal) and the contractors (the agents) depends primarily on what is contracted.

The following propositions can therefore be formulated:

Proposition 12: *To apply multilateral centralized project contractual governance, the sponsoring company must possess domain-specific and domain-agnostic project management knowledge and project capability.*

Proposition 13: *In a multilateral centralized project contractual governance the accountability for the project outcome, overall responsibility for delivering the project outcome, responsibility for project management functions and tasks, and project risk remain with the sponsoring organization.*

Proposition 14: *Contracting of specific parts of the project or specific task is motivated by the lower cost of contracting the appropriate, structured combination of resources, knowledge, skills, and capabilities from external entities compared to acquiring, configuring, integrating, and maintaining this combination of resources and knowledge in-house.*

There are several theoretical scenarios which involve contracting of specific parts of the project.

3.5.1 *Contracting a Specific Skill Set*

The first scenario involves contracting a specific skill set. The sponsoring organization hires an individual, several individuals, or an organized group of people to address a gap in its structured combination of resources, knowledge, skills, and competences required to deliver a project. Such individuals must be therefore fully integrated into the project organizational structure, meaning they are assigned roles and responsibilities and become familiar with the processes and procedures in effect for the project. They operate as if they were internal employees of the sponsoring organization: they are directed and controlled by the project management and have to obey authority much like members of the hiring organization. In this scenario, suitable contract types include behavior-based or resource-based contracts. Since the individuals hired are under the daily direction and control of the hiring organization, it is unnecessary to invest effort in crafting a detailed behavior description. Assuming the hired individuals possess the requisite skill set, their behavior can be guided by management. Therefore, a resource-based, full-time contract, outlining the desired skill set, specifying individuals who possess this skill set, and defining the timeframe during which they are available to the client, is adequate. The viable control mechanism is monitoring, and it is done via standard project governance structure and mechanisms, exactly the same way as in the internal project setup. In this scenario, the attributes of the contractual setup are similar to those of a hierarchy, i.e. strong coordination mechanisms, coordinated adaptations to disturbances, and strong administrative control. The coordination of project participants is achieved via authority (fiat) of the project hierarchy as all the participants are obliged to obey this authority.

In summary, contracting individuals with a specific skill set and integrating them into the internal project hierarchy is similar to hiring internal employees and assigning them to the project. The distinction lies in the fact that contractors acknowledge and accept the temporary nature of their engagement upfront, whereas employees are on permanent contracts. Consequently, contractors may be more motivated to contribute to the project's goals; however, they may be less cooperative, especially when facing unexpected disruptions.

Proposition 15: *Contracting a specific skill set in a multilateral centralized project contractual setup has the following attributes:*

- Resource-based, full-time contract specifying the skill-set and time-frame.
- Medium-powered incentives.
- Lower-level of motivation to cooperate as compared to employment contract.
- High level of coordinated adaptation to disturbances as the sub-contractors are integrated into the project organizational structure and are directed by the project authorities.
- High level of administrative control performed via monitoring of the sub-contractor behavior by the project authorities on a daily basis.
- Governance performed via non-contractual project governance structure and mechanisms within the project hierarchy.

3.5.2 *Contracting a Partial Outcome of a Project*

The second scenario involves contracting a partial outcome of a project. The feasible types of contracts and contractual governance mechanisms depend on:

- How well the partial outcome can be defined.
- How well the partial outcome can be measured (Eisenhardt, 1989). This measurement requires separating the outcome from other partial outcomes within the project in terms of its definition, responsibility, task assignment, and interdependence.

Well-defined and easily measurable outcome

For a well-defined and easily measurable (well-separated) outcome, an outcome-based contract is the best fit. From the principal's perspective (the buyer), it shifts accountability, responsibility, and risk to the contractor, and the transaction cost of implementing a governance based on metering is relatively low. Additionally, for the contractor, if the outcome is well defined and can be easily separated from other parts of the project, the risk of not meeting the contractual conditions is also relatively low. Classical contracting, with a close to complete contract, can be achieved quite easily by detailing the definition of the outcome and the time-frame, thereby limiting uncertainty and minimizing the potential for future disputes. This can be summarized in the following proposition.

Proposition 16: *Contracting a well-defined, easily measurable and well-separated partial outcome(s) of a project in a multilateral centralized project contractual setup has the following attributes:*

- Outcome-based contract with detailed definition of the desired outcome and the time-frame.
- High-powered incentives – the compensation is tightly linked to the result of work (or effort) – as the result of work is well-defined and well-separated from other partial outcomes of the project.
- Low level of coordination, with the contract as the main point of reference – As the outcome is well-defined and well separated from other outcomes, and the accountability, responsibility and risk is attributed to the sub-contractor, they do not need to coordinate their actions with other project participants on a daily basis. What has to be coordinated is the entry point and the exit point in time. In case of unexpected changes to the schedule or the scope of work, those can be managed by re-negotiation of the contract terms.
- Control done via metering – i.e. the actual result of the work is compared to the description of the outcome in a contract.
- Contract as the main point of reference for governance of contractual relations. With regards to non-contractual governance mechanisms, it is enough to include the starting and ending point of the delivery in the project schedule.

Well-defined and not easily measurable outcome

Next, the outcome may be well defined but not easily measurable. Intuitively, a well-defined outcome should be also easy to measure, as one can compare the detailed definition of this outcome with its actual features once it is finished. However, when considering partial outcomes and/or outcomes produced jointly by several legally separate entities, the situation is not as straightforward. The separation of the sub-outcomes and/or efforts made by individual entities may, in such cases, be problematic.

Firstly, any partial outcome is interrelated with other partial outcomes of a project. The nature of these interrelations and the clarity of the boundaries between the partial outcomes influence the ability to measure the outcome, and assign responsibility and accountability. The simplest situation involves sequential dependence between the sub-outcomes delivered by distinct entities. In other words, the work on sub-outcome β by contractor B cannot begin until contractor A finalizes their work on sub-outcome α. The outcome-based contract can still be effective in such a situation, provided that it is supplemented with conditional clauses reflecting the possible contingencies resulting from the dependence of work (e.g., what happens if contractor A delays, fails to deliver, or delivers an outcome with faults that prevent contractor B from delivering their part or make this delivery more costly). The level of coordination and administrative control is also higher because project management must evaluate the progress of each partial outcome to foresee and prevent possible delays and assess their impact on other contractors. A non-contractual governance mechanism suitable for this purpose would be periodic status meetings, during which contractors report the progress in their work, the issues they face, potential risks they foresee. Status meetings, involving project management and representatives of all contractors should also be the first instance for resolving possible disputes. Another governance mechanism is inspection, during which the project management physically assesses the progress of the work. For this to be possible, the definition of the outcome must not only be detailed but also disaggregated into smaller elements (e.g., by using the work breakdown structure) and placed on the time axis so that the progress can be easily traced at any moment. A consolidated project schedule, including all sub-products has to be produced and made available to all project participants.

Therefore:

Proposition 17: *Contracting well-defined sub-outcomes produced jointly by several legally separate entities, with sequential dependence between the sub-outcomes in a multilateral centralized project contractual setup has the following attributes:*

- Outcome-based contract with detailed definition of the desired outcome, the delivery schedule and conditional clauses reflecting the possible contingencies resulting from the dependence of work;
- High-powered incentives – the compensation is tightly linked to the result of work (or effort) – as the result of work is well-defined;
- Moderate level of coordination – the contract is still the main point of reference, but it has to be supplemented with non-contractual governance mechanisms, including status meetings and inspections to continuously track progress, promptly identify issues and risks, and initiate corrective actions before the contractual clauses become effective.
- Control is achieved through metering, characterized by a continuous, partial, and detailed approach, rather than a discrete and holistic one.
- Governance is achieved through a mix of contractual and non-contractual mechanisms. The outcomes are defined in the contracts, so the acceptance of the work is done with the use of the contract. The contracts also include contingency clauses related to the performance of other contractors. The

contracts, however, are rather the last point of reference than a tool allowing for coordinated achievement of the project goals. Non-contractual governance mechanisms, including status meetings and inspections must be put in place to proactively manage possible issues so that the contracts do not have to be used to resolve disputes.

Things get more complicated when the work on delivery of specific sub-outcomes is mutually permeating, i.e. contractor A needs to deliver part of the sub-outcome α_1 so that contractor B can proceed with the part of their sub-outcome β_1 after which contractor Z needs to deliver part of the sub-outcome $\mathfrak{z}_1$ so that A can start delivering α_2 and so on. For example, construction works related to laying floors and ceilings intertwine with installation tasks, such as laying cables and pipes. For contracting reasons, it would make sense to merge the sub-outcomes into a larger one and select one contractor as accountable and responsible. This way, all the possible conflicts on the boundaries between the partial outcomes could be resolved inside the contractor organization (as stated earlier, allowing for cooperative behavior to resolve disputes through authority within a hierarchy). However, due to the diverse skill sets the partial outcomes require, this is not always possible. Each contractor is a specialist accountable for a specific, clearly defined outcome. These outcomes are interrelated with those of other contractors, each having their own responsibilities. Consequently, a contractor cannot be held responsible for a failure to deliver their outcome if other contractors do not meet their obligations. One way of handling this situation is by drafting a complete contract that not only outlines the desired outcome but also delineates all potential interdependencies with other sub-outcomes, possible contingencies, and the corresponding actions. However, this approach may prove to be prohibitively costly or even unfeasible due to the multitude of unpredictable interdependencies among the permeating sub-outcomes. Alternatively, another approach involves entering into a behavior-based contract. If the sponsoring organization possesses the requisite knowledge and competence to effectively monitor the behavior of all contractors within their specialized domains and is willing to bear all project risks, this becomes a viable option. In this scenario, however, it makes even more sense to revert to the contracting of a specific skill set, drafting a resource-based contract, fully incorporating the contractors into the project structure, and directing and controlling them directly through the authority of the project organization. Assuming the transfer of all risks and the sponsoring organization's possession of the necessary knowledge, such an approach would minimize transaction costs, given that the cost of setting up a project organization is incurred anyway. The question arises: how should the contractual relationship be governed if the sponsoring organization lacks knowledge or expertise in the specialized domains of the contractors and/or is unwilling to bear the risks associated with their work? Such a scenario calls for a specific combination of contractual and non-contractual governance mechanisms. First, contracts must specify the respective outcomes in detail so that contractors may be held responsible in case the quality of their outcomes does not meet the required standards. Therefore, an outcome-based contract, which is complete in terms of the definition of the outcome should be implemented. Secondly, significant interactions between contractors and the resulting consequences should also be explicitly addressed in the contracts. This requires incorporating a behavior-based, incomplete contract component defining both desirable and undesirable behaviors in most common, foreseeable situations between the project parties. As this component is intentionally left incomplete, non-contractual governance measures must also be implemented. Project coordination, control, and adaptation to unforeseen contingencies should be managed through project governance structures and mechanisms. Within the boundaries of their contracts, contractors should adhere to the authority of the project management, which is empowered to coordinate their activities in the event of unforeseen disruptions or interference with other contractors. All contractor activities should be consolidated in the project schedule, visible to all participants, and under the control of project management. Contractors are expected to report partial progress, anticipated risks, and identified issues during regular status reporting events. In the face of unforeseen events requiring adaptation, project management should be the primary authority to coordinate and direct adaptive activities. This also applies to the resolution of disputes between contractors. Contracts should, therefore, incorporate slack or tolerance zones to facilitate these actions. Only in extreme cases should the contract be the point of reference, as relying solely on it risks project stoppage and hinders coordinated efforts to achieve project goals. This results in the following proposition:

Proposition 18: *Contracting well-defined sub-outcomes produced jointly by several legally separate entities, with permeating sub-tasks executed by various contractors in a multilateral centralized project contractual setup has the following attributes:*

1. Providing that the sponsoring organization possesses the necessary knowledge and competence to effectively monitor the behavior of all contractors within their specialized domains and is willing to bear all project risks:
   - Resource-based, time and materials contract specifying the skill-set and time-frame.
   - Low-powered of incentives, similar to those in employment contract within a hierarchy,

- High level of coordinated adaptation to disturbances as the sub-contractors are fully integrated into the project organizational structure and are directed by the project authorities.
- High level of administrative control performed via monitoring of the sub-contractor behavior by the project authorities on a daily basis.
- Governance performed via non-contractual project governance structure and mechanisms – project hierarchy.

2. Providing that the sponsoring organization lacks knowledge or expertise in the specialized domains of the contractors and/or is unwilling to bear the risks associated with their work:
   - Mix of complete, outcome-based contract specifically defining the outcome and incomplete, behavior-based contract, describing both the desirable and undesirable behaviors in most common, foreseeable situations between the project parties.
   - High-powered incentives – the compensation is tightly linked to the result of work – as the result of work is well-defined and the payment is done for the result. However, there are conditions outside of the control of the contractor which may affect their ability to deliver or influence the quality of the outcome. This may lead to problems with association of responsibility and related risk, and, consequently – to disputes. The mechanisms to prevent and eventually solve the disputes include the behavior-based part of the contract and non-contractual governance mechanisms.
   - High level of coordination – Project coordination, control, and adaptation to unforeseen contingencies is managed through project-related governance structures and mechanisms – the project hierarchy. Within the boundaries of their contracts, contractors must adhere to the authority of the project management, which is empowered to direct contractors in the event of unforeseen disruptions or interference with other contractors.
   - High level of administrative control – metering the result (continuous and at the end) plus monitoring of behavior – to coordinate and eliminate risks, including risks of disputes.
   - Governance is achieved through a mix of contractual and non-contractual mechanisms. The outcomes are defined in the contracts, so the acceptance of the work is done with the use of the contract. On a daily basis, however, coordination and control is done via project hierarchy, which is also the first instance for resolving possible disputes. The contracts, are the last point of reference in case other mechanisms fail.

Thirdly, the outcome may require some extent of joint effort involving resources out of control of the contractor: either the resources of the sponsoring organization or resources of the other contractor. It may be difficult to measure the exact contribution of each participant into the final outcome, and thus lead to disputes regarding the relevance of the remuneration. Some participants may also intentionally attempt to minimize their effort and transfer as much effort as possible to others. Projects involving joint effort, co-production or value co-creation (Lech, 2022b; Lehrer et al., 2012; Bettencourt et al., 2002; Ranjan & Read, 2016) is a norm in consulting, marketing, Information Systems and other knowledge-intensive business service (KIBS) projects. In such situations the outcome-based contract becomes unfeasible and the solution is to contract a specific skill set basing on the resource-based contract.

The hired resources work under the direction and control of the sponsoring organization project management structures, and are paid a lump sum for a specified period of time, offering 100% availability. Alternatively, they may be subject to part-time, time and materials contract according to which the contractors are paid for their actual time spent on the project. Such approach needs tight coordination, direction and monitoring from the sponsoring organization but minimizes the cost of agency, opportunism, disputes, responsibility conflicts, appropriation problems etc.

Proposition 19: *Contracting a well-defined outcome which requires co-production of several contractors in a multilateral centralized project contractual setup has the following attributes:*

- Resource-based, full-time contract specifying the skill-set and time-frame.
- Medium-powered incentives.
- Lower-level of motivation to cooperate as compared to employment contract.
- High level of coordinated adaptation to disturbances as the contractors are integrated into the project organizational structure and are directed by the project authorities.
- High level of administrative control performed via monitoring of the contractor behavior by the project authorities on a daily basis.
- Governance performed via non-contractual project governance structure and mechanisms within the project hierarchy.

Also, a mix of the outcome-based and behavior-based contract with non-contractual governance based on project hierarchy may be set up, as in the case of mutually permeating outcomes described above. This mix, however, becomes far more problematic than in the case of permeating outcomes as the boundaries regarding partial outcomes and effort are difficult to set.

Ill-defined outcome

The last scenario in a multilateral centralized setup, involves contracting of partial outcomes of a project to independent entities which are not well defined. The ill definition of the outcome may result from the negligence of the parties involved (which will not be discussed here) or from objective factors, including:

- Ambiguity of the outcome definition – i.e. different interpretations between the stakeholders of what the outcome is, which cannot be eliminated through the simple exchange of information (Atkinson et al., 2006; Thiry, 2002);
- Knowledge asymmetry between the project stakeholders preventing the common understanding of the project outcome, and causing ambiguity (Lech, 2022a);
- Cost of the exact outcome definition close to- or exceeding the cost of gradual outcome development, evaluation and necessary adjustments – e.g. in Information Systems development projects;
- Frequent changes of the outcome definition during the project, accompanied by relatively low costs of implementing the changes – e.g. in Information Systems development projects;
- Problem-solution entanglement (Lech, 2022a) – i.e. the situation in which the solution to one of the sub-problems modifies the set of the remaining sub-problems and/or alters the set of available solutions to the remaining sub-problems – e.g. in management consulting projects and Enterprise System implementation projects;
- Lack of commonly accepted and unequivocally understood conventions for defining the project outcome – e.g. in marketing or management consulting projects.

The above-mentioned factors, preventing from detailed definition of the project outcome before or during the initial phases of a project are characteristic for the projects with intangible outcome, with knowledge-intensive business service (KIBS) projects, such as management consulting, marketing and Information Systems being the prominent examples.

In a multilateral centralized setup the solution minimizing the transactional cost is the resource-based contract and incorporating of the hired resources into the project hierarchy.

Proposition 20: *Contracting an ill-defined outcome in a multilateral centralized project contractual setup has the following attributes:*

- Resource-based, full-time contract specifying the skill-set and time-frame.
- Medium-powered incentives.
- Lower-level of motivation to cooperate as compared to employment contract.
- High level of coordinated adaptation to disturbances as the contractors are integrated into the project organizational structure and are directed by the project authorities.

- High level of administrative control performed via monitoring of the contractor behavior by the project authorities on a daily basis.
- Governance performed via non-contractual project governance structure and mechanisms within the project hierarchy.

With regards to non-contractual governance mechanisms, agile methods were designed to deal with projects characterized by the ill-defined outcome.

3.6 Prime-Contractor Hybrid Governance Setup

The second type of hybrid project contractual setup, arguably the most complex and interesting in terms of governing contractual relations, is the prime-contractor (bilateral) setup. In this arrangement, the financing organization outsources the project to a prime-contractor, who assumes the majority of responsibility and risk.

The primary reasons for choosing a prime-contractor setup include a lack of project capability within the sponsoring organization or an unwillingness to bear project risk. As mentioned earlier, executing a project independently requires project capability, i.e., the ability to acquire, integrate, configure, and deploy resources effectively to achieve desired outcomes.

If this capability is lacking, the organization should compare the costs of developing it in-house against the cost of contracting it. If the organization does not anticipate repeatedly executing similar projects, the limited reuse of domain-specific project capability and project management knowledge may justify outsourcing to a specialized entity.

Therefore, the sponsoring organization may opt for a prime-contractor (bilateral) setup, transferring some or all responsibility and risk to the prime-contractor. The prime-contractor then acquires, configures, integrates, maintains, and deploys the necessary domain-specific resources and knowledge, charging a premium, and executes the project on behalf of the sponsoring organization. In many cases, prime-contractors, being project-based organizations, already possess the required project capacity and can deploy it directly to the project. The prime-contractor may either execute the project using its own resources, establishing a unilateral (internal) project governance, or contract parts of the work, creating a multilateral centralized contractual relationship with its contractors. Both governance structures have been previously discussed. This can be summarized in the form of the following proposition:

Proposition 21: *In case of a lack of project capability in the sponsoring organization, it should compare:*

- The cost of developing the project capability in-house, options for its future re-use, and the alternative cost of its underutilization with
- the transaction cost of contracting the project capability from an expert entity, as a prime-contractor,

and choose the least costly option.

Proposition 22: *In the prime-contracting governance setup, the responsibility and risk is transferred to the prime-contractor whose responsibility is to acquire, configure, integrate, and maintain the combination of resources and knowledge necessary to perform the project, and to perform the project on behalf of the sponsoring organization.*

Still, there are multiple governance variants, depending on the characteristics of the projects involved, viable and preferable governance/control mechanism as well as preferences and abilities of the parties involved.

The viable contractual scenarios depending on the definability and measurability of the outcome will be presented below, together with their major attributes. As in the previous cases those include:

- Feasible types of contracts;
- Power of incentives;
- Required level of coordinated adaptation to disturbances and available coordination mechanisms;
- Level of administrative control and the available control tools;
- Equilibrium between contractual and non-contractual governance mechanisms.

However, in contrast to the multilateral centralized setup, where the sponsoring organization retains primary and active ownership of the project, assumes accountability, coordinates and directs project activities, and bears overall risk, the prime-contractor setup is distinguished by the distributed allocation of accountability, responsibility, empowerment, and risk among contractual parties. Consequently, the following challenges highlighted by agency theory, information and knowledge asymmetry, and stewardship theory become more pronounced and need attention:

- Information asymmetry – i.e. situation when one party of a transaction possesses better information than the other party or parties, which puts her in a potentially favourable situation, in particular:
  - deliberately hiding information crucial to the transaction to the benefit of oneself;
  - ways of minimizing information asymmetry – both voluntary and forced by one of the parties;
  - impact of knowledge asymmetry of the parties on the possibility to reduce information asymmetry;

- Goal conflict between the principal and the agent – and the ways of aligning the goals;
- Distribution of risk between the principal and the agent;
- Hidden-action/opportunistic behavior – i.e. and benefitting from the hidden information in an opportunistic way, after the transaction has been made;
- Governance mechanisms constraining opportunistic behaviors of the parties.

3.6.1 *Prime-Contractor Projects with Well-Defined Outcome*

The first scenario involves a well-defined and easily measurable outcome. If the outcome can be precisely defined before the project at an acceptable cost, an outcome-based, complete contract would be the most suitable choice. Under such a contract, the responsibility for delivering the project outcome, along with the corresponding risk, is entirely transferred to the contractor (the agent). The contractor, in turn, has the freedom to shape the project's operational approach according to their discretion. S/he establishes the project governance structure and mechanisms, plans, organizes, directs, and controls the project on a daily basis.

Prior to signing a contract, a supplier must be selected. For a well-defined outcome, the classical tendering process may be used:
- a tender document, containing the detailed definition of the outcome, as well as other project terms and evaluation criteria (such as expertise with similar projects) is issued by the client;
- the potential suppliers review the tender document and, if interested, prepare and submit a formal tender response;
- the client evaluates the tender responses and shortlists the best proposals;
- the client further discusses the details of the tender proposals and negotiates the contract terms with the shortlisted suppliers;
- based on the above evaluation the client selects the winning bidder, finalizes the negotiations, and signs the contract.

This process can be lengthy and complex, as evaluations may be based on multiple additional criteria (Leśniak and Plebankiewicz, 2015), and negotiating the final contract terms can also be challenging. The costs associated with the bidding process contribute to the Total Cost of Project. Nevertheless, the comparison of offers, guided by the detailed project outcome specified in the tender documents, provides an objective basis for selecting the contractor based on measurable criteria. The search for contractors may be streamlined, as well-designed tender documentation will attract suitable suppliers, and the evaluation process will filter out those unable to perform the job.

During the realization, under the outcome-based contract, the sponsoring organization's control is limited to metering – that is, comparing the actual results of the project with the outcomes specified in the contract. The frequency of this control may vary from continuous, periodical (at the end of the project stages defined in the contract), to one-time – at the end of the project. To be able to:

– unambiguously define the project outcome in the contract, in accordance with the sponsors' requirements,
– and control the outcome of the project by comparing the planned and actual results,

the sponsoring organization needs the knowledge regarding the project domain and the technical means of expressing the requirements (the notation). The absence of the appropriate knowledge (i.e. knowledge asymmetry) may, at best, result in unintentional ambiguities in the understanding of requirements between the project stakeholders. Consequently, this could give rise to disputes regarding the actual meaning of the contract provisions. Furthermore, the contractor may also be inclined to exploit the knowledge asymmetry via opportunistic behavior by intentionally hiding crucial information or by shaping the contract to its advantage. In fact, under knowledge asymmetry, the contractor does not even have to hide the crucial information to gain opportunistic advantage. It is enough that s/he does not explain the consequences of crucial technical details and interrelations in the project outcome definition which the sponsor, due to the lack of knowledge, is unable to interpret by themselves. Therefore, the project sponsor (principal) must either already possess the knowledge necessary to define the project outcome and control the results versus the plan or acquire it prior to the project. The acquisition of knowledge may be performed via learning or by hiring independent, knowledgeable professional(s) who would act in the name of the sponsor.

In some cases, the process of requirements definition may be outsourced to an external expert. In a design-bid-build (DBB) setup, the preparation of design documentation based on the client's requirements is undertaken by this external expert company. Their role is to translate the client's general requirements into a detailed format, adhering to the formal rules of the project's domain. This process may involve creating a detailed design document that includes not only the requirements but also specific solutions that consider existing constraints. These documents must then be executed with 1:1 accuracy. The client uses this documentation to initiate a second tendering process, resulting in the selection of another specialized company to execute the project (Hale et al., 2009).

Another possibility for a client lacking domain knowledge is the design and build (DB) approach, in which both the design and execution of the project are contracted to a single entity (Hale et al., 2009). However, the level of the requirements' detail, and thus the level of client domain knowledge, must be higher than in the design-bid-build scenario to assure the comparability of the offers in a single tendering process.

Both approaches have their pros and cons (Hale et al., 2009; Hasanzadeh and Esmaeili, 2022; Lee et al., 2020; Minchin et al., 2013; Shrestha et al., 2012).

The advantages of the design-bid-build approach include possible lower costs due to competitive bidding for the build phase of the project, comparability of the build offers due to the clarity of expectations in the previously completed design (same for all bidders), and the lack of incentive to opportunistically shape the design in the contractor's favor (as the designer and the executor are distinct companies). The disadvantages include possible loss of information during the translation of the client requirements into the design document, and then during translating the design into execution, lack of the executor's responsibility for errors in the design, and possible opportunistic behaviors of the bidders in the build phase, who may lower the price to win the project and then renegotiate the contract later. The study by Minchin et al. (2013) provides examples of lower costs of DBB compared to the DB approach.

The advantage of the design-build delivery method is the lower chance of information loss, misunderstandings, and misinterpretations during the translation of the requirements into the design and the translation of the design into execution, as the process is performed by a single entity. It is also simpler to clarify differences in interpretations, as a single company is responsible for the entire process, from requirements gathering to final build. The project duration may be decreased due to the elimination of the bidding process for the build phase and the possibility of performing some of the design and build activities in parallel. The disadvantages include the lack of competitive bidding for the build phase and the possibility of opportunistic shaping of the design to the contractor's favor. The studies by Hale et al. (2009) and Shrestha et al. (2013) provide evidence that DB projects may be superior in performance compared to DBB ones.

Providing that the knowledge asymmetry problem is solved, the information exchange between the principal (the sponsoring organization) and the agent (the contractor performing a project) can be done in an asynchronous way. The principal outlines the detailed requirements regarding the scope of the project in the contract. As the appropriate notation used to express the requirements is known to both parties (there is no knowledge asymmetry), the requirements are unambiguous. This way the contractor has all the necessary information to produce the desired outcome. After an agreed stage of the project is completed, the contractor informs the sponsor so that s/he can check it, perform the approval procedure, or submit remarks if the outcome does not meet the requirements from the contract.

Regarding the unforeseen contingencies, which require adaptations, they may be divided into two basic categories:
- changes in the scope of the project,
- new/changing conditions in which the project is performed.

The first category can be managed by the amendment of the contract. Providing that the initial scope of the project was described in enough detail, the change to the scope would be unambiguous to both parties of the contract. The change in the scope should be manageable by extending the existing terms of the contract to the new scope, providing the project has not yet faced the irreversible stage (Flyvbjerg and Gardner, 2023, p. 34). If the project has advanced into the stage that the effects of prior decisions regarding the scope are irreversible (e.g. construction of a physical site has advanced), the changes of the scope may not be possible at all (or, to be precise, possible at an unacceptably high cost).

As the contract is outcome-based, the adaptation to the previously unknown conditions or an unexpected change of the conditions under which the project is performed is the responsibility of the contractor (the agent). If the change is in the price of resources, it will affect the project's profitability for the contractor unless the contract contains indexing clauses. However, there may also be changes in project conditions that implicate adaptations to the project methods/structure and/or changes in the resource base. As a rule, these adaptations should be made within the contractor's project hierarchy and do not require involvement from the sponsoring organization unless they affect the project's boundary conditions – for example, if they impact the project schedule in such a way that the project's final delivery date is postponed. At this point it is worth mentioning the possibility of opportunistic behavior of a principal. During the definition of the project scope in the contract, the sponsoring organization (the principal) may deliberately hide specific information regarding the conditions of the project from the contractor (the agent) if the principal knows that these conditions would increase the project price. The contractor may take the following preventive actions against the possible opportunistic behavior of the principal:
- Include the higher risk margin in the contract price – As the project risk is on the contractor, s/he would typically include some risk margin for unexpected events even if s/he does not expect the principal to behave unethically. If there is a high probability of the principal's opportunistic behavior, the risk margin could be higher.

- Specify the acceptable range of conditions under which the project is supposed to be accomplished in the contract. Consequently, if the project conditions go outside the specified range, the contract has to be re-negotiated or terminated. Although it may be difficult to foresee all possible future contingencies, an experienced contractor should be able to specify the conditions crucial from the perspective of delivering the project outcome. However, this requires the contract to be nearly complete, which may incur additional costs.
- Attempt to obtain the hidden information regarding the actual project conditions prior to signing the contract. This, however, may be prohibitively costly or even impossible.

If the project conditions deviate significantly from the standard expectations set by the contractor, whether due to the principal hiding crucial information or as a result of objective events, the contractor may need to consider extending the project resources, budget, and schedule to such extent, that it is either necessary to re-negotiate the contract or to abandon a contract despite the sunk project costs, lost revenues, penalties, and possible loss in reputation.

On the side of the principal, the tendency to re-negotiate the contract will depend on the level of specific investments into the relationship with the current contractor, and the cost of switching to another one. In the currently discussed scenario the specific investments of the principal are relatively low. The definition of the requirements can be done independently from the contractor, is prepared in accordance to the unified, commonly understood notation, and therefore any contractor would be able to comprehend it without significant clarification effort. In other words, the requirements definition is explicit, the boundaries between the requirements definition and the solution are sharp, and the requirements definition is contractor-independent. Once the requirements are defined by the principal, they can be understood and analyzed by any contractor without significant additional effort from the principal. The project execution neither requires current involvement from the principal and any work-in-progress should be fairly easily transferrable between various contractors. Therefore, transaction costs of terminating the contractual relationship with one supplier and switching to another one during the project involve possible contractual penalties or excessive payments in favor of the current contractor, search and negotiation costs with the new contractor, possible additional fees for taking over the work-in-progress by the new contractor, and the alternative cost of extending the project schedule due to the take-over.

The possibility of opportunistic behavior of the agent is related to the level of knowledge asymmetry. If the principal does not possess sufficient knowledge regarding the project domain, the contractor may deliberately offer cheaper solutions of lower quality hoping that the principal would not be able to asses that fact. The solution for the principal is to mitigate the knowledge gap, which was already discussed above. In the absence of knowledge asymmetry the possibility of the opportunistic behavior of the agent is limited providing that the scope of the project is defined properly and in sufficient detail, and control mechanisms are properly designed and implemented. Control mechanisms involve quality inspections of work-in-progress which need to be done frequently enough so that a given piece of work is not covered by another one, and, in case of defects, they can be corrected. For example: the quality of the piping has to be checked before the floors are laid down. Otherwise, the correction of the piping system would involve the destruction of the floors. In summary, the following proposition may be formulated:

Proposition 23: *Prime-contractor setup for projects with a* ***well-defined*** *and* ***easily measurable*** *outcome has the following attributes:*

- The outcome-based contract is a natural fit;
- The relationship is characterized by high-powered incentives – i.e. the compensation is tightly related to the outcome of the contractor's work;
- The risk is entirely on the contractor;
- The requirement for coordinated adaptations to disturbances is low, as the responsibility and risk for the entire work and the outcome lies solely on the contractor. The coordination mechanisms between the sponsor and the contractor in the face of unexpected contingencies are the contract and contract re-negotiation.
- The principal's administrative control is limited to metering of the actual results versus the definition of the results in the contract. The control tools include inspections and status meetings with the contractor.
- The governance mechanisms are contract-based.
- Setting aside the willingness of the parties to behave opportunistically, the potential for information asymmetry is low. There exists a unified, commonly understood notation, which allows for detailed and unambiguous definition of the project outcome.
- The principal may behave opportunistically by hiding crucial information regarding the specific conditions under which the project is to be executed. The contractor may prevent it by including the acceptable range of conditions in the contract, increase the risk margin or attempt to acquire the hidden information independently.
- The contractor may exhibit opportunistic behavior by hiding information regarding the quality of resources used in the project and masking deficiencies in project sub-outcomes with other work. The former can be addressed by a sufficiently knowledgeable principal through independent disclosure of resource characteristics. The latter necessitates careful planning and execution of inspections throughout the entire project duration.

The above scenario assumed contracting the entire project of a well-defined and easily measurable scope to one contractor, who bears the risk and responsibility for the entire work basing on the outcome-based, close to complete contract.

3.6.2 *Prime-Contractor Projects with Not Well-Defined Outcome*

The projects with not well-defined (and thus not easily measurable) outcomes will now be discussed, acknowledging that the level of definability and measurability of outcomes may vary among specific projects.

As previously discussed, the definability of the project goal or outcome depends on intrinsic factors (arising from the physical characteristics of the project goal) and/or extrinsic factors (influenced by the project's environment). Intrinsic factors include the physical nature of the outcome (tangible or intangible), existence of the commonly accepted, mature notation for describing the outcome, and complexity of the outcome, which determines the amount of time and effort needed to prepare the detailed definition. It can be assumed, with a probability close to certainty, that every tangible (physical) outcome can be defined in detail. There also exist commonly accepted, mature, engineering notations for describing any tangible outcome. Furthermore, most, if not all, tangible outcomes should be designed in detail, and their production planned carefully a priori due to the 100% irreversibility of decisions once their execution has progressed (Flyvbjerg and Gardner, 2023). If you want to alter advanced construction work once it has begun, you have to demolish it and start over again, not only losing all the effort and resources invested up to that point, but also investing additional resources into the demolishing process. Summing up, the outcome of engineering projects can and should be defined in detail, and the project should be planned carefully, taking into consideration all possible contingencies that can be foreseen, regardless of the contractual setup the parties intend to go for. Therefore, the problem of definability concerns primarily intangible outcomes. First of all, it is generically more difficult to visualize and understand an intangible outcome due to the lack of its physical manifestation. Following that, it is harder to develop an unambiguous notation for modelling intangible entities, and such notations do not always exist. Even if they exist, it is far more difficult to unambiguously model the intangible outcome due to the already mentioned difficulty with visualization and understanding of non-material entities. Take software development and implementation projects as an example, as they are one of the most researched type of projects with intangible outcome. There are books on requirements specification and modelling (e.g. Laplante and Kassab, 2022; Wiegers and Beatty, 2013), multiple notations for representing requirements and system design, such as Unified Modelling Language (UML) (Wrycza and Marcinkowski, 2011) or Business Process Modelling Notation (BPMN) (Marcinkowski and Kuciapski, 2012), and despite that, poor requirements definition and misinterpretation of requirements pop up as top failure factors in software projects (e.g. Al-Ahmad, 2009; McManus and Wood-Harper, 2007; Yeo, 2002).

Still, software systems are an example of intangible outcomes that can be defined in detail, although not without significant effort and challenges. There are, however, types of projects with intangible outcomes, for which a detailed a-priori definition of an outcome is unfeasible.

Firstly, some projects lack a widely accepted and unambiguous notation for modeling their intangible outcomes because providing a detailed definition of the outcome would essentially be equal to completing a project. Consider the creation of a company's visual identity as an example: the only reasonable way to define it is to actually create it, or at least mock it up. Or consider a legal or management advisory project in which the outcome is an expert opinion on a complicated subject matter. Such projects also suffer from the appropriability problem. "Appropriability refers to the ability of the owner of a resource to receive a return equal to the value created by that resource (Teece, 1987; Levin et al., 1987)" (in: Grant, 1996). Having the concept disclosed before the transaction may encourage the customer to use it for free (Arrow, 1962; Grant, 1996; Pollock, 2008).

Secondly, there are projects with a prevalent diagnostic phase. Such projects, as any other project in fact, aim at solving a problem (or define a solution for a problem at least), but contrary to other types of projects, the problem is not defined a-priori. The diagnosis and subsequent definition of a problem form a significant part of a project. Business improvement projects are a good example. When a management consultancy receives an order to suggest solutions for improving a process or a business area of a company, they cannot determine a-priori what problems they will encounter that should be solved. A project consists of a diagnosis of existing problems, and a report with suggested solutions. Prior to performing the diagnosis the consultant is unable to define what the suggested solutions would be, if any. All of the examples above are instances of Knowledge-Intensive Business Services (KIBS) which are delivered by knowledge-intensive firms. The activities of a knowledge-intensive company consist of "locating, developing, combining and applying various types of generic knowledge [...] to the local and specific problems, issues and contexts of their clients" (Miles, 2005). What these companies deliver to their customers is a concept, or a concept and its implementation. Rarely, it may also involve the implementation of someone else's concept. They include law and accounting firms, management and information technology consulting firms, market research and advertising companies, and research and development companies (Muller and Doloreux, 2009).

The examples mentioned above are projects that result in delivering a 'concept only'. These are projects that involve performing a diagnosis or requirements analysis, defining the problem, and designing its solution, but without implementation, such as:

- Preparing a company's visual identity without implementing it on the company's outlets.
- Providing legal or management advice.
- Creating a business improvement concept without implementing it in practice.

Such projects will be discussed in detail first.

Concept only projects

'Concept only' projects face an extreme measurement problem (Gallouj, 1997), not only regarding the output but also regarding the behavior of the contractor and the effort needed. First, the output cannot be defined in detail due to the reasons already mentioned above. Second, the quality of an output, the behavior and effort needed from the contractor to deliver it, is difficult for the client to asses due to the so-called opaque quality. Opaque quality means that "the quality of an expert's output is hard for nonexperts (i.e. customers) to evaluate, even after the output is produced and delivered" (Von Nordenflycht, 2010). The same refers to the contractor behavior and the extent of effort needed (Sharma, 1997). Opaque quality results from a knowledge asymmetry between the client and the agent, who is significantly more knowledgeable in the project's domain area. This knowledge asymmetry between the knowledge-intensive firm and its less knowledgeable client means that the client faces difficulties in interpreting the information provided by the service provider. To be able to interpret the information, the client would have to "invest significant time, effort and money to obtain the specialized knowledge, similar to the knowledge possessed by the knowledge-intensive service provider. This can be done only at extremely great cost or, as in most cases, not at all" (Sharma, 1997). Therefore, the client may face challenges in assessing key characteristics of the outcome, including scope, quality, and the necessary effort. Knowledge asymmetry and opaque quality have significant consequences for both knowledge-intensive business service firms and their clients. These consequences manifest even before the contract negotiation phase, influencing decisions during partner selection and tendering process. The contractors encounter the challenge of a vaguely defined subject in the request for quotations. Because of the limited definability of the intangible and conceptual nature of the expected outcome, there exists a significant level of ambiguity regarding the project's desired output. Additionally, as the conditions under which the project would unfold remain unknown to the contractor (and revealing them would be prohibitively costly), there exists a high level of uncertainty regarding the amount of work required to achieve the vaguely defined outcome. This, coupled with clients having limited knowledge about the subject matter of the contract, gives rise to challenges when comparing offers. Firstly, the offers may encompass incomparable scopes. Secondly, due to their restricted understanding, clients might struggle to assess which scope aligns with their needs and whether the planned effort and assumptions in the offers are accurate.

Some suppliers may attempt to behave opportunistically by offering a limited scope and effort for a price that would consequently be lower than that of honest competitors. This may lead to adverse selection, as in Akerlof's (1970) seminal example of used cars, where sellers of good-quality products (cars in Akerlof's paper, services here) are not able to obtain a fair price because clients are unable to differentiate between their product and low-priced, low-quality products offered by others. The result would be a market failure, as the good sellers would be pushed out of the market by the bad ones. Akerlof was analysing the situation of information asymmetry, in which the sellers intentionally hide information about the real condition of a used car from the buyers.

Information asymmetry can, to some extent, be reduced at a given cost. The buyer of a used car can perform screening: they can hire an expert to assess the car's condition. They may use a paint thickness gauge to reveal whether the car was repainted (which suggests it was repaired after a crash). They may also look for opinions from other buyers regarding the seller's reputation on the Internet. The seller may perform signalling: e.g. offer a warranty for a certain period. The problem with knowledge-intensive, intangible services is even more severe than the one with used cars. First, there is a problem of definability which does not exist in case of cars. Everyone understands how a car should look like and operate. This is not the case for knowledge-intensive, intangible services. Secondly, there is knowledge asymmetry which makes the evaluation of the quality of the outcome even more tricky. Remember that we are discussing the 'concept only' projects here. For such projects not only the client would have problems in comparing the offers from different vendors ex-ante, but the quality of the project outcome would also be difficult to evaluate ex-post, both by the client, and by external entities, such as courts. This makes adverse selection even more difficult to eliminate. The screening and signalling options are also limited comparing to the tangible product, such as a car. For 'concept suppliers' the only thing a prospective buyer can screen for is reputation (Greenwood et al., 2005). The sources for evaluating reputation can be classified as private or public. Private sources are embedded within an individual's reputation network (Dellarocas, 2006). A reputation network is built upon trust among its members and represents an ancient solution to the challenge of trust-building. Such networks possess the ability to foster cooperation without relying on expensive enforcement institutions and have existed long before the formal establishment of legal and contractual enforcement systems (Dellarocas, 2006). A key foundation of trust is repeated interpersonal interaction (Adler, 2001, Czakon and Czernek, 2016). Therefore, the first choice for a buyer would be to select a vendor whom s/he trusts due to the past successful interactions. However, trust can also be acquired "by reputation through a network of other trusted parties" (Adler, 2001). In other words, an individual would seek information from people s/he trusts to identify someone within their network who they trust as an expert in a specific domain.

Public sources of reputation include signals from vendors and other customers published in publicly available sources, such as social networks, industry outlets, web pages, and dedicated online reputation mechanisms (Dellarocas, 2003; Resnik et al., 2000). Public sources of reputation are less reliable than private ones because the receiver is unable to verify their veracity. They can be both positively and negatively biased. Vendors prefer to highlight their strengths rather than weaknesses. Even if a positive opinion comes from a customer, the receiver cannot be sure of the interests that connect the customer with the vendor. The customer may have incentives to promote the vendor, such as future discounts, or they may be in a hostage situation of some kind. A customer may also publish negative information that is not objective due to difficulties in assessing the service's quality resulting from knowledge asymmetry and opaque quality, as mentioned earlier. The number of opinions regarding idiosyncratic project outcomes would also be relatively small, making it difficult to base judgments on these opinions. There is little chance that an online reputation mechanism similar to those implemented in online shopping or hotel reservation platforms exists, with hundreds of opinions (which may also be biased, of course), allowing for judgments based on the average or dominant views from a large population of opinions.

With regard to signalling, vendor's options are limited due to the intangible, idiosyncratic, and often confidential nature of their output. Vendors may attempt to signal their competence either indirectly, by building reputation, or directly, by sharing parts of their knowledge. The sources of reputation have already been discussed. Private reputation is established through successful cooperation with clients who gain trust in the vendor, involve them in subsequent engagements, and spread the vendor's reputation within their private network. A vendor has little influence on this process, except by consistently delivering excellent work for clients. Public reputation building involves communicating achievements, success stories, competencies, and the portfolio of offerings through various public channels such as social media, conferences, trade fairs, websites, and industry outlets.

Reputation holds significant importance for vendors of intangible, knowledge-intensive outcomes, given the challenges in applying other measurable selection criteria by prospective buyers. As highlighted by Greenwood et al. (2005), reputation enables lower marketing costs as clients actively seek higher-status firms (Podolny 1993, 1994), and the ability to charge premiums due to brand recognition (Beatty 1989, Krishnan and Schauer 2000). Clients are often hesitant to switch from large professional service firms due to uncertainty about competitors' quality and comparability. On the other hand, a vendor's concern for reputation serves as a safeguard against fraud and opportunistic behavior (Dellarocas, 2006; Wolinsky, 1993). Acting unethically can damage a vendor's reputation and significantly impact its future market position.

Direct signalling of competence and knowledge may also be public or private. Public signalling may be performed by creating freely accessible knowledge centers and forums, publishing of white papers and reports, involving in academic publishing, active participating in industry and academic conferences. These activities also contribute to reputation building. Due to the already mentioned idiosyncratic and confidential nature of the specific outputs, the knowledge shared by the public channels must be generalized and high-level. In other words, it would rarely be specific enough so that a potential new customer could apply it to solve their problem without external help. In addition to that, only explicit knowledge can be presented, and significant part of the company's knowledge is tacit – i.e. embedded in the vendor's personnel. Summing up, sharing general, high-level knowledge via public channels does not hurt the company's competitive advantage or its bottom line, because there is little chance anyone (competitors or prospective clients) would be able to effectively apply this knowledge to actually solve any real-life problems – there is no appropriability problem. The disadvantage is that due to its limited usefulness, public signalling of competence has also limited effectiveness: anyone can do it and there is little possibility of verifying whether the communication is true or false.

Private signalling of knowledge and competence involves demonstrating a dedicated piece of work to a potential customer. This poses several problems for the supplier. Firstly, for 'concept-only' projects, there is often no other way than showing the concept to the customer, which causes the appropriability problem. As Pollock (2008) puts it: "Knowledge, by its nature, tends not to be a homogeneous good, and thus a buyer is unlikely to be willing to pay much for a piece of knowledge whose properties are unknown. However, if the seller reveals the knowledge to the buyer in order to demonstrate its value, the very act of disclosure serves to transfer the knowledge and eliminate the seller's market".

Secondly, the effort to prepare the concept for demonstration constitutes a sunk cost for the vendor unless the transaction is completed afterward. The solution to both problems is the offering of a paid proof of concept. However, this approach also brings sunk costs to the future buyer, who must pay several potential suppliers for delivering the same piece of work.

Screening and signaling costs can be minimized if **there is trust** between the parties. Trust is defined as "the subjective probability with which an actor assesses that another actor or group of actors will perform a particular action, both before she or he can monitor such action (or independently of his or her capacity ever to be able to monitor such action) and in a context in which it affects his or her own action" (Gambetta,1988 as cited in Adler, 2001). In fact, trust between the contractual parties lowers not only the screening and signaling costs, but other transaction costs as well (Noteboom, 2000; Müller et al., 2013). As it was mentioned in Chapter 1, transaction costs are the administrative costs for agreeing and following up on contracts (Müller et al., 2013) which include search and information costs, bargaining and decision costs (Coase, 1988), costs of drafting, negotiating, and safeguarding an agreement (Williamson, 1985), mal-adaptation and haggling costs, costs of running of governance structures (including monitoring and/or metering), and the economic bonding costs of effecting secure commitment (Williamson, 1985).

The sources of trust can be categorized into direct repeated interaction, reputation within a network of other trusted parties, and adherence to values and norms (Adler, 2001). Among these, direct repeated interaction is the strongest. If a buyer has successfully completed similar projects with a particular vendor in the past and had positive experiences, they may bypass market screening and information searches to engage directly with the trusted vendor. Reputation endorsed by other trusted parties can also influence vendor selection, although to a lesser extent, which was already discussed above. Values and norms represent the weakest source of trust as it is not directly verifiable. Trust plays a crucial role in governance across various project types, even those with clearly defined goals (Yan and Zang, 2020). However, its significance grows when project goals are less defined, and there is greater knowledge asymmetry between partners. In such cases, other governance mechanisms may become challenging, costly, or even unfeasible. The role of trust in subsequent phases of project contractual relations will be covered further in this chapter. The above can be summarized in a form of the following proposition.

Proposition 24: *The process of search and selection of a partner for a 'concept only', knowledge-intensive projects in a prime-contractor contractual setup has the following characteristics:*

- The detailed definition of the outcome of a 'concept only' project is unfeasible as:
  - They lack unambiguous and generally accepted notation;
  - And/or providing a detailed definition of an outcome would be equal to completing the project;
  - And/or diagnostic phase constitutes majority of the anticipated project work.
- Ambiguity of the outcome poses problems:
  - for the buyer to define the expected outcome in the request for quotation;
  - for the seller to address the vague and ambiguous requirements in the offer;
  - for the buyer to compare the offers as they may have addressed the ambiguities in the definition of scope in completely different manners.
- The search for prospective vendors is therefore based on:
  - Trust resulting from past direct interactions;
  - Private reputation disseminated through the network of other trusted parties;
  - Public reputation built through public signaling of competencies, achievements; success stories, and the portfolio of offerings through various public channels such as social media, conferences, trade fairs, websites, and industry outlets.
  - Private signalling of knowledge and competence involves demonstrating a dedicated piece of work to a potential customer.

Once a partner is chosen, a contract and other governance mechanisms must be established for the project. As mentioned earlier, 'concept only' projects face challenges in measuring output, evaluating supplier behavior, and assessing required effort. Knowledge asymmetry between the supplier and the buyer makes it difficult for the buyer to effectively evaluate the output, behavior, and effort of the supplier even after successful delivery of the project. Therefore, implementing effective metering or monitoring control strategies becomes challenging. Furthermore, neither outcome-based nor behavior-based contracts are entirely feasible due to difficulties in specifying outcomes and evaluating both outcomes and supplier behavior, related to the knowledge asymmetry (Sharma, 1997; Gallouj, 1997). Indeed, buyers of 'concept-only' projects face unfavorable conditions. Except from very particular situations, buyers of knowledge-intensive, intangible outcome projects should avoid 'concept only' projects and shift towards 'concept and implementation' ones, as they reduce the options of opportunistic behavior of the vendors and facilitate the assessment of the final outcome. Bernis (2022) interviewed CEO's of McKinsey and BCG consulting enterprises, who both agreed that this is happening: clients tend to shift from "advising to advising and building". The situations in which 'concept only' projects are justified include:

- An outside opinion of knowledgeable experts is needed to make a highly consequential and/or controversial decision (Cole, 2022);
- The implementation of a concept is straightforward and may be executed with the use of less expensive (possibly internal) resources.

Due to the limited definability of the intangible outcomes in 'concept-only' projects, the contracts will inherently be incomplete. The specific content of these contracts depends on the nature of the project outcome. If the outcome is an intangible product (like a written report or visual company branding), the contract will likely outline the general features of this product.

This creates an incomplete outcome-based section within the contract. Conversely, transactions that do not involve the delivery of any product, such as continuous advisory services over a period, representing a client in court, or ongoing project supervision will not have the outcome-based section. Such activities, however, do not meet the definition criteria of a project, i.e. temporary organization set up to achieve a specified goal or output under the constraints of time, budget and other resources. They can only be contracted on a resource-based, time-and-materials basis, where personnel with defined knowledge, skills, and capabilities are delegated for a specified number of hours or days. Payment is based on the hours or days spent on the assignment, irrespective of the specific activities performed. Many professional service firms, including law and accounting firms, commonly adopt this model.

Returning to projects, it can be assumed that every project, per definition, has an outcome, and a general description of this outcome should be included in the contract. However, the definition of the outcome is ambiguous, and due to the knowledge asymmetry, clients may struggle to assess the necessary skills, competencies, and effort required to achieve it. In many cases, both parties in the transaction would benefit from a description of the process for achieving the outcome – a behavior-based section. Describing the vendor's behavior helps reduce the opacity of the supplier's efforts to some extent and provides justification for billing. It also aids in conveying the level of complexity of the services being procured to the vendor.

On the other hand, knowledge-intensive projects often require active client participation to achieve their goals. This is especially crucial for 'concept and implementation' projects but also for some 'concept only' projects the client co-production is necessary. Consider managerial diagnosis as an example: detailed information from the client regarding the subject of the diagnosis is essential for its completion. In other words, suppliers of many knowledge-intensive projects rely on their clients' participation to deliver the promised output. Therefore, a contract should include a section defining the client's required behavior for successful delivery of the output.

There is another crucial element for the success of knowledge-intensive projects, which is the specific combination of knowledge, expertise, and skills possessed by the individuals delivering the project, which is in-line with the Knowledge Based View (Grant, 1996. Lech, 2014). Certainly, knowledge, expertise, and skills are important in any project, not only in knowledge-intensive ones. For instance, when building a ship, a combination of highly knowledgeable engineers and various skilled workers is required. However, the difference lies in the verifiability of their expertise, which can be relatively easily assessed through inspections of their work and related outputs. Moreover, competence, skills, and related behaviors are largely standardized through industry norms and regulations in such projects.

In contrast, knowledge-intensive projects, especially those focused solely on concepts, present a different scenario. The quality of the output is challenging to assess, and the supplier's behavior may remain opaque to the buyer. Therefore, the knowledge and expertise of the personnel involved become crucial determinants of the output quality. A buyer should consider including a resource-based section in the contract, detailing the level of expertise and knowledge required from the supplier's personnel. In extreme cases, this section of the contract may take the form of a list of named individuals, along with their CVs, who are guaranteed to be involved in the project. This provision protects the client from the vendor's opportunistic behavior when experienced and qualified experts are presented during the offering process, while juniors are sent to execute the job. Summarizing, the following proposition can be formulated:

Proposition 25: *The contract for 'concept-only' projects should include up to three key elements:*

- **Outcome-based element**: This defines what will be delivered. Due to the limited specificity of the outcome, its description may be somewhat general and may not serve as a definitive basis for evaluating project completion.
- **Behavior-based element**: This section outlines how the work will be performed and specifies the activities involved. It adds credibility and structure to the more ambiguous outcome-based component. It allows the client to monitor, to some extent, whether the work is being performed with due diligence and/or, at least according to the plan. In cases of knowledge asymmetry between the buyer and the vendor, this section demonstrates to the less knowledgeable buyer the level of effort and complexity required to accomplish the project goal. The behavior-based part should also detail the

activities expected from the buyer, such as promptly providing all required information or evaluating partial project outcomes without delay.
- **Resource-based element:** This details the level of expertise and knowledge required from the supplier's personnel. This ensures that the project is executed by the right individuals, which is crucial for delivering proper quality given the limited specificity of the outcome.

The inclusion of one or more of the above elements influences the available options for billing. The first possibility is an outcome-based fixed-price contract, where the payment of the full project price is executed upon delivery of the project outcome. The advantage of this approach to the buyer is that they only pay if the project outcome is delivered. It minimizes the risk that the supplier will withdraw from the project in the middle of work after receiving partial payments, which could be difficult to recover even with the use of courts, given the vagueness of the contract and the likely clauses in the contract regarding co-production requirements that the vendor could opportunistically exploit. However, the intangible outcome of a knowledge-intensive, 'concept-only' project is impossible to define in detail, both in terms of its particularities and quality. Therefore, relying solely on the outcome as the determinant of payment poses a risk that the vendor would provide a low-quality outcome with minimal effort just to receive payment. This risk can be reduced by adding a behavior-based and resource-based parts to the contract, which will be covered later. Also, the vendor would risk its reputation which could affect its future options to sell to other clients. On the other hand, the buyer may not properly assess the outcome due to knowledge asymmetry or behave opportunistically by questioning its particularities and/or quality, even if both are correct. One remedy could be to split the payments between partial outcomes over time, although not every final outcome is divisible. Another more feasible option is to introduce a behavior-based payment structure, where payments are made after certain activities are accomplished. This option will be discussed in more detail later.

An outcome-based fixed-price contract poses severe risks to both sides, albeit greater to the vendor. No matter how diligently the vendor does its work, the buyer may always question the result, and the verifiability of this result by external parties such as courts is limited. One possible safeguard is adding clauses to the contract regarding copyright transfer only after payment has been made. Therefore, an outcome-based contract should be avoided as it poses issues to both parties.

The second possibility is a combined outcome-based and behavior-based fixed-price contract. Payments are made upon completion of specified activities and after the delivery of the project outcome. Additionally, the buyer should include a resource-based section in the contract detailing the knowledge and expertise of the vendor's personnel involved. This section does not affect billing but provides additional assurance of the outcome's quality.

One can envision a contract with a single payment made after all activities specified in the contract are finalized and the outcome is delivered. This approach gives more control to the buyer compared to a purely outcome-based contract. The buyer can monitor the activities performed by the vendor's personnel, reducing the possibility of minimizing effort and delivering a low-quality product to some extent. In most cases, there is a knowledge asymmetry between the buyer and the vendor, so the buyer will not be able to assess the substantive nature of the vendor's effort. However, they will at least be able to verify that the effort has been made. Combined with the assurance of the vendor's personnel qualifications, this constitutes at least a partial guarantee of the service quality involved.

A single payment scenario does not reduce any risks for the vendor, who still faces the possibility that the buyer may refuse payment regardless of the actual quality of the outcome or effort made. This risk is due to the limited definability and verifiability of the outcome. At most, what a single payment scenario does for the vendor is increase credibility in case of a legal dispute, as they can prove that the necessary activities to deliver the outcome were performed. However, engaging in any legal process, regardless of the outcome, can negatively impact a vendor's reputation, which most vendors would prefer to avoid. Including a behavior-based component in the contract, which specifies the required activities, also reduces flexibility in fulfilling contractual obligations. There may be instances during the project where certain tasks specified in the contract become unnecessary. Nevertheless, the vendor would still be obligated to perform them. For these reasons, it would be unreasonable for a vendor to accept a single payment scenario.

The solution that balances the risks resulting from limited definability of the outcome and knowledge asymmetry between the client and the supplier, while also limiting the possibility of opportunistic behavior from both sides, is the combined outcome-based and behavior-based fixed-price contract with partial payments. Under such a contract, fixed partial payments are executed after certain activities have been accomplished, and a final payment is made after the delivery of the project outcome. If project activities result in partial outcomes, payments should be associated with the delivery of these outcomes, as they can be measured and approved. However, as stated earlier, not every final outcome is divisible, especially in the case of 'concept-only' projects.

As in the previous case, the buyer should also include a resource-based section in the contract detailing the knowledge and expertise of the vendor's personnel involved, as it serves as an additional important mechanism for ensuring the proper quality of the outcome. This setup also allows the buyer to monitor the completion of the project tasks compared to their specification from the contract. Additionally, the buyer has greater motivation to actually check the status of the activities (rather than shirk) as there is a payment associated with it. The vendor is protected from not being paid due to the buyer's limited understanding of the outcome or opportunistic behavior with the use of partial payments. Also, possible misunderstandings regarding cooperation surface more quickly due to periodical assessments of progress related to partial payments. These misunderstandings can be addressed sooner or, in the worst case, cooperation may be terminated earlier, minimizing the loss of effort and money.

All the above variants are fixed price, so they do not account for a change in scope or effort. Any variance in effort must be covered by the vendor. In case of the change in scope, it may be either also covered by the vendor or subject to the scope change management procedures. The issue of changes in scope after the contract has been signed are more relevant for the 'concept and implementation' projects, so they will be discussed in detail later.

The payment terms which leave more flexibility in reaction to the changes in scope are time and materials, when the actual working hours or days are billed. Time and materials contracts put far more pressure on the buyer, who needs to closely monitor the consumption. Otherwise the planned effort may be burned down on unproductive activities, or the vendor may opportunistically exaggerate their involvement. There is little advantage of such contracts for the buyers of 'concept only' projects otherwise than in the situations when an outcome is completely undefined. Such situations, however, do not meet the definition of a project and are rather a kind of operations outsourcing. Again, a resource-based section should be added to the contract detailing the knowledge and expertise of the vendor's personnel involved.

Due to their short to medium duration and lack of physical implementation, 'concept only' projects, by definition, are not subject to a high level of disturbances, provided that the participants do not create them themselves. However, they do require active participation from the client's personnel, which needs to be coordinated.

Most if not all 'concept only' projects follow the pattern:

> (1) Diagnosis -> (2) Agreement on the problem definition -> (3) Design of the solution proposal(s) -> (4) Presentation, selection, and sign-off of the solution proposal

The steps 1 and 2 and 4 require tight cooperation between the supplier and the client, while development of the solution (or alternative solutions) proposal(s) can either be done solely by the supplier or in iterative, agile mode, depending of the substance of the project.

During the diagnostic phase of a project (which constitutes a significant part of the project work), there is a need for the provision of information from the client to the supplier. Unlike projects with well-defined, tangible outcomes discussed earlier in this chapter, asynchronous provision of information in the form of documentation is not sufficient. First of all, there is no commonly accepted, unambiguous notation for conveying the information. Furthermore, information presented in documents may be influenced by biases. In some cases, the specific goal of a project could involve identifying and mitigating these biases and their impact. Therefore, a combination of information sources and means of gathering information should typically be used. These include analysis of documentation, workshops with various stakeholders, one-to-one interviews, field observation of physical processes, demonstrations, among others. Activities related to information exchange must be coordinated in time and space. This requires, at minimum:

- A procedure and tool for scheduling work, meetings, and workshops, informing stakeholders about their required presence, and booking relevant infrastructure.
- Physical and/or virtual infrastructure for conducting work, meetings, and workshops.
- A dynamic list of stakeholders with specifications of the knowledge areas from which they should provide information and/or other roles they play in the project.
- Project manager(s) or coordinator(s) who will oversee the above tasks.
- Authority to ensure all stakeholders provide their input in a timely and high-quality manner. This authority should be established by fiat within each participating organization. One approach to achieving this is by appointing two project managers, one from the supplier's organization and one from the client's organization, each possessing the authority to manage their respective sub-teams.
- Established procedures, document templates, and a repository for documenting the project inputs and outputs.

The project activities and outputs must also be reviewed and approved, both contractually and substantively. First, the findings during the information gathering/diagnostic activities need to be confirmed and signed off by the stakeholders to ensure that the supplier's understanding of the phenomenon/requirements is comprehensive and compatible with what the supplier intended to convey, thereby achieving agreement on the problem definition. This step does not necessarily have anything to do with the contractual agreements, but it constitutes a crucial part of the diagnostic phase of the project. Secondly, the final outcome of the project also needs to be signed off by the stakeholders, involving both substantive and contractual approval. Both sign-offs require approval procedures to be put in place, and adherence to these procedures must be ensured by the project manager(s). Depending on the type of contract involved, there must be respective governance mechanisms in place.

An outcome-based contract (or part of the contract) requires a procedure to determine who and on what basis evaluates the compliance of the actual outcome with its contractual definition. The approval procedure for the outcome would typically cover both substantive and contractual sign-off. Substantive approvals would take place gradually during the project, and at the end of the project, substantive approval would come first followed by the contractual approval. Since the outcome is not defined in detail, the evaluation must be based on the judgment of the stakeholders. The procedure would involve, at a minimum, a list of approvers, means of submitting remarks, methods of addressing remarks (e.g., clarification meetings), and methods of approval (e.g., sign-off of the paper document, email notification, change of status in the workflow system). The behavior-based component necessitates a mechanism for evaluating and approving the activities outlined in the contract. This requires implementing a status reporting system, such as a RAID (Risks, Activities, Issues, Decisions) log or another task-tracking tool, along with an approval procedure to determine who, how, and based on what criteria decides that tasks are considered complete. A task-tracking tool is essential not only for contractual governance but also to assist project managers in their daily operations. For a time and materials contract, a time reporting system is required, followed by an approval procedure.

In most 'concept-only' projects, the co-production between the client and the supplier is typically limited to the exchange of information and approvals. Nonetheless, governance mechanisms must ensure the following:

- Coordination of the work of each party separately, necessitating a project manager or coordinator with an appropriate level of authority. The source of this authority depends on the contractual setup within the project team. For the client team, this typically relies on hierarchy (fiat), as the individuals assigned to the project are employees of the client organization. For the supplier team, it may involve hierarchy if the work is performed by the supplier's employees, or a combination of contractual and non-contractual governance mechanisms if subcontractors are involved. In either scenario, the teams must function as a single temporary organization, in which members accept authority from their respective project manager.

- Ongoing coordination of work between the two parties on a daily basis, achievable through non-contractual governance mechanisms such as scheduling tools, task management tools, project manager meetings, and project team meetings.
- Timely resolution of disputes and tensions between the parties, which may or may not necessitate reference to the contract.
- Monitoring, measuring, and approval of contractual provisions.

The above requirements necessitate a combination of contractual and non-contractual governance mechanisms, each of equal importance. Specifically, it becomes natural to have two project managers, one for each project party, who collaborate daily to plan, organize, direct, and control the project work. They must actively resolve ongoing issues and streamline activities within their respective project sub-teams to ensure coordinated contribution towards achieving the project goal.

This leads to the following proposition:

Proposition 26: *For projects that are characterized by ill-defined, intangible, and conceptual outcomes, and are executed under a prime-contractor setting, there are certain aspects that remain consistent regardless of the implemented contract regime:*

- Conceptual projects face substantial information asymmetry, which is too costly to mitigate before project execution. The diagnostic phase, during which this asymmetry is addressed, constitutes a major part of these projects.
- Due to their nature (typically short to medium duration with conceptual rather than functional outcomes), such projects are not subject to significant disturbances. However, the nature of the work anyhow necessitates coordinated actions, requiring ongoing information exchange among project parties.
- Coordination is achieved through a combination of contractual and non-contractual governance mechanisms, with non-contractual mechanisms being equally or more critical. Non-contractual governance mechanisms encompass a suite of tools and procedures for planning, organizing, directing, and controlling project activities, including the involvement of project managers from both parties who coordinate work within and between their respective sub-teams. These non-contractual mechanisms are essential components of project management, independent of the specific contract type, as they stem from the project's nature rather than its contractual framework.
- Additionally, non-contractual mechanisms provide a foundational basis for governing contractual relationships, facilitating project effort monitoring and outcome assessment through continuous information exchange and cooperation.

Besides the above-mentioned common attributes, there are also characteristics of contractual relationships, which vary based on the contract regime.

Proposition 27: *Viable contractual governance setups for 'concept only' projects are as in table 5.*

TABLE 5 Contractual governance for 'concept-only' projects

	Type of contract		
	Outcome-based fixed-price (single or partial payments)	**Combined outcome-based and behavior-based fixed-price (single or partial payments), with resource-based section**	**Resource-based time and materials**
General remarks	This approach is advisable only when there is a high level of mutual trust between the parties, as the contract itself provides limited coverage or protection to either party.	A single payment approach provides more protection for the principal compared to a pure outcome-based contract, but it increases the risks for the agent, who should avoid such an approach. A partial payment setup balances the positions of the principal and the agent in the contractual relationship. A resource-based section detailing the knowledge and expertise of supplier personnel increases the probability of achieving the expected quality.	This is the only feasible scenario when an outcome is completely undefinable, such as during ongoing consultations or legal advice. Such assignments do not meet the criteria of a project, as there is no defined outcome.
Power of incentives	The definability of the outcome is low, with payment directly tied to the outcome. The client faces challenges in verifying the outcome's conformity to the vague contractual definition and assessing its quality. Consequently, the **power of incentives** appears paradoxically **low**.	The low definability of the outcome is compensated to some extent by listing the activities needed to accomplish it in the contract. The **power of incentives is highest** compared to other contractual setups, as the agent is motivated to accomplish all the desired tasks and deliver the contracted outcome.	Incentives are low because the agent is paid for every hour spent on the assignment, regardless of what they do or accomplish.

TABLE 5 Contractual governance for 'concept-only' projects (*cont.*)

	Type of contract		
	Outcome-based fixed-price (single or partial payments)	**Combined outcome-based and behavior-based fixed-price (single or partial payments), with resource-based section**	**Resource-based time and materials**
Goal conflict between the principal and the agent	The level of goal conflict is high. The supplier has an incentive to minimize effort and interpret the outcome definition in a way that favors them. Meanwhile, the client may have a different interpretation of the outcome definition.	Provided that the activities detailed in the contract are aligned with the project outcome, the goal conflict is low. The agent is interested in performing the activities as described in the contract, as this is a condition for partial (or final) payments. The realization of all the activities should lead to the accomplishment of the project goal.	The nature of the goal conflict is that the agent wants to bill as many hours as possible, while the principal wants to minimize them.
Ways of aligning the goals between principal and agent	The contract does not provide mechanisms of aligning the goals. The alignment of goals can be achieved with the use of trust, reputation and non-contractual project governance mechanisms.	Goal alignment can be achieved by ensuring that the list of activities in the behavior-based part of the contract includes all activities necessary to attain the project outcome and excludes any obsolete tasks. The resource-based part of the contract, which specifies the knowledge and expertise of the supplier personnel, serves as an additional safeguard for the outcome quality.	The way to align the goals is through tight cooperation between the principal and the agent, allowing the principal to direct and closely monitor the agent's actions.
Distribution of risk between the principal and the agent	Both supplier and client are at risk. The client is at risk of obtaining a low-quality output while the supplier is at risk of not being paid.	In a single payment scenario, most of the risk is transferred to the agent, who may find themselves in a situation where all activities are performed and the outcome is delivered, but the principal opportunistically questions the outcome to avoid payment.	The entire risk is on the principal

TABLE 5 Contractual governance for 'concept-only' projects (*cont.*)

	Type of contract		
	Outcome-based fixed-price (single or partial payments)	**Combined outcome-based and behavior-based fixed-price (single or partial payments), with resource-based section**	**Resource-based time and materials**
		A partial payment scenario distributes risk between the agent and the principal. The principal can continuously monitor the agent's behavior by comparing the tasks actually performed with their definitions in the contract, as well as evaluate the final outcome. The agent is paid in parts after the agreed sets of activities have been performed, which protects them from the risk of not being paid at the end of the project.	
Opportunistic behavior of the agent	The agent may attempt to minimize their effort and/or assign individuals with low expertise (and therefore lower employment costs). The resulting low quality of the outcome would be difficult for the client to prove and challenging for external entities, such as courts, to evaluate.	The possibility of opportunistic behavior by the agent is significantly reduced, provided that all three parts of the contract are properly constructed. The resource-based part of the contract ensures that the qualifications of the agent's personnel are appropriate for the tasks assigned to them and for achieving the project's objective. The behavior-based part ensures that all tasks necessary to accomplish the project objective are performed. The outcome-based part is the least important due to its inherent vagueness, but it ensures the final outcome is delivered.	The agent may tend to overbill and/or perform activities which are not necessary to achieve the outcome to add billing hours.

TABLE 5 Contractual governance for 'concept-only' projects (*cont.*)

	Type of contract		
	Outcome-based fixed-price (single or partial payments)	**Combined outcome-based and behavior-based fixed-price (single or partial payments), with resource-based section**	**Resource-based time and materials**
Governance mechanisms for constraining opportunistic behavior of the agent	The contract provides limited mechanisms for constraining the agent's opportunistic behavior. Loss of reputation, in the event that the low quality of the output becomes public, is the main constraint.	The governance mechanisms that constrain the opportunistic behavior of the agent include: – The resource-based part of the contract, which guarantees the involvement of people with appropriate qualifications. – The behavior-based part of the contract, which ensures that all tasks needed to attain the project goal are performed. – The outcome-based part of the contract, which ensures the final outcome is delivered.	The governance mechanism is continuous monitoring of the agent's actions.
Opportunistic behavior of the principal	Due to the vague definition of the outcome in the contract, the principal may question its conformance with the description and/or quality even if they are objectively correct to avoid payment.	In the single payment scenario, the possibility of opportunistic behavior by the principal is similar to that of a purely outcome-based contract. The only difference is that the agent's chances in court are higher, as they can attempt to prove that the activities defined in the contract have been performed and, therefore, the outcome is correct. In the partial outcomes scenario, the possibility of opportunistic behavior by the principal is greatly reduced, as they must pay after certain sets of activities have been accomplished.	The principal may tend to question the billed hours even though they are legitimate.

TABLE 5 Contractual governance for 'concept-only' projects (*cont.*)

	Type of contract		
	Outcome-based fixed-price (single or partial payments)	**Combined outcome-based and behavior-based fixed-price (single or partial payments), with resource-based section**	**Resource-based time and materials**
		Therefore, the intention not to pay is revealed much sooner, before the delivery of the final outcome, which allows the agent to react appropriately.	
Governance mechanisms for constraining opportunistic behavior of the principal	Property rights may prevent the principal from using the outcome of the project in some cases. Partial payments for sub-outcomes can protect the agent from losing the entire value of the contract.	The opportunistic behavior of the principal is reduced by introducing partial payments eligible after defined sets of activities have been performed and by implementing the behavior-based part of the contract, which specifies the activities the principal must perform as input to the project.	Tight cooperation with the principal and frequent billing reduce the possibility of the principal to behave opportunistically.
Additional aspects and remarks		The single payment scenario should not be chosen by the agent. The partial payments scenario provides a balance between the parties.	

It is important to reiterate that the potential loss of reputation is a significant incentive to reduce the temptation for opportunistic behavior by the agent under any of the above contractual setups. Trust is a crucial governance mechanism that reduces the need for complex contractual arrangements. Still, as previously highlighted, 'concept-only' projects with ill-defined, intangible outcomes should be approached with extreme caution. Contracting both the conceptual part and implementation to the same entity can solve some problems caused by the low definability of the outcome.

Concept and implementation projects

Concept and implementation is equivalent to a design and build delivery method, commonly known in 'hard' projects. In 'hard' projects with well-defined outcomes, there is a balance of pros and cons between 'design and build,' where all activities are contracted to one entity, and 'design-bid-build,' where the design and construction are contracted to separate agents. The design-bid-build approach protects against an agent's attempt to opportunistically steer the design to favor themselves during construction (e.g., making it cheaper, requiring less effort, or yielding a better margin). Additionally, it allows for competitive bidding among potential constructors, which can result in a lower project price. However, this requires the project scope to be detailed and unambiguous, meaning every actor in the market understands it the same way. Since perfect unambiguity is hard to achieve even for projects with tangible, well-defined outcomes, a drawback of the design-bid-build approach is that the constructor may interpret ambiguities in their favor. Moreover, if the designer makes a mistake, the constructor cannot be held responsible for the consequences. Furthermore, the designer may have less incentive to prepare the design diligently, knowing they will not be responsible for construction.

The cons and pros of a design and build approach are exactly the opposite. The contractor, responsible for both the design and the build, may attempt to shape the design in a way that is more beneficial to themselves rather than to the principal during the build phase. Additionally, there is no competitive bidding, as one contractor is assigned both the design and construction phases (although there may be a bidding process in which the designer competes with other entities for the construction phase). On the other hand, the contractor ensures that the design is feasible, as they are held responsible for both the design and the construction based on that design.

It is important to note that the literature on 'hard' projects' design-and-build versus design-bid-build delivery methods (e.g., Hale et al., 2009; Hasanzadeh and Esmaeili, 2022; Lee et al., 2020; Minchin et al., 2013; Shrestha et al., 2012) implicitly assumes that a client's requirements are translated into a feasible blueprint in a single step – i.e., the design phase. This assumption is valid for 'hard' projects as the requirements tend to be unambiguous due to their basis in the physical world, and there exists a commonly accepted notation for translating requirements into design. Furthermore, the separation between the requirements (i.e., the 'what') and the design (i.e., the 'how') is small, as it is constrained by the number of well-defined and proven technical options for achieving a particular goal in the physical world. For example, there are a limited number of technical options for building a road or a bridge.

In contrast, in 'soft' projects, the requirements may be unclear not only to future contractors but also to the client. Therefore, an additional diagnostic step: requirements elicitation or requirements definition may be necessary, during which an expert partner works with the client to gather and accurately represent the requirements. This leads to the following proposition:

Proposition 28: *'Soft' projects involve define, design, and build phases, which can be combined into the following delivery methods:*

- Define and design-bid-build (concept-bid-build): In this scenario, one entity prepares the design and another executes the project after winning a bidding process. This method is the equivalent of design-bid-build in 'hard' projects but rarely makes sense for 'soft' ones due to the lack of standard, commonly accepted notation and the resulting loss of information as well as risk of imposing a specific solution while there exist many of them.
- Define-design-build: These are 'concept and implementation' projects type 1, in which the entire process is contracted to a single entity.
- Define-bid-design-build: These are 'concept and implementation' projects type 2, where competitive bidding is used for the design and build of a solution based on previously defined requirements. The definition of requirements may be performed by the client themselves or by a separate expert company.

For 'soft' projects with intangible and not well-defined outcomes, the balance of pros and cons shifts dramatically towards the 'concept and implementation' approaches. The advantages of 'concept-bid-build' diminish due to the low definability of the outcome. Even assuming zero opportunism from either of the two agents, the agent responsible for implementation may not be able to understand the concept prepared by the other agent without ambiguity. Since there is no commonly accepted, unambiguous notation for representing the project outcome, the implementing party may interpret the concept (the design) differently than intended by the designing party. Furthermore, as the notation is ambiguous, it does not convey information without loss: partial loss of information occurs during the transfer from document to people. Therefore, the implementing party may build something that is far from what the designing party intended, not to mention the intention of the client, as the information exchange between the client and the designing party also involves ambiguity and information loss at the people-to-document interface. Moreover, due to the low definability and ambiguity of the design, in the case of bidding, offers from various bidders are incomparable as they may propose completely different outcomes based on their understanding of the design.

In addition, bidders may behave opportunistically and deliberately interpret the design in a way that allows for a cheap solution, even if they understand that the client intended otherwise. This approach enables the bidder to win the contract by offering a low price, progress the work enough so that it becomes costly for the client to withdraw, and then re-negotiate the contract. Similarly, the contractor responsible for the design may also act opportunistically by including solutions or mechanisms that do not work in a given practical setting, are extremely costly, or are otherwise suboptimal, knowing they will not be responsible for the implementation – a classic agency problem. These risks are eliminated in the 'concept and implementation' approaches, although this comes at the cost of a possibly higher project price due to the lack of competitive bidding after the design phase.

Let's return to the initial assumptions: the client/buyer wants to execute a project with an outcome that is intangible and difficult to define. Since the project is outside the client's area of expertise, they lack the necessary domain-specific knowledge, domain-specific project management knowledge, and project capability necessary to perform or at least lead the project by themselves. Due to the one-time or occasional nature of the project, the client decides that the cost of developing this capability in-house, as well as the cost of acquiring, configuring, integrating, maintaining, and deploying the required resources and knowledge, is too high. Therefore, the client opts to outsource the project to a specialized contractor who possesses the appropriate combination of resources, knowledge, skills, and capabilities to perform the project.

The project outcome is not well-defined prior to execution due to intrinsic factors, extrinsic factors, or a combination of both:

- There is no unambiguous, commonly accepted notation for defining the outcome.
- The problem to be solved is not well-defined a priori, and diagnosing and describing the problem constitutes a significant part of the project.
- The requirements for the outcome are unclear or unstable.
- The cheapest (or only) way to define the outcome is through demonstration.
- Problem-solution entanglement occurs (Lech, 2022a), meaning the choice of a particular partial solution changes the definition of the problem and vice versa.

For example:

1. In Information Systems development projects, there are unambiguous notations, but in some cases, the requirements are unclear and unstable. The most cost-effective way to clarify these requirements may be through presenting prototypes.
2. In business process improvement and business change projects, diagnosing and describing the problem constitutes a significant part of the project.

3. There is no unambiguous notation for defining the outcome of a project aimed at creating a company's visual identity, and demonstration is the only way to define the outcome.
4. Implementing a company-wide Enterprise System, such as an Enterprise Resource Planning (ERP) system, involves both organizational changes and the introduction of new technology. The solutions made in the system shape the organizational processes and, therefore, alter the problem to be solved. This results in problem-solution entanglement.

Furthermore, many of these projects involve co-production that goes beyond the provision of information. Client personnel must not only provide requirements and assess their completion but also make decisions that influence the company's operations, implement organizational changes, and cooperate with the contractor's staff during daily project activities. These project characteristics and situational conditions shape the contractual relations between the parties, from partner selection to project closure.

With regard to the tendering and partner selection process, similar to 'concept-only' projects, the ambiguous definition of the project outcome poses challenges in identifying and proposing relevant solutions by the suppliers, as well as in evaluating and comparing the offers by the client. Even setting aside the possibility of opportunism, suppliers may interpret the client requirements differently and, as a result, offer solutions to different problems. Furthermore, they may offer solutions to the same problem that significantly differ in comprehensiveness. Some may also opportunistically interpret the requirements to their favor, hoping for a later renegotiation of the contract. On the other hand, the client would struggle to compare the inherently incomparable offers. Furthermore, due to a lack of appropriate domain knowledge, they may not be aware that the offers address completely different scopes.

As 'concept and implementation' projects result in something that works, the achievable level of project goal definability may be greater than for 'concept-only' projects. Certainly, the verifiability is greater because, even if one cannot evaluate how the project outcome works, they can assess whether it yields the expected results. However, in most cases, the client would need to modify the classical tendering process used for well-defined outcomes. In the classical process, potential suppliers responded to a tender document containing the detailed definition of the outcome, along with other project terms and evaluation criteria (such as expertise with similar projects). This approach allowed for an objective evaluation of the offers and the formulation of a nearly complete, outcome-based contract.

The extent to which this process needs to be changed depends on the clarity, level of detail, completeness, and stability of the requirements. Possible situations range from a very general problem statement to a fairly clear and complete list of requirements (though not 100% clear, complete, and unambiguous), and fall within the following generic scenarios:

1. Only a general problem/outcome definition is known prior to the project – type 1 projects
2. Detailed requirements specification is known prior to the project – type 2 projects.

They will be discussed in detailed below.

1. General problem definition is known prior to the project

The first scenario assumes that only a general or broad definition of the problem is known before starting the project: neither the 'what' nor the 'how' is known in detail prior to the project's commencement. The reasons include the following:

- Diagnosing and defining the problem form a significant part of the project, making it impossible or unreasonable to separate the diagnosis from the solution.
- The cheapest (or only) way to define the outcome is through demonstration.
- It is prohibitively costly to prepare a complete and detailed definition of the project outcome (including situations where problem-solution entanglement occurs).
- Only incremental problem definition/ requirements specification during the project is possible as the requirements are unclear, incomplete and/or unstable.

The projects with general or broad definition of the problem would continue a path outlined when discussing the 'concept only' diagnosis projects, which is:

> (1) Diagnosis -> (2) Agreement on the problem definition -> (3) Design of the solution proposal(s) -> (4) Presentation, selection and sign-off of the solution proposal -> (5) Implementation of the agreed solution

Compared to the 'concept only' project, a fifth step: implementation of the agreed solution is added. For some projects, one iteration may be sufficient, while in others, the above steps will be repeated iteratively in agreed time-boxes (sprints) in an agile/hybrid approach. Additionally, in an agile/hybrid approach, the design and implementation of the solution would intertwine.

The **partner selection and tendering** process in this scenario faces similar problems as those for 'concept only' projects. Due to the vague definition of the outcome, it is difficult to perform the tendering process in a classical way, i.e. through the objective comparison of the offers posed by the bidders. The contractors may have different understandings of the problem the project aims to solve and, therefore, may offer incomparable solutions. Some suppliers may attempt to behave opportunistically by offering a limited scope and effort for a price that would consequently be lower than that of honest competitors, and then aim for re-negotiation during the project, hoping that the client's sunk investment in the relationship would prevent them from breaking the contract (the hold-up problem).

Similar to 'concept only' projects, for 'concept and implementation' projects with a general outcome definition, the reputation of a contractor is a significant factor to screen for. The first choice for a buyer is to select a vendor whom they trust due to past successful interactions. The second choice would be a contractor who is trusted within the buyer's reputation network which means, a buyer would seek information from people they trust to identify a company that is trusted as an expert in a specific domain. If private sources of reputation fail to identify a suitable contractor, the client may turn toward public sources: signals from vendors and other customers published in publicly available sources such as social networks, industry outlets, web pages, and dedicated online reputation mechanisms.

Unlike 'concept-only' projects, the evaluation opportunities for 'concept and implementation' projects extend beyond reputation. These projects deliver tangible outcomes, such as an information system, a reorganized company, re-engineered business processes, or a won lawsuit. Therefore, a supplier should be able to signal a reference list of successfully completed similar projects. Reviewing this list, speaking with the companies involved, and organizing reference visits to observe the results of the vendor's prior engagements are valuable ways to assess a potential contractor. However, the main drawback of reference talks and visits is that former clients' time and willingness to participate are limited resources for the vendor. Former clients are unlikely to welcome frequent requests from potential clients. The reference visits are a scarce resource for the vendor, so they would reserve them for potential deals with high value and probability of success.

In other words, the vendor would estimate the expected value of the deal – i.e., the value of a contract multiplied by the estimated probability of winning the contract – and agree to invest in a reference visit only if the expected value of the deal exceeds the alternative cost of losing a future deal due to the limited number of available reference visits.

Consequently, clients should request reference visits only after shortlisting potential contractors. Otherwise, they risk being declined by some vendors and prematurely eliminating promising contractors, potentially leading to suboptimal decisions.

If the project outcome can be divided into smaller parts, potential contractors can also be asked to deliver a small, partial outcome in the form of a **proof of concept** (POC). This is the most tangible way to verify whether the contractor can deliver an outcome that meets the client's needs. However, it is also the most costly method.

One possibility for the client is to ask every vendor in the tendering process to prepare the POC free of charge. Nevertheless, the client would still need to invest time and resources to detail the requirements and collaborate with all the vendors during the POC creation process. On the other hand, vendors would weigh the expected value of the contract against the cost of delivering the POC, which would be lost if they do not win the deal. This consideration might exclude some contractors from the tendering process. Often, the best contractors in the market have the weakest incentive to compete under these conditions.

Besides the cost of utilizing resources to prepare the POC free of charge, the vendor will also assess the opportunity cost of not involving those resources in other potentially profitable activities. This is especially important since knowledge-intensive project businesses are non-scalable. Not only can a given combination of resources be utilized for only one assignment at a time, but it is also difficult to expand the resource base at a constant marginal cost.

The situation with most knowledge-intensive project businesses is that their projects are non-repetitive and rely predominantly on highly knowledgeable people who need to gain specific knowledge through experience (Lech and Zamojska, 2017). Therefore, the possibility of acquiring people with the appropriate level of knowledge and skills to be immediately assigned to a new project is very limited. In the short term, the capacity of a knowledge-intensive project business is constrained by its available personnel. The best companies on the market have a network of former clients who trust them and hire them for new assignments. They also acquire new clients through the private reputation networks of their former clients. Consequently, they may not have the capacity to engage in costly and uncertain tendering processes.

Another option for the client is to pay several potential contractors to prepare a Proof of Concept (POC). This option is favorable for the suppliers as they, at a minimum, get their costs covered. However, it increases the client's search and information costs. The investment in the POC of the winning bidder may be recovered, as the result of the POC can be included in the final product. However, the investment in the POCs of the losing bidders would be lost, along with the time and resources the client spent cooperating with them. The advantage of this approach is that it does not potentially exclude the best suppliers, who might otherwise refrain from bidding due to the high cost. This can be summarized in the following proposition:

Proposition 29: *The process of search and selection of a partner for 'concept and implementation', knowledge-intensive projects with general problem* *definition known prior to the project, in a prime-contractor contractual setup has the following characteristics:*

- To minimize search and information costs, a client would select a partner they trust based on previous successful engagements.
- If such a partner does not exist, the client would shortlist possible contractors based on their reputation (within their private reputation network and from public sources).
- For the shortlisted group of possible contractors, the client would conduct reference talks, reference visits, and, if possible, paid proofs of concept.

The signaling possibilities of suppliers derive from the above-mentioned screening options of clients. First and foremost, suppliers must maintain trustful relationships with their past and current clients. The most straightforward way to achieve this is by delivering what they promise with good quality. Secondly, suppliers should convert this trust into both private and public reputations. This can be done by involving past clients in success stories, which are then shared through joint presentations at conferences and other forums, as well as in podcasts and publications. The latter is an infinitely expansible digital good, while the former is a scarce good, as the time former clients are willing to invest in in-person events is limited.

Another step is to ensure the possibility of reference talks and visits, which, as mentioned earlier, are also scarce assets. In the case of 'concept and implementation' projects, the outcome is an intangible solution working in a specific environment. Therefore, by sharing high-level knowledge in their area of expertise with the general public free of charge, suppliers do not face attribution problems. Their value stream is realized by applying their knowledge and expertise to specific problems, in specific environments, and under specific constraints, which are only known during the specific project engagement. So, sharing general knowledge in the form of white papers, presentations, podcasts, etc., is another valuable way to signal competence.

Once the project partner is initially selected, a contract must be prepared and signed, and the project must be planned and kicked-off.

The available ways of shaping the contractual relations between the parties are similar as for 'concept only' projects, although not without differences. In the currently discussed scenario, the detailed definition of the project outcome is not known prior to the project's start. Consequently, the outcome-based section of the contract will likely outline only the general features of this outcome, which may not serve as a definitive basis for evaluating project completion.

However, 'concept and implementation' projects result in a working solution: a system, a process, an organization, or an artifact. Therefore, although the scope of this solution is not known in detail before the project begins, it must be defined and approved during the project.

The procedures and activities leading to the incremental outcome definition, the form of representing the partial results, as well as the criteria, procedure, and schedule for approving project partial results and the final outcome must all be specified in the contract. These elements augment the outcome-based and behavior-based sections of the contract, respectively and can be shortly names as 'incremental outcome definition and approval procedure'.

Its structure depends on the project management approach applied, which in turn depends on the characteristics of the outcome and the intrinsic and extrinsic factors affecting its definability.

For projects with outcomes that fit the waterfall approach, the following should be specified at a minimum:

- Definition and schedule of the activities comprising the diagnosis stage.
- Form of the presentation of the results of the diagnosis stage.
- Procedure and criteria for acceptance of the results of the diagnosis stage, including the dispute resolution procedure.
- Schedule for the preparation and the form of the presentation of the design.
- Procedure and criteria for acceptance of the design, including the dispute resolution procedure.
- Schedule of the implementation phase.
- Criteria for acceptance of the final solution and acceptance procedure, including:
  - The definition and schedule of partial acceptances, if they exist
  - The schedule for final acceptance
  - The dispute resolution procedure
  - Procedure for handling changes in scope made after the design sign-off.

The above list is supported by stage gate waterfall project management methodologies as described in PMBOK (2013–2021), PRINCE2 (2009), or PM^2 (2023). What the contract includes should be aligned with the specific project management methodology applied.

It must be noted that due to the imperfect information transfer between people and documents, the intermediate results of the project, such as the problem definition document and the design document, are not easily transferable to entities other than the one that prepared them. If the client decides to terminate the contract with the supplier after the diagnosis phase is completed, and hand over the problem definition document to another contractor, the diagnosis phase would need to be repeated to some extent, as the new contractor would require clarifications to properly understand the problem. The same applies to the design document. Despite these transferability issues, the intermediate project outcomes can be used as milestones for partial payments.

Agile/hybrid approaches assume that every time-box results in a working increment and includes a full cycle: from in-depth diagnosis and definition of a problem, through design and implementation of the solution, to testing and sign-off of the increment. Therefore, if a project is to be executed using an agile/hybrid approach, the contract should include, at minimum, the following:

- Number and duration of time-boxes (sprints).
- Assignment of items from the product backlog to the sprints (in hybrid approach).
- Acceptance criteria for the increment.
- Definition of roles and responsibilities within the agile team.
- Procedure for handling changes to the product backlog during the project (in hybrid approach).

The major difference between hybrid and agile approaches is that in a hybrid approach, the scope is fixed before the project begins. Any changes to the scope later in the project must go through a strict change management procedure. In contrast, agile approaches welcome changes to the scope even late in the project. Therefore, a hybrid approach involves assigning items from the backlog to sprints in advance, ensuring that all scope is distributed across the sprints beforehand. It also includes a scope change management procedure. Agile methodologies define all aspects that need to be established before the project starts, so the contract should follow the guidelines of the chosen agile methodology.

Most knowledge-intensive business projects require a high level of co-production. First of all, since the project outcome is not unambiguously defined in detail prior to the project, the client must cooperate throughout the entire project duration. This involves gradually providing detailed information on the nuances of the scope, verifying the contractor's understanding, approving the resulting design, and testing the effects of the implementation. If the project involves problem-solution entanglement, the client must not only check and approve the conformance of the design with their requirements but also assess the impact of design decisions on their operations, and possibly manage organizational change and requirements changes in other areas of the project scope. If the project requires changes in the organizational structure, processes, or procedures, the client must actively execute them.

The need for co-production significantly impacts both the governance of contractual relations and non-contractual, project governance. The client's responsibilities should be included in the behavior-based part of the contract, as failure to adhere to them can prevent successful project completion. However, co-production, as the name suggests, involves continuous cooperation between parties in pursuit of the project goal. It is unrealistic to expect parties to constantly refer to the contract to verify their duties. Moreover, since the project outcome is not well-defined, achieving it may require adjustments in the behavior of both parties compared to the initial plan. The contract should serve as the last point of reference in case of disagreements that cannot be resolved otherwise or in the event of premature termination of cooperation and subsequent legal action.

Successful co-production requires establishing non-contractual governance mechanisms that enable the parties to function as a single temporary organization, regardless of their position in the contractual relationship. A unified project structure must be set up to facilitate prompt decision-making, planning and task assignment, task execution, response to changes and issues, and progress control. Roles and responsibilities must be clearly defined and filled by individuals from both parties. Procedures for planning, decision-making, coordination, communication, risk and issue management, and project status control must be designed and implemented.

The need for co-production also influences how project relationships can be explained by dominant theories. In a classical agency setup, the principal delegates tasks, responsibility, and authority to the agent so that the agent acts on behalf of the principal, either executing designated activities or achieving the desired outcome. In the case of co-production in a bilateral, prime-contractor setup, the high-level situation is similar: the client (the principal) hires a contractor (the agent) to accomplish a project. However, at the operational level, co-production changes the relations between the parties.

The contractor, as the more knowledgeable party, is hired by the client to perform the project because the contractor possesses the necessary domain-specific project management capabilities and expertise. The specificity of the project requires constant cooperation between the client and the contractor, extending far beyond the initial presentation of requirements and final assessment of the outcome. Since the contractor knows what needs to be done to accomplish the project, the contractor often directs the client on a daily basis. Furthermore, the contractor cannot deliver the project if the client fails to cooperate.

Thus, at the operational level, the roles of principal and agent are reversed: the contractor directs the client, supervises their behavior, and evaluates the results of their work, while at the project level, the client remains the principal who pays the contractor to deliver the project. On the high level, the client is the principal who sets the requirements, evaluates the results, and pays for them. On the operational level, the contractor acts as the principal who plans, directs tasks, and supervises their execution.

An attempt to explain the relationship between the parties of projects with poorly defined outcomes, executed in a prime-contractor setup and subject to co-production with the use of agency theory leads to the theoretical paradox. Such projects:

1. Involve two parties with a conflict of interest.
2. This conflict of interest cannot be resolved in the contract, as the contract is incomplete and the outcome is not defined in sufficient detail.
3. The nature of the project outcome requires the parties to cooperate as if the conflict of interest did not exist.

The cooperation of the parties is facilitated by the implementation of non-contractual governance mechanisms, such as a unified project structure, roles, responsibilities, processes, and procedures. An open question remains as to why the parties agree to set aside their self-interest to some extent and cooperate towards the project goal, and how potential conflicts of interest are resolved in a non-contractual manner.

The answer may be provided by stewardship theory (Derakshan et al., 2019; Müller et al., 2013). Stewardship theory challenges the assumptions regarding human nature that underlie agency theory, specifically the idea that people (and organizations) are purely profit maximizers. It assumes that at least some people, in certain situations, maximize their utility through means other than profit maximization. Regarding the classical agency problem, where managers are hired to run a company on behalf of the shareholders, stewardship theory posits that some managers may prefer to "do a good job, to be a good steward of the corporate assets" even if their interests are not perfectly aligned with those of the principal. This behavior stems from a sense of duty (Davis et al., 1997) and a motivation driven by "a need to achieve, to gain intrinsic satisfaction through successfully performing inherently challenging work, to exercise responsibility and authority, and thereby to gain recognition from peers and bosses" (Donaldson and Davis, 1991). In the context of projects, stewardship theory suggests treating project managers as stewards who are willing to act in the best interest of the project sponsors (Derakshan et al., 2019), and implementing trust as the governance mechanism (Müller et al., 2013).

The situation under analysis here is different, as it involves two separate legal entities: the client (principal), who orders a project, pays for it, and benefits from its outcome, and the supplier, who executes the project on behalf of the client using their own resources. Additionally, the project requires co-production, meaning the client must actively participate in the project activities. The supplier is more knowledgeable in terms of the project domain, so they direct the project activities toward successful completion. Since the project outcome is not well defined prior to the project, the contract is incomplete and does not provide sufficient governance for either party. The parties must develop non-contractual governance mechanisms to deliver the project.

Regardless of the contractual situation, the parties must cooperate as a unified project organization. Stewardship theory suggests that at least some entities will choose to complete the project even if doing so involves actions that are not perfectly aligned with their self-interest. These entities are motivated by factors other than their own self-interest, such as a sense of duty or commitment to the project's success.

The client's motivation is (at least theoretically) straightforward: they are the party who deliberately initiates the project, benefits from its results, and is directly interested in its successful completion. However, potential issues can arise. First, the client may understand their participation in the project differently than the supplier. They may assume a smaller involvement of their resources than the supplier expects. They might also assume that certain activities will be performed by the supplier, while the supplier assumes otherwise. Such issues can and should be resolved in the behavior-based and resource-based parts of the contract. The contract should explicitly define what resources are needed, for how long, and with what intensity from the client. Furthermore, the contract should list the activities that require client involvement, possibly in the form of a RACI (Responsible, Accountable, Consulted, Informed) matrix (e.g., Smith & Erwin, 2005). The behavior-based part of the contract should prevent opportunism from both sides regarding the imposition of tasks on the other party.

Secondly, the client may face challenges in motivating their personnel to diligently participate in the project. The ways of managing this problem are similar to those used in projects conducted within a single organization. Lastly, there may be politics and conflicts between different factions within the client organization, some of which may support the project, while others may jeopardize it (Flyvbjerg, 2021). Stakeholder theory addresses the situation where different interest groups affect and are affected by the project. Nevertheless, the client's dedication to the project is key to its successful completion. Without the client's real involvement, the project cannot succeed. In summary, in projects requiring co-production the issue of client's incentive to accomplish the project goal becomes crucial.

For the supplier, the project is the core of their operations. They are a project-based organization specifically set up to handle such projects. In most contractual arrangements, the supplier has an incentive to complete the project, as part of their remuneration depends on it. Non-contractual incentives include the potential loss of reputation in case of a project failure. Court cases, even if won, are not welcomed by suppliers of knowledge-intensive business services. Typically, suppliers would go the extra mile for their clients to avoid public failure, even if it means acting against their own profit. Therefore, suppliers maintain a buffer of goodwill to use before resorting to court or halting the project. However, this buffer can be depleted by an opportunistic or unmotivated client, leading the supplier to take legal action, even at the risk of losing reputation.

In regular situations, the relationship between the parties should be governed through non-contractual mechanisms and mutual trust. Contractual mechanisms should be reserved for extreme situations, after the buffer of trust and goodwill is depleted on one or both sides.

Nevertheless, both parties in the contractual relationship have the potential for opportunistic behavior. Since the project outcome is not precisely defined, it cannot serve as a clear basis for evaluating success. This ambiguity allows the client to exploit the supplier by demanding an increased scope or refusing payments, claiming dissatisfaction with the outcome. On the other hand, the supplier, having a knowledge advantage, may minimize their effort and deliver the minimal scope by interpreting vague descriptions to their benefit. To minimize the potential for opportunistic behavior, a mix of contractual and non-contractual governance mechanisms should be implemented.

In projects requiring co-production, non-contractual governance mechanisms play a more significant role than contractual ones. These mechanisms are crucial not only for ensuring successful project completion but also for preventing opportunistic behaviors.

In waterfall-based projects, the project management structure typically includes two project managers, one from each project party. These project managers closely cooperate to coordinate project activities, each directing the part of the project team from their respective organizations. Continuous, frequent, and close cooperation between the project managers allows for mutual control of behavior. Thus, any attempt of opportunistic behavior can be quickly identified and addressed. The steering committee, the highest element of the project structure, also includes participants from both project parties to resolve issues that the project managers cannot.

In agile-based projects, the rules of agile team composition require that all project participants work in multidisciplinary teams. These teams consist of members from both parties. Furthermore, the product owner is a member of the client organization, while the scrum master (or project manager, in some approaches) is from the supplier organization. Alternatively, the parties may choose to appoint two scrum masters or project managers to balance power within the team. In any case, the team is also capable of identifying attempts of opportunistic behavior.

In both co-production projects and those without co-production (although the latter are less common), contracts should include mechanisms to constrain opportunistic behavior. Firstly, as previously mentioned, the contract must specify the roles and responsibilities of the parties, possibly using a RACI matrix. This helps prevent opportunistic behaviors by ensuring neither party shirks responsibilities or transfers tasks inappropriately.

Additionally, payment terms can act as a mechanism to reduce opportunistic behavior. 'Concept and implementation' projects, which last longer than 'concept only' projects, produce intermediate outcomes and conclude with the delivery of a working solution. Therefore, it makes sense to relate payments to the achievement of project outcomes. Given the project's duration and the often vague definition of outcomes, a single payment at the end of the project would place the contractor in a highly unfavorable position. The client could refuse payment, claiming the outcome does not meet the (vague) requirements. For the contractor, an acceptable form of outcome-related payments involves partial payments for intermediate project results.

In agile or hybrid approaches, payments can be tied to the accepted increment of each sprint. In waterfall approaches, payments would be related to intermediate products such as the problem definition document, solution design document, prototype, and final solution, following the incremental outcome definition and approval procedure discussed earlier. Relating payments to intermediate products has an additional advantage: it incentivizes client personnel to carefully verify project results, as they need to formally sign them off and take responsibility for this fact. This benefits all parties and the project itself, as possible misunderstandings can be identified and corrected early. Introducing partial payments for intermediate products also provides control mechanisms for the client. However, clients, typically less knowledgeable about the project domain, may face challenges in assessing the quality of these intermediate products.

These problems are less significant in a hybrid/agile approach, as each time-box results in a working increment that can be evaluated against the client's expectations of how the solution should function. In contrast, in a waterfall approach, the client may struggle to verify whether the solution design meets their requirements without actually seeing the solution itself. This leads to an important conclusion: if the project outcome can be divided into smaller working parts, the hybrid or agile approach should be chosen. The choice between a hybrid or agile approach depends on whether the scope is fixed prior to the project or not.

For the client, it is extremely important to ensure the highest possible quality of supplier personnel in terms of their knowledge and skills. Therefore, the client should include a resource-based section in the contract detailing the supplier's personnel's qualifications and the degree of involvement. This section aims to reduce the likelihood of the supplier replacing experts with less knowledgeable, junior staff. The more detailed this section is, the better. Instead of stating that two senior consultants will be available for 30% of the project duration, it is preferable to specify that named person A will be available for the project every Monday and Tuesday, and named person B will be available every Wednesday and Thursday. This section should also include the conditions under which personnel can be replaced. Junior staff should, of course, also be involved in the project, as they need opportunities to learn and grow.

The scenario described above assumes that payments are related to the intermediate products of the project, i.e., the payment terms are fixed price. For this to be possible, the project scope must be fixed at a high level and only detailed during the project in terms of specifics. Therefore, it would need to follow either a hybrid or waterfall approach. As mentioned previously, if the project outcome can be divided into smaller, working parts, a hybrid approach gives the client better control and reduces ambiguities.

In the current scenario, where only a general problem definition is known before the project, it may sometimes be impossible or unproductive to fix the high-level scope beforehand. In such instances, a purely agile approach may be implemented. The project goal is described in very general terms, and an initial list of outcome features is gathered in the form of a backlog with the explicit assumption that it will not only be detailed but also changed, decreased, or increased. In this case, the backlog does not constitute the outcome-based part of the contract.

Instead, the contract may include a mix of behavior-based and resource-based sections, specifying that a certain group of people will complete a certain number of sprints within a given timeframe. Payment can be based on time and materials or fixed. In the latter case, the fixed amount can be paid for a given period of time (e.g., monthly) or related to the acceptance of an increment after each sprint. It is important to note that in a pure agile approach, the scope is neither fixed nor distributed among the sprints before the project starts. The agile team selects the items from the product backlog to be completed in a given sprint during sprint planning. Additionally, the scope in the product backlog may change after each sprint as a result of the sprint review. Therefore, the trigger for payment would be the fact that the increment has met the acceptance criteria (definition of done) rather than conformance to a rigid project plan (which does not exist). Time-and-materials and time-related fixed-price contracts provide weak incentives for the supplier, who is paid regardless of the outcome. In contrast, increment-related payments offer strong incentives for the supplier, as payment is contingent upon the formal sign-off of each increment. This scheme also incentivizes the client, who is obliged to formally sign off on an increment and cannot reverse this decision. While the increment-related payment scheme provides an optimal level of incentives, it requires discipline from both parties. If the client delays signing off on the increment, the project halts, or the entire risk shifts to the supplier.

In any case, agile setup requires very tight cooperation and coordination using non-contractual governance mechanisms to ensure that people do not lose motivation due to the lack of tangible control of their progress against the plan. Agile frameworks provide guidelines on how to achieve this. As always, the challenge lies in implementing these guidelines in a specific, real-life setting. This can be summarized into the following proposition:

Proposition 30: *For projects characterized by ill-defined, intangible outcomes, for which only a general goal description exist, and which are executed under a prime-contractor setting, there exist attributes of the contractual relationship that are shaped by the nature of the project itself, regardless of the implemented contract regime:*

- The projects are subject to high levels of volatility, uncertainty, and ambiguity.
- Therefore, they require a very high level of coordinated adaptation to disturbances, often involving co-production.
- Co-production and coordination are achieved predominantly through non-contractual governance mechanisms. The project parties must work together within a unified project structure.
- The implication of co-production is that the supplier is unable to accomplish the project without the client's active participation. Thus, the required behaviors of the client must be detailed in the contract. Additionally, the problem of incentivizing the client to accomplish the project arises.
- The project is subject to a high level of two-sided information asymmetry: the supplier does not know the client's detailed requirements, and the client does not know the definition of the project outcome.
- Reducing information asymmetry and controlling the project should be executed through the incremental outcome definition and approval procedure included in the contract, and continuous cooperation within the unified project structure.
- The main mechanism of mutual control is continuous cooperation within the project structure, which allows for natural monitoring of each other's actions.
- Client control is limited by knowledge asymmetry; due to a lack of knowledge, the client may not be able to properly assess the supplier's behavior and/or intermediate outcomes of the project.
- Trust is an important additional governance mechanism, which, if present, reduces the transaction costs of running the project.

- The goal conflict and temptation for opportunistic behavior are high on both sides. As the goal is not well-defined, the supplier may attempt to deliver as little as possible at a high cost. The client may attempt to impose their tasks on the supplier and refuse to pay for the project outcome, claiming it does not meet their needs.
- Ways to reduce the goal conflict include the incremental outcome definition and approval procedure included in the contract and continuous cooperation within the unified project structure.
- The risk is distributed between the parties.

The nature of the project favors non-contractual governance mechanisms. Continuous cooperation within the unified project structure is essential for project success. Although most attributes of the contractual relationship are influenced by the project's nature, the parties should still secure their interests through contractual mechanisms.

***Proposition 31:** Viable contractual governance setups for 'concept and implementation' projects with general goal description are as in table 6.*

TABLE 6 Contractual governance for 'concept and implementation' projects with general goal description

	Combined outcome-based, behavior-based, resource-based – partial payments fixed price – hybrid	**Combined outcome-based, behavior-based, resource-based – partial payments fixed price – waterfall**	**Behavior-based and resource-based – agile**
Related project management methodology	Hybrid	Waterfall	Agile
Prerequisites	Scope must be fixed on a general level – the backlog is fixed prior to the project. Backlog items are initially distributed between sprints before the project.	Scope must be fixed on a general level	Scope is fluid

TABLE 6 Contractual governance for 'concept and implementation' projects (*cont.*)

	Combined outcome-based, behavior-based, resource-based – partial payments fixed price – hybrid	**Combined outcome-based, behavior-based, resource-based – partial payments fixed price – waterfall**	**Behavior-based and resource-based – agile**
Construction	Behavior-based part defines: – number and duration of sprints – roles and responsibilities within the agile team – procedure for handling changes to the product backlog during the project – issue resolution procedure in case of non-acceptance of an increment Outcome-based part defines: – general description of the final project outcome – assignment of items from the product backlog to the sprints – acceptance criteria for the increment Resource-based part lists the supplier's personnel's qualifications and the degree of involvement	Behavior-based part defines: – incremental outcome definition and approval procedure – roles and responsibilities of both parties (e.g. RACI) Outcome-based part defines: – general description of the final project outcome – intermediate products of the incremental outcome definition and approval procedure Resource-based part lists the supplier's personnel's qualifications and the degree of involvement	Behavior-based part defines: – number and duration of sprints – roles and responsibilities within the agile team – issue resolution procedure in case of non-acceptance of an increment Resource-based part lists the supplier's personnel's qualifications and the degree of involvement Acceptance criteria for the increment must be defined.

TABLE 6 Contractual governance for 'concept and implementation' projects (*cont.*)

	Combined outcome-based, behavior-based, resource-based – partial payments fixed price – hybrid	**Combined outcome-based, behavior-based, resource-based – partial payments fixed price – waterfall**	**Behavior-based and resource-based – agile**
Payment scheme	Payment is done for each accepted increment. Every time-box results in a working increment that can be evaluated against the client's expectations of how the solution should function.	For intermediate products, such as problem definition document, design document, solution prototype, and final solution.	– time and materials – or fixed price for period of time – or fixed price after acceptance of each increment
Power of incentives for the contractor	As the payment is related to the acceptance of every increment, the power of incentives for the contractor is high.	As the payment is related to the acceptance of partial outcomes, the power of incentives for the contractor is high.	Time and materials and fixed price for a period of time offer low-powered incentives for the contractor, as the payment is not tied to the outcome. In contrast, with fixed price after the increment acceptance, payment is related to the outcome, providing strong incentives for the contractor. However, without a prior definition of the outcome against which sprint results can be evaluated, there is a risk of disputes over acceptance. To minimize the probability of such disputes and reduce the risk of client opportunistic behavior, the acceptance criteria, acceptance procedure, and issue resolution procedure must be detailed thoroughly.

TABLE 6 Contractual governance for 'concept and implementation' projects (*cont.*)

	Combined outcome-based, behavior-based, resource-based – partial payments fixed price – hybrid	**Combined outcome-based, behavior-based, resource-based – partial payments fixed price – waterfall**	**Behavior-based and resource-based – agile**
Power of incentives for the client	The client is motivated to put effort into evaluating each increment because it has financial consequences. The incentives for the client are strong.	The client is motivated to put effort into evaluating each intermediate product because it has financial consequences. The incentives for the client are strong. However, due to knowledge asymmetry, the client may have difficulty assessing the quality of intermediate products, leading to two potential issues: they might either accept a low-quality outcome or question a properly executed one.	The client is motivated to put effort into evaluating each increment because it has financial consequences. The incentives for the client are strong.
Opportunistic behavior of the agent and constraining mechanisms	Frequent evaluation of partial outcomes, along with the fact that these outcomes take the form of a working partial solution, significantly limits the potential for opportunistic behavior. Additionally, the	The agent may attempt to benefit from the knowledge asymmetry and offer solutions which require less effort although they do not meet client's expectations. Due to lack of	Under time and materials and periodical fixed price payment schemes the contractor may attempt to limit their engagement. The remedy is non-contractual control through tight cooperation. Under the fixed price after the increment acceptance

TABLE 6 Contractual governance for 'concept and implementation' projects (*cont.*)

	Combined outcome-based, behavior-based, resource-based – partial payments fixed price – hybrid	**Combined outcome-based, behavior-based, resource-based – partial payments fixed price – waterfall**	**Behavior-based and resource-based – agile**
	resource-based section of the contract restricts the possibility of replacing experienced staff with less experienced individuals.	appropriate knowledge the client may face difficulties in identifying such attempts in the early stages of the project and therefore accept solution design of low quality. The solution may be to hire external experts to help evaluate the intermediate project outcomes.	frequent evaluation of partial outcomes, along with the fact that these outcomes take the form of a working partial solution, significantly limits the potential for opportunistic behavior. Additionally, the resource-based section of the contract restricts the possibility of replacing experienced staff with less experienced individuals.
Opportunistic behavior of the principal and constraining mechanisms	Due to the vague definition of the outcome and the fact that payments are tied to this outcome, the client may refuse to pay, claiming that the result does not meet their expectations. Since the outcome is not clearly defined before the project begins, such refusals cannot be contractually prevented. However, making frequent payments after each sprint	Due to the vague definition of the outcome and the fact that payments are tied to this outcome, the client may refuse to pay, claiming that the result does not meet their expectations. Since the outcome is not clearly defined before the project begins, such refusals cannot be contractually prevented. However,	Under the time and materials and periodical fixed price payment schemes the possibility for principal's opportunistic behavior is limited. Under the fixed price after the increment acceptance, the client may refuse to pay, claiming that the result does not meet their expectations. Since the outcome is not defined before the project begins, such refusals cannot be contractually prevented. However, making frequent payments after each sprint

TABLE 6 Contractual governance for 'concept and implementation' projects (*cont.*)

	Combined outcome-based, behavior-based, resource-based – partial payments fixed price – hybrid	**Combined outcome-based, behavior-based, resource-based – partial payments fixed price – waterfall**	**Behavior-based and resource-based – agile**
	reduces the contractor's risk of non-payment to the final sprint only.	making frequent payments for intermediate outcomes limits the contractor's risk to the last payment only.	reduces the contractor's risk of non-payment to the final sprint only.
Additional aspects and remarks	The acceptance criteria for the increment (definition of done) must be precise and unambiguous. There must be a procedure for issue resolving. The acceptance criteria and procedure should be included in the contract.	Since the waterfall approach provides the client with fewer opportunities to control the supplier's opportunistic behavior and ensure the proper quality of the project outcome, it should only be used when the project outcome cannot be divided into smaller working parts. Otherwise, a hybrid approach should be used.	The acceptance criteria for the increment (definition of done) must be precise and unambiguous. There must be a procedure for issue resolving. The acceptance criteria and procedure should be included in the contract.

Theoretically, there are other contractual options. The two extremes are:
- Outcome-based fixed-price.
- Resource-based time and materials.

Outcome-based fixed-price with a single payment upon project completion is highly risky for the contractor. If the project goal is not well-defined, there is no way to compare the actual outcome with the planned one. There is no contractual or other mechanism to protect the contractor from an opportunistic client who refuses to pay, claiming the outcome is not what they expected.

On the other hand, resource-based time and materials is very risky for the client. Without appropriate knowledge to direct and monitor the supplier's behavior, the client cannot verify whether the contractor's efforts are justified. The contractor may opportunistically consume resources and request budget extensions. However, actual man-days can be used as a measure of effort against the planned effort in projects with poorly defined scopes. For example, in an agile approach, it can be predefined that a group of five individuals from the supplier's side will work in ten sprints, each lasting two weeks. The planned effort is 500 man-days, which cannot be exceeded unless additional people are added to the project or the schedule is extended. Linking payment to the actual consumption of man-days under such circumstances is a safe option.

Another approach to managing a project with only a general problem definition known beforehand is to convert it into a project with a complete problem definition and requirements specification through a separate diagnosis subproject. This method is viable for projects where the diagnosis and subsequent phases are sequential and do not overlap. The project is then contractually divided into two parts.

The diagnosis subproject results in a complete and fairly detailed problem definition. The contract for this subproject would follow one of the contractual schemes for 'concept only' projects. The contractor then prepares a proposal for the design and implementation of a solution based on the problem definition document. If the proposal is rejected, the project is terminated, or the problem definition document can be used as a basis for competitive bidding. If the proposal is accepted, the contract for the design and implementation phase is signed with the original contractor. This contract will likely be outcome-based and follow the contractual governance of projects with complete problem definitions/requirements specifications known beforehand, as covered later in this section.

The disadvantage of this approach is the lack of competitive bidding after the diagnosis phase. However, the advantage is the elimination of information loss due to imperfect information transfer, as the same contractor handles both the diagnosis and the subsequent phases of the project.

2. Requirements specification is known prior to the project

The second scenario for concept and implementation projects with intangible and difficult-to-define outcomes is to attempt to define them before the project begins. The reason behind this step is to gain more tangible control over project progress and enable competitive bidding prior to project commencement. This approach, named here as define-bid-design-build, involves competitive bidding for the design and build of a solution based on previously defined requirements. These requirements can be outlined by the client themselves or with the help of a separate expert company. The goal is to obtain a fairly clear, detailed, and comprehensive list of requirements before the project starts which serves as the basis for competitive bidding, outcome-based contracts, and further progress control by comparing actual results with planned ones (i.e., metering). This method mimics the classical approach, successfully used for 'hard' projects with tangible and well-defined outcomes. However, there are inherent differences due to the nature of the project outcome. These differences were discussed earlier, but are also summarized here:

– The project outcome is intangible and abstract, making it difficult for stakeholders to envision. Its form is not constrained by the laws of mechanics.
– Consequently, the requirements regarding the project outcome may be unclear not only to future contractors but also to the client.
– There is no unambiguous, commonly accepted notation for defining the outcome.
– Information transfer between people and documents is imperfect. Each time information is transferred from a person to a document or vice versa, some information may be lost or misinterpreted. Therefore, the problem definition document and the design document are not easily transferable to entities other than the one that prepared them. If one contractor (or the client) performs the diagnosis phase and then hands over the problem definition document to another contractor, the diagnosis phase would need to be repeated to some extent, as the new contractor would require clarifications to properly understand the problem.
– The separation between the requirements (i.e., the 'what') and the design (i.e., the 'how') is significant, as the design options are not limited to a set number of well-defined and proven technical solutions for achieving a particular goal in the physical world. The same requirement may be fulfilled in many ways, some of which may affect other requirements (problem-solution entanglement).

Under such conditions, it is impossible to obtain a definition of requirements that is 100% clear, complete, and unambiguous. However, one can attempt to get as close to this ideal as possible.

In a define-bid-design-build approach, the client, either independently or with the help of a specialized partner, performs the requirements definition stage. Given the significant separation between the requirements and the design, the requirements should be design-agnostic: they should specify WHAT needs to be accomplished, not HOW it should be accomplished. The requirements definition document is then used for selecting the implementation partner, facilitating bidding, and signing the contract.

As previously mentioned, the information transfer is imperfect, so the requirements specification document will not be unambiguous for the winning contractor. Therefore, unlike in 'hard' projects, the contractor will not be able to realize the project outcome asynchronously without further participation from the client. Firstly, the requirements will need further clarification. Secondly, the design options will have to be presented to the client, discussed, and decided upon. Furthermore, most projects will require co-production, i.e., active involvement from the client beyond merely providing information. Consequently, the project will be performed according to the following scheme:

> (1) *Definition of requirements and constraints* – (2) *Bid and contract* – (3) Detailed diagnosis – (3) Solution design – (4) Presentation and sign-off of the solution proposal (5) Solution implementation

The definition of requirements and constraints is done by the client themselves or, more likely, with the help of an expert company. The list of requirements is then distributed among prospective contractors who submit their offers. After the winning supplier is selected, final negotiations and contract signing take place. The project starts with the detailed diagnosis phase, during which the winning supplier clarifies any ambiguities regarding the requirements. As in previous scenarios, the detailed diagnosis, solution design, and, in some cases, implementation phases may intertwine and/or be performed iteratively in agile time-boxes.

Given the existence of a list of requirements defining the project scope, there are additional options in the partner selection and tendering process compared to projects with a general goal definition. The core of the process involves comparing offers that respond to the requirements specification and additional conditions included in the formal request for quotation (RFQ). Since the requirements cannot always be presented unambiguously, several issues arise in this process, unlike in 'hard' projects with commonly accepted, rigid design notations and methodologies. Simply put, ambiguous requirements may lead to ambiguous responses from prospective contractors. Even if a requirement is clear to the contractor, the response might be ambiguous to the client. Furthermore, some contractors may opportunistically interpret the requirements to their advantage, offer a low price, and then renegotiate during the detailed diagnosis and design phases, claiming they only then understood the proper meaning of the requirement. This raises the question of how detailed the requirements should be and in what form the answers should be given. More detail is not always better. Firstly, overly detailed requirements risk entering design mode, specifying not only what the solution should provide but also how it should be provided. This can eliminate potentially better solutions at the start. Secondly, responding to hundreds of pages of detailed requirements is time-consuming for contractors. The same applies to the required mode of response, which may vary from a simple yes/no for each requirement to an actual initial design of the future solution.

At first glance, this might not seem like a problem for the client. However, as previously stated, knowledge-intensive businesses are non-scalable. This means that a prospective contractor would need to allocate their valuable expert resources to the unpaid task of answering the request for quotation (RFQ), which represents an opportunity cost for the contractor. If the contractor has no other assignments, they might respond to the detailed RFQ. However, the best contractors in the market are usually the busiest. Therefore, requiring detailed answers to a detailed RFQ can lead to an adverse selection scenario, where the client receives responses only from mediocre contractors.

Since detailed diagnosis will involve the client's personnel anyway, the requirements list at the bidding stage serves more as a basis for comparing offers and as a safeguard in the future contract rather than as a firm basis for solution implementation. Therefore, a medium level of detail and a yes/no answer, possibly with a short description of the proposed solution, seems to be a good balance. To assess the possible level of ambiguity of the requirements, it makes sense to ask for a valuation range rather than a single quote, for example:

- Please provide the quote for the simplest solution you can imagine for our requirements.
- Please provide the quote for the most comprehensive solution you can imagine.

As the offers will likely be ambiguous anyway, reference visits and paid proofs of concept for selected requirements are valuable options to confirm the capabilities of shortlisted contractors. Since the contractual relationship is based on a predefined list of requirements, the role of trust is smaller than in previous cases. The transactional cost of defining, addressing, maintaining, and controlling the requirements is incurred regardless, and trust can only reduce these costs to a limited extent. The reputation of the contractor plays a similar role as in previous scenarios: it is a good indicator for pre-selecting the contractors who would be invited to place offers and serves as a safeguard against opportunistic behavior during the project.

The pros and cons of a process based on a detailed list of requirements compared to a general problem definition are as follows.

Pros

- It allows for a more structured and informed bidding process. The winning offer can be selected based on a set of criteria that appear objective (though

they are not completely objective due to inherent ambiguity). This is particularly important when the client is unfamiliar with the market or contractors and lacks trusted contractors from previous assignments. Additionally, some organizations require this approach as part of their corporate governance.
- It provides a solid foundation for project management and control. Even if the requirements change, some become obsolete, and new ones emerge, the process can be managed using the initial list of requirements. Project management can clearly identify changes and act accordingly. In projects with a general scope description, especially agile ones, the risk of scope creep is higher. Nonetheless, both types of projects require a disciplined approach to managing change.

Cons:
- Projects of the nature discussed here are often subject to high levels of volatility, uncertainty, and ambiguity. This means requirements will likely evolve and change during the project. The critique of waterfall approaches in Information Systems and the rise of agile methodologies address this issue. It is prudent to assume that pre-specified requirements will evolve. A change management process must be in place to address such situations. However, this process increases transaction costs and thus the total project cost. In organizations attempting to apply uniform project governance mechanisms to every project, this can lead to a significant rise in transaction costs or even project failure.
- It may provide a flawed perception of objectivity and control. While requirements and criteria appear objective, they are only partially so due to ambiguity. They must be treated with caution and often with a significant degree of tolerance. Literal interpretation of the criteria may lead to unnecessary disputes or the implementation of unwanted project features, both of which increase the total project cost.
- It requires more effort, as the diagnostic stage occurs twice: once before the project and again as the project's first phase.
- If project scope management is not conducted properly and lacks sufficient flexibility, there is a risk of excluding valuable solutions and implementing solutions with less value.

The project contract and governance of contractual relations would be primarily outcome-based. The contractor commits to delivering the project features listed in the requirements specification. Control is executed mainly by comparing the requirements specification with the actual project outcome. It is important to highlight that, in the type of projects discussed here, the requirements define what the solution should do or achieve, but not how it should be done or achieved. The 'how' is elucidated during the design phase of the project, collaboratively by the client and the contractor.

Therefore, the final assessment of the scope's conformance with the contract involves checking whether all features listed in the requirements specification are delivered. The detailed nature of these features is not included in the contract and is elaborated by the project team during the project. This has several implications. First, co-production is crucial to ensure that the project outcome features meet the client's expectations. Secondly, if the client does not adequately co-produce and leaves the contractor to guess how the features should work, differences in understanding the requirements will inevitably occur. This, in turn, leads to disputes and increases transactional and total project costs.

Disputes may end with the client accepting functionality that does not meet their needs, the contractor changing the functionality and being compensated or not, or, in the worst-case scenario, the dispute may end up in court. As co-production eliminates these problems, it is in the client's best interest to engage. However, the contract should still include a behavior-based section detailing the required client engagement. Additionally, an 'outcome detailing and approval procedure' should be included. Since the outcome is fixed a priori, this procedure includes the necessary steps to detail the requirements, design the solution, and approve both.

For projects with outcomes that fit the waterfall approach, the following should be specified at a minimum:
- Definition and schedule of the activities comprising the detailed diagnosis stage.
- Form of the presentation of the results of the detailed diagnosis stage.
- Procedure and criteria for acceptance of the results of the detailed diagnosis stage, including the dispute resolution procedure.
- Scope change management procedure.
- Schedule for the preparation and the form of the presentation of the design.
- Procedure and criteria for acceptance of the design, including the dispute resolution procedure.
- Schedule of the implementation phase.
- Criteria for acceptance of the final solution and acceptance procedure, including:
  - The definition and schedule of partial acceptances, if they exist,
  - The schedule for final acceptance,
  - The dispute resolution procedure.

As the scope is fixed, the currently discussed scenario is not eligible for agile. It may, however, benefit from hybrid approach. In case the outcome can be divided into smaller working parts, hybrid approach is a way to go. In such case the following parameters should be included in the contract:

- Number and duration of time-boxes (sprints).
- Assignment of items from the product backlog to the sprints.
- Acceptance criteria for the increment.
- Definition of roles and responsibilities within the agile team.
- Scope and schedule change management procedure.

Since the scope, in terms of the definition of the requirements, is fixed prior to the project, the requirements should also be assigned to the sprints a priori to ensure the project plan realizes the entire scope. During the sprints, the detailed diagnosis, design, implementation, and sign-off of the requirements selected for a given sprint take place.

Switching features between sprints, including new features in the product backlog, or removing features cannot be at the discretion of the agile team. There must be a high-level governance mechanism to ensure that either the initially agreed scope is delivered or that any changes in the scope are agreed upon by both project parties at the contractual level. Any change to the scope or schedule must go through the change management procedure, including amendments to the contract.

This applies to both hybrid and waterfall-managed projects. Defining the scope prior to the project provides better control and manageability, but it comes at the cost of reduced flexibility and higher transactional costs if a scope change is needed, requiring a complex change management procedure.

In a hybrid approach, every sprint results in a working increment. This is an advantage over the waterfall approach, as it is easier for the client to approve a working solution rather than diagnosis and design documents.

Since client engagement is crucial to project success, the contract should include a behavior-based section specifying the minimum required involvement of the client's personnel. A behavior-based section can possibly take the form of the RACI matrix, determining the behaviors of both contractual parties. From the client's perspective, it is essential to ensure the contractor staff possesses the proper knowledge and capabilities. Therefore, a resource-based section detailing the personnel engaged in the project should also be included.

As in the previous scenario, the parties must cooperate within a unified project structure, regardless of the contractual relationships. Therefore, non-contractual mechanisms are more significant than contractual ones. These mechanisms include a unified project structure, clearly defined roles, responsibilities, processes, and procedures, and their implementation on a daily basis throughout the project.

Regarding payment terms, they would rather be related to intermediate and final outcomes. Otherwise, the effort to define the requirements prior to the project would be useless. A single payment upon project completion is highly risky for the contractor. Although the requirements are set before the project, disputes can arise regarding their interpretation in the final solution. A single payment does not incentivize the client to verify the design gradually during the project either. Therefore, single payments are only suitable for simple and short projects. Longer projects should involve partial payments for intermediate products. For projects following a waterfall approach, these include detailed diagnosis, design documents, a prototype, and the final solution. For projects following a hybrid approach, each timebox results in a working increment that can be verified and form the basis for payment.

Summing up, the nature of the projects under consideration here is the same as in the previously analyzed scenario, where only a general problem definition was known before the project. What differentiates these two scenarios is the approach to defining the scope and managing the project. The above can be summarized by the following proposition:

Proposition 32: *For projects characterized by ill-defined, intangible outcomes, for which the requirements specification exist, and which are executed under a prime-contractor setting, there exist the following attributes of the contractual relationship:*

- Projects are subject to high levels of volatility, uncertainty, and ambiguity.
- Therefore, they require a high level of coordinated adaptation to disturbances, often involving co-production.
- Co-production and coordination are achieved predominantly through non-contractual governance mechanisms. The project parties must work together within a unified project structure.
- The implication of co-production is that the supplier cannot accomplish the project without the client's active participation. Thus, the required behaviors of the client must be detailed in the contract. Additionally, the issue of incentivizing the client to complete the project arises.
- Due to imperfect information transfer, the requirements must be detailed, and the solution must be gradually designed during the project.
- The governance mechanisms that allow this to happen include the approval procedure in the contract and continuous cooperation within the unified project structure.
- The main mechanisms of mutual control are:
  - metering of the realization of the requirements included in the contract,
  - continuous cooperation within the project structure.
- The temptation for opportunistic behavior is high on both sides. Given the ambiguity in interpreting the requirements, the supplier may attempt to deliver as little as possible, while the client may try to impose additional tasks on the supplier and refuse to pay for the project outcome, claiming it does not meet their needs.

- Ways to reduce goal conflict include the incremental detailing of requirements, the approval procedure in the contract, and continuous cooperation within the unified project structure.
- The risk is distributed between the parties.

Proposition 33: *Viable contractual governance setups for 'concept and implementation' projects with requirements specification are as in table 7.*

TABLE 7 Contractual governance for 'concept and implementation' projects with requirements specification

	Combined outcome-based, behavior-based, resource-based – partial payments fixed price – hybrid	**Combined outcome-based, behavior-based, resource-based – partial payments fixed price – waterfall**
Related project management methodology	Hybrid	Waterfall
Prerequisites	The scope, defined by the requirements, is fixed before the project begins. The backlog is established and backlog items are assigned to sprints in advance. Any changes to the scope, schedule, or budget must go through the change management procedure.	The scope, defined by the requirements, is fixed before the project begins. Any changes to the scope, schedule, or budget must go through the change management procedure.
Construction	Outcome-based part defines: – requirements specification of all the features – the product backlog – assignment of items from the product backlog to the sprints – acceptance criteria for the increment Behavior-based part defines: – number and duration of sprints – roles and responsibilities within the agile team – procedure for handling changes to the product backlog during the project	Outcome-based part defines: – requirements specification of all the features – intermediate products of the outcome detailing and approval procedure Behavior-based part defines: – outcome detailing and approval procedure – roles and responsibilities of both parties (e.g. RACI) Resource-based part lists the supplier's personnel's qualifications and the degree of involvement

TABLE 7 Contractual governance for 'concept and implementation' projects (*cont.*)

	Combined outcome-based, behavior-based, resource-based – partial payments fixed price – hybrid	**Combined outcome-based, behavior-based, resource-based – partial payments fixed price – waterfall**
	– issue resolution procedure in case of non-acceptance of an increment Resource-based part lists the supplier's personnel's qualifications and the degree of involvement	
Payment scheme	Payment is done for each accepted increment. Every time-box results in a working increment that can be evaluated against the client's expectations of how the solution should function.	Payment is done for intermediate products, such as problem definition document, design document, solution prototype, and final solution. For short projects with uncomplicated outcome single payment upon completion is viable, although risky for the contractor.
Power of incentives for the contractor	As the payment is related to the acceptance of every increment, the power of incentives for the contractor is high.	As the payment is related to the acceptance of partial outcomes, the power of incentives for the contractor is high.
Power of incentives for the client	The client is motivated to put effort into evaluating each increment because it has financial consequences. The incentives for the client are strong.	The client is motivated to put effort into evaluating each intermediate product because it has financial consequences. The incentives for the client are strong. However, due to knowledge asymmetry, the client may have difficulty assessing the quality of intermediate products, leading to two potential issues: they might either accept a low-quality outcome or question a properly executed one.

TABLE 7 Contractual governance for 'concept and implementation' projects (*cont.*)

	Combined outcome-based, behavior-based, resource-based – partial payments fixed price – hybrid	**Combined outcome-based, behavior-based, resource-based – partial payments fixed price – waterfall**
Opportunistic behavior of the agent and constraining mechanisms	Frequent evaluation of partial outcomes, along with the fact that these outcomes take the form of a working partial solution, significantly limits the potential for opportunistic behavior. Additionally, the resource-based section of the contract restricts the possibility of replacing experienced staff with less experienced individuals.	The agent may attempt to benefit from the knowledge asymmetry and offer solutions which require less effort although they do not meet client's expectations. Due to lack of appropriate knowledge the client may face difficulties in identifying such attempts in the early stages of the project and therefore accept solution design of low quality. The solution may be to hire external experts to help evaluate the intermediate project outcomes.
Opportunistic behavior of the principal and constraining mechanisms	As the outcome is defined only in terms of the requirements, and the payments are tied to this outcome, the client may refuse to pay, claiming that the result does not meet their expectations. However, making frequent payments after each sprint reduces the contractor's risk of non-payment to the final sprint only.	As the outcome is defined only in terms of the requirements, and the payments are tied to this outcome, the client may refuse to pay, claiming that the result does not meet their expectations. However, making frequent payments for intermediate products limits the risk of the contractor.
Additional aspects and remarks	The acceptance criteria for the increment (definition of done) must be precise and unambiguous. There must be a procedure for issue resolving. The acceptance criteria and procedure should be included in the contract.	Since the waterfall approach provides the client with fewer opportunities to control the supplier's opportunistic behavior and ensure the proper quality of the project outcome, it should only be used when the project outcome cannot be divided into smaller working parts. Otherwise, a hybrid approach should be used.

Regardless of the contractual setup, the primary governance mechanisms for projects with ill-defined outcomes are non-contractual. A temporary project organization must be established with appropriate structure, roles, responsibilities, processes, and procedures for planning, task coordination, control, and issue resolution. Even if project participants come from multiple legal entities with potentially conflicting interests, they must work in a coordinated manner within the temporary project organization on a daily basis. Contractual mechanisms serve as the ultimate means of resolving conflicts when non-contractual mechanisms fail.

3.7 Alliance

An alliance project is a collaborative endeavor between two or more parties that share risks and rewards to achieve a common goal by pooling resources, expertise, and efforts (Ross, 2003; Walker et al., 2015; Walker et al., 2022). The key characteristics of alliance projects include the following (Ross, 2003; Walker et al., 2002):
- Risks and rewards are shared among the project participants.
- The project is governed by a joint body, and decisions are made collectively.
- Issues are resolved within the alliance rather than through arbitration or in court, except for a very limited class of clearly defined events.
- The project follows an "open book approach," with financial information shared transparently among the parties.
- "Day-to-day management of the project is conducted by a seamlessly integrated project team, where all members are assigned to the team on a 'best-for-project' basis, regardless of which party employs them" (Ross, 2003).
- The project is based on trust and cooperation among the project parties.

The natural candidates for alliance project contracting are research and development projects, but a variant of this approach is also used in large-scale infrastructure projects where a public sector agency works collaboratively with private sector parties. The Australian government has issued a normative document detailing how to develop such kind of an alliance project: National Alliance Contracting Guidelines. Guide to Alliance Contracting (National Alliance Contracting Guidelines, 2015). It provides the key features of alliance contracting:
- risk and opportunity sharing;
- commitment to 'no disputes';
- best-for-project unanimous decision-making processes;
- 'no fault – no blame' culture;

– good faith;
– transparency expressed as open book documentation and reporting;
– joint management structure.

Alliance contracting is an attempt to introduce the principles of co-production and value co-creation, realized by a joint, integrated project temporary organization, into 'hard' projects. The alliance involves a public sector agency, which is the project owner, and private sector parties – non-owner participants (NOPs). This setup differs from research and development projects, where there may be no 'owner', and risks and rewards can be distributed among the alliance members based on effort, cost, or other proportional measures included in the contract. In the case of a public alliance project the owner and non-owner participants are not completely equal, as the public project owner pays the NOPs and leads the project in certain ways. Therefore, it makes sense to differentiate between two types of alliances:

– No-owner alliance: Several parties join resources and efforts and share risks and potential rewards proportionally.
– Owner alliance: The (public) owner allies with the non-owner participants (NOPs).

Both types of alliances are built upon the features of alliance contracting listed above, but there will also be differences resulting from the leading role of the owner in the latter setup.

In both cases, the idea is that most governance is executed through non-contractual governance mechanisms, such as a joint management structure, joint decision-making, and resolving disputes internally within the temporary hierarchy, using joint teams built on a "best-for-project" basis. However, the alliance still requires contractual governance, which is executed through the Project Alliance Agreement (PAA) intended to drive alignment between the participants.

At the core of the Project Alliance Agreement is the sharing of risks among the participants. The National Alliance Contracting Guidelines. Guide to Alliance Contracting (National Alliance Contracting Guidelines, 2015) states that: "The alliancing principle of 'collective assumption of risks' and the approach to remunerating the NOPs arising from risk and opportunity sharing is fundamental to understanding the alliancing culture." However, "the NOPs' painshare is capped, and the owner will bear 100% of the designer/contractor risk (or 'pain') beyond the cap."

In a no-owner alliance, the proportional share of the 'pain or gain' rule is implemented in the contract. This means that either all the participants win or all lose. In the owner alliance, the owner pays the NOPs based on the following scheme (Ross, 2003):

1. Project costs and project-specific overheads reimbursed based on audited open-book actual costs.
2. A fee to cover corporate overheads and "normal" profit.
3. An equitable share of the "pain" or "gain" depending on how actual project outcomes compare with the pre-agreed targets. The "pain" may be capped at the loss of the fee mentioned in point 2.

The management and control of the project are executed using non-contractual governance mechanisms through a joint project management structure, comprising individuals from all parties, on a 'best-for-project' basis. The alliance project is intended to function as a single, integrated temporary organization, regardless of the participants' origins.

In addition, the National Alliance Contracting Guidelines (2015) provide a template for the Project Alliance Agreement, which includes principles such as commitment to no disputes, good faith, open book documentation and reporting, joint management structure, and risk and opportunity sharing. While the scope of works is fixed, the guidelines allow the project owner to direct participants to change, increase, or decrease the works. Only 'significant' changes are subject to the change management procedure, which may lead to misinterpretations of what constitutes a significant change. Many of these provisions are unenforceable and may only be effective if all parties act in good faith for reasons beyond the contractual terms.

Indeed, alliance project governance, as described by the National Alliance Contracting Guidelines (2015) and other authors citing it (Ross, 2003; Walker et al., 2015; Walker et al., 2022), is an attempt to contractually sanction project execution using a joint, integrated temporary organization, akin to a project within a single company. This approach is naturally compelled by the nature of projects with ill-defined outcomes or those requiring co-production and value co-creation. Such projects are well-suited for owner alliances, whether the owner is a public or private entity. However, the governance of these projects is primarily achieved through non-contractual mechanisms, with the contract serving as the last resort for appeals and lawsuits. Applying the principles of governing a project as a single, integrated temporary organization to 'hard' projects, which do not require co-production, appears promising from a project management perspective. Nevertheless, this approach raises potential issues regarding the unenforceability of some contractual provisions in case of disputes.

It also requires the owner to take on more risks, more responsibility for project completion, and to engage far deeper in continuous project management than in the case of traditional contracting.

The above can be summarized into the following proposition:

Proposition 34: *Alliance project contracting is characterized by the following features:*

- In a no-owner alliance:
  - Several parties combine resources and efforts, sharing risks and potential rewards proportionally.
  - The outcome of a project is uncertain and can only be defined in general terms or goals.
  - The contract should specify the resources and engagement of each party.
  - In justified cases, a behavior-based section detailing each party's responsibilities may be included.
  - The contract defines the mechanisms for sharing risks and rewards among the project parties.
  - Incentives are weak – the remuneration is related to the outcome, but based on an 'all win – all lose' principle, and is not tied to the outcome achieved by any given party.
  - Decisions are made by a joint committee comprising all engaged parties.
  - Coordination is carried out through a joint, integrated temporary organization.
  - Information asymmetry and opportunistic behaviors are reduced through non-contractual governance mechanisms that rely on full transparency within the joint, integrated temporary organization.
- In an owner alliance:
  - A project owner selects one or several non-owner participants (NOPs) to jointly perform a project.
  - The outcome of the project is defined prior to its start and refined by the participants of the alliance.
  - The non-owner participants have their project direct costs and project-specific overheads reimbursed, while the payment of the additional fee depends on meeting the project goals, thereby sharing the risk among the participants.
  - The contract specifies the project outcome, schedule, and target outturn cost (TOC), which must not be exceeded.
  - Incentives are strong – the remuneration is linked to the outcome. Failure to meet the project criteria incurs penalties, while exceeding the criteria results in rewards.
  - Decisions are made by a joint committee comprising all engaged parties, with the owner having a leading voice.
  - Coordination is carried out through a joint, integrated temporary organization, with the project owner managing the coordination.

- Information asymmetry and opportunistic behaviors are reduced through non-contractual governance mechanisms that rely on full transparency within the joint, integrated temporary organization.
- Risk is distributed among the project parties. The owner assumes more risk compared to traditional contracting for 'hard' projects.

In fact, only the first instance precisely meets the definition of an alliance, where the parties have similar rights and obligations, jointly decide on the course of actions to meet a commonly accepted goal, and share pain or gain. The second instance has a leader (the owner) who has the final say in crucial aspects of the project. The owner may terminate the project prematurely, expel a participant due to poor performance, deny the acceptance of the project outcome, etc. However, it is a valuable attempt to address the paradox of parties with different interests needing to work jointly in a coordinated manner to meet the project goals.

CHAPTER 4

Towards a Project Governance Framework

So far, this book has discussed the available options for governing contractual relations in projects, along with the determinants and consequences of their selection in light of the dominant organizational theories. This chapter takes a different perspective: that of individuals, who are tasked with planning, organizing, and delivering a project. Setting aside possible variations and complications, assumption is made, that they are a group of individuals who:

- Are accountable and responsible for overall project success.
- Act on behalf of the project client, i.e., the entity that pays for the project and benefits from its results.
- Communicate with other internal stakeholders regarding the project scope but has the final say.
- Make binding decisions on behalf of the client before and during the project.
- Manage the project on a daily basis on behalf of the client.

While this group may consist of various individuals, including project sponsors, business owners, process owners, product owners, and (in some cases) client project managers, they will be referred to simply as a *project owner*. The question this chapter aims to address is the following: What contractual setup and what combination of governance mechanisms should a project owner apply to a project, given different sets of project characteristics and other project attributes?

Like the previous one, this chapter builds upon the existing theories and practices presented in Chapters 1 and 2. It also utilizes the metatheoretical framework developed in Chapter 3. Its added value lies in the comprehensive, deductive presentation of possible variants of project governance, depending on project attributes and the capabilities of the sponsoring organization. It also provides discussion on pros and cons of each of the presented variants.

4.1 The Paradox of the Interfirm Project Management

As defined earlier in this book, project management is the process of acquiring, configuring, integrating, maintaining, and deploying people, knowledge, and other resources (tangible, intangible, and financial) using planning, organizing, commanding, coordinating, controlling, and motivating to achieve a project goal in a coordinated manner within the constraints of time, budget, and other resources.

Therefore, the primary role of a project manager is to **ensure coordination**, regardless of the origin of the people, knowledge, and other resources, and the contractual relationships they are subject to.

Contract theory and Transaction Cost Economics suggest that strong coordination is achieved through hierarchy, while market-based and hybrid contractual mechanisms provide lower to moderate levels of coordination.

However, in the context of projects, hierarchy in operations-based organizations does not always offer effective coordination mechanisms. This is because the dynamics of projects differ from those of ongoing operations, requiring distinct, and sometimes conflicting cultural settings, incentives, and governance approaches.

Projects require both their own temporary organization, as well as a specific form of supporting hierarchy within the permanent organization, which results in the existence of project capability. These are typically found in project-based organizations, for which projects are their core activity. However, establishing such a structure within an operations-based organization is only justified if it executes certain types of projects on a repetitive basis. In other cases, it is reasonable to outsource the project to a specialized, project-based company. As a result, many projects are carried out through interfirm collaboration under hybrid contractual arrangements.

The paradox of project management is that it must ensure strong cooperation and coordination within contractual frameworks that frequently do not inherently support these elements.

When two or more separate legal entities participate in a project under any type of hybrid contractual setup, they typically have different, often conflicting interests. For example, in a simple client-supplier relationship, the client wants the output delivered at the lowest possible price while maintaining quality, whereas the supplier wants to earn as much as possible. Under a complete contract that clearly defines the output in detail, and covers all possible future contingencies, the parties could negotiate the price and other key contractual conditions before the project begins. Although preparing and negotiating such a contract adds to the Total Cost of Project, it would prevent disputes later on. However, as mentioned many times earlier in this book, such an ideal situation is rarely possible. Many projects are 'soft' and their scope is difficult to define beforehand and evolves as the incremental solution is developed. In some cases, the cost of defining the scope in detail is comparable to the cost of delivering the solution, making detailed definition economically unjustified. Additionally, even projects with clearly defined outcomes ex-ante may be subject to high levels of volatility and uncertainty.

Nevertheless, project owners and project managers worldwide successfully deliver various types of projects, ensuring cooperation and coordination. In some cases, this is primarily (but not only) based on contract provisions; in others, it relies on a balanced mix of contractual and non-contractual governance mechanisms. In extreme cases, cooperation and coordination are achieved not in accordance with, but rather in spite of, contractual provisions.

4.2 Project-Based versus Operations-Based Organizations

While one might imagine a project as a standalone, isolated, independent, and temporary entity, created entirely on its own, separate from any other organizational structure, this is rarely the case. Projects are almost always embedded into existing organizations (Sydow et al., 2004).

The first type of organization a project may relate to is a project-based organization. A project-based organization delivers its outputs in the form of projects. In other words, it creates projects to produce outcomes that it sells to its customers. In the terms used in this book, such an organization functions as the supplier of a project. Project-based organizations are found in a wide range of industries, including consulting and professional services (accounting, advertising, architecture, law, management consulting, public relations), cultural industries (film-making, video games, publishing), software production and implementation, information systems, construction, and infrastructure development (Sydow et. al, 2004). Up to this point, this book has focused on the relationships between the supplier and the client, treating the internal activities of the supplier organization as a black box. Also this chapter takes the perspective of the project owner, i.e., the one who pays for and benefits from the project's outcome.

It is rarely the case that a project owner is a project-based organization, as the primary purpose of these organizations is to deliver projects for their clients, not for themselves. Therefore, most project owners are operations-based organizations, institutions, or private individuals.

Consequently, this book does not aim to explore in detail the internal structure of project-based companies. However, it makes sense to cover the topic in general to highlight the differences between project-based and operations-based organizations. These differences often pose challenges for operations-based project owners when they attempt to manage projects within or alongside their organizations.

There is existing research and literature on the topic of project-based organizations dating back to the early 2000s (Turner & Keegan, 2000; Lindkvist, 2004; Sydow et al., 2004). Turner and Keegan (2000) support the idea that project-based organizations require different management mechanisms compared to operations-based companies. Miterev, Mancini and Turner (2017) provide general directions regarding the design of project-based organizations such as:

- The project-based organization needs a specific form of organization design, which addresses the fact that "the definition of the agents of the organization and their assignment is constantly changing."
- The main business processes of a project-based organization are built around project management, program management and project portfolio management frameworks.
- "The project-based organization needs to adopt a project-oriented culture, where everybody working in the organization recognizes that is the organization's way of doing business and adopts appropriate behaviors. Reward structures within the organizations should reflect the nature of project-based working".

Huemann (2024) distinguishes between project-based and project-oriented organizations. A project-based organization is "an organization that carries out contract projects for external customers," whereas a project-oriented organization manages its activities through projects as a strategic choice. Therefore, project-based organizations form a subset of the broader category of project-oriented organizations.

Both project-oriented and project-based organizations deliver their outcomes in the form of projects, so their culture, attitudes, structure, processes, knowledge, skills, resources, and capabilities must all revolve around successfully delivering projects to internal or external customers. The permanent structure and processes of such organizations must focus on acquiring, developing, and maintaining the following:

1. Domain-specific procedural (explicit) knowledge;
2. Human resources with both explicit and implicit domain-specific knowledge and skills;
3. Non-human tangible and intangible resources necessary to execute a project of a given type;
4. Project capability – the organization's ability to acquire, integrate, configure, maintain and deploy the above resources so that a project of a given type can be planned, prepared, executed, and successfully completed. This requires both domain-agnostic and domain-specific project management knowledge.

In other words, the company must either possess or be able to quickly acquire all the knowledge and resources necessary to plan, set up, and execute a project. In addition, the project-based organization must develop the ability to acquire project contracts from their clients.

Once a project contract is acquired, people and resources are assigned to the temporary project organization, which then becomes their primary organizational assignment (in addition to their role in the permanent organizational unit). The role of the permanent units is to acquire, develop, and maintain relevant resources, and deploy them into projects as needed. Once assigned to a project, individuals report primarily to the project manager, not their line manager. Being assigned to a project is the natural state for every employee, and employee evaluations are based on project performance.

This core function of a project-based organization must, of course, be supported by secondary functions such as research and development, human resources management, legal support, marketing and sales, financial management, and infrastructure management. In a project-based organization all these functions revolve around supporting the company's ability to acquire, set up, and successfully execute projects within its domain of expertise.

Summing up: the core competence of a project-based organization is the ability to effectively perform projects of a given type and core capability is the ability to acquire, integrate, configure, maintain and deploy these competence and related resources in a way that they successfully accomplish these projects.

The situation is different in operations-based organizations, whose core competence is the ability to produce relatively standard products in a relatively repetitive way. Their design is based around permanent hierarchy and repetitive processes, while the secondary functions are concentrated on supporting these repetitive processes. Therefore, in the operations-based companies projects are a side activity and are not at the center of the organization culture, processes and procedures.

Of course, they also must react to the changes in the business environment and possess the ability to re-configure their resources accordingly (which is called dynamic capability). And of course, there are also many industries whose operations scheme is based on a make-to-order, which sits somewhere between the pure project-based and pure operations-based dichotomy. Still, performing a project in an operations-based organization is a major cultural and organizational challenge.

4.3 Setting Up a Project Governance Framework

A project is a temporary organization established to achieve a specific goal or output within a defined constraints of time, budget, and other resources. Like any other organization, it must have established standards and rules of operation. Consequently, it can be assumed that every project requires some form of governance framework to ensure the coordinated achievement of its objectives. If it doesn't, due to its short duration and simplicity, it would likely be considered a service rather than a project.

A governance framework is necessary regardless of the contractual relationships between the parties, as projects, due to their medium to long duration, require ongoing coordination, direction, and control. Contracts between project parties do interact with the governance framework, potentially influencing its form. Contractual arrangements may be incorporated into the procedures of the governance framework. Conversely, a governance framework, whether generic for a specific project type or preferred by the parties involved, may influence the contract or be included as part of the contractual arrangements.

In some cases, such as when a contract is heavily influenced by standardized corporate policies, it may not fully align with the specific needs of the project. In such instances, the governance framework may be designed independently of the contractual provisions.

As the aim of project governance is to provide the standards, mechanisms and tools allowing for structured management of a project, the form of a governance framework primarily depends on the nature of the project outcome and methods, with contractual relationships serving as a secondary determinant of its structure.

Projects with clearly defined outcomes and methods, where a detailed specification of both the outcome and task plan is justified, can be governed using a plan-and-control, waterfall approach. Regardless of the contractual setup, governance mechanisms would focus on precisely defining the scope and schedule, implementing control mechanisms to verify progress, and establishing intervention mechanisms in case deviations from the plan occur.

The precise and detailed definition of the scope and tasks can be fairly easily transferred into an outcome-based contract, whether it's an internal one or a contract with external suppliers. Such contract can be a major point of reference in governing a project.

On the other end of the spectrum are projects with poorly defined outcomes and/or methods, which require governance mechanisms centered on continuous and frequent coordination. When project goals are subject to VUCA (volatility, uncertainty, complexity, ambiguity), they need to be gradually refined and frequently revised, while project tasks must be continuously adjusted. Achieving continuous and frequent coordination is only possible through non-contractual governance mechanisms. Project participants must form a temporary organization, regardless of their legal status or contractual relationships. Contracts are of minor relevance in this situation.

The secondary determinant of the project governance structure is the contractual relationship, which includes the contractual setup (i.e., the number of contracting parties involved in the project and their interrelations) and the type of contract signed between them. The contractual setup primarily depends on the availability of the required combination of knowledge, skills, capabilities, and resources for the sponsoring company within the desired time frame. It may also depend on the project owners approach to project involvement (or project involvement orientation). The latter aspect has not been discussed yet. Regardless of other factors, such as the type of project outcome and resource availability, the project owner may have a particular stance on project management. They may choose an active (hands-on) involvement approach, taking accountability and responsibility for the project's success, and actively participating in or leading project and management activities on a daily basis. Alternatively, they may prefer a results-oriented (hands-off) approach, delegating much of the project responsibility and activities to other entities. The type of contract is influenced by the attributes of the project outcome, the contractual setup, the project owner's attitude towards risk, and project involvement orientation.

While the contractual relationship does impact the form of the project governance framework to some degree, the project owner's goal remains consistent regardless of the contractual arrangements. The objective is to acquire, configure, integrate, maintain, and deploy people, knowledge, and other resources (tangible, intangible, and financial) through effective planning, organizing, directing, coordinating, controlling, and motivating, in order to achieve the project outcome within the constraints of time, budget, and other resources.

To achieve this goal, the project owner requires a governance framework shaped by the following factors:

- The type of project outcome, ranging from well-defined to poorly defined.
- The programmability of project methods, from highly programmable to unknown.
- The project's contractual setup, including the number of independent legal entities involved and their interrelations, which, in turn is dependent on:
  - availability of the required combination of knowledge, skills, capabilities, and resources for the sponsoring company within the desired time frame,
  - owners attitude to risk,
  - owners project involvement orientation.
- The types of contracts between the project participants.

These determinants of the project governance framework are not entirely independent of each other. Their interrelations, particularly in terms of contractual relationships, were discussed in the previous chapter. For example, a project with a poorly defined outcome cannot be governed by an outcome-based contract. If the methods are undefined, the project will require a trial-and-error approach, which limits the contractual setups to internal, alliance, or (less commonly) bilateral, based on time and materials contracts. The interplay between these determinants shapes the form of the governance framework. Specifically, it influences the overall project management approach – whether waterfall, agile, or hybrid – and determines the balance between contractual and non-contractual mechanisms necessary to successfully complete the project.

As the governance framework must exist regardless of the contractual relationships between the project parties, the cost of establishing it is, to a great extent, independent of the project's contractual setup. Regardless of whether the governance framework is primarily contract-dependent or independent, and whether the project is carried out internally by the sponsoring organization or through a hybrid collaboration involving multiple legal entities, all of its elements must be developed for each new project. The cost of setting it up will depend on whether the project parties have access to a governance framework template that can be adapted to the specific project, or if they need to design it from the ground up based on generic project management frameworks.

The ongoing costs of maintaining the project governance structure and execution of governance during the project may vary significantly depending on:

- The necessary level of continuous coordination,
- Interest alignment between the project parties.

The required level of continuous coordination is inversely proportional to the definability of the project outcome and programmability, independence, and stability of the project tasks.

The governance framework for a project is formulated through two key steps:

1. Identifying a generic project management methodology: waterfall, agile, or hybrid.
2. Adapting the selected methodology based on the specific characteristics of the project, including the nature of contractual relationships and the required level of co-production.

Chapter 2.2, "Project Governance," outlined the generic project management frameworks and the criteria used to select the most suitable one. The primary criterion for choosing between waterfall and agile (or hybrid) is the feasibility and economic justification of defining the project outcome in detail, assuming the delivery methods are known. Projects with unknown delivery methods are inherently exploratory and require governance mechanisms typically associated with research and development initiatives.

The waterfall approach is selected when the project's goals can be clearly defined, and such definition is either necessary or economically justified. This is typically the case for projects with a physical outcome, including most construction and engineering projects, as well as those with critical intangible outcomes.

For projects with non-critical intangible outcomes, which are either poorly defined or subject to volatility, agile or hybrid methodologies are recommended. The choice between agile and hybrid depends on the nature of the contractual relationships among project stakeholders. If the relationship between the project owners and the project team requires a clearly defined contract, whether a legal agreement between independent parties or an internal agreement between departments, a hybrid approach is more appropriate.

4.5 Governance of a Waterfall Project

As previously mentioned in this book, waterfall is a traditional, plan-based project management methodology that originates from operations research. It relies on thorough planning, monitoring, and control to achieve defined goals.

Waterfall methodologies follow a sequential, stage-gate approach, where each phase's output serves as the input for the next. These phases are ordered sequentially and typically include project initiation, planning, execution, and closure. During the initiation and planning phases, the project's scope, budget, and schedule are carefully defined and detailed.

In the execution phase, the focus is on implementing the plan and minimizing deviations from it. If a deviation, or the need for one, arises, it must be carefully assessed for its root causes, necessity, and impact on the project. If the deviation is deemed justified, the plan must be adjusted accordingly. This may happen for two main reasons:

- The original plan was incorrect and did not accurately reflect the actual situation, even though this situation was anticipated and remained unchanged.
- The project's outcome or the surrounding conditions have changed compared to the initial assumptions and plans.

Re-planning is costly, and the more complex the plan, the higher the cost of re-planning. Additionally, re-planning often requires a reallocation of resources in both space and time. As a result, frequent changes to project parameters are generally discouraged.

If a deviation is deemed unjustified, a problem-solving procedure must be implemented. While there are various sophisticated problem-solving frameworks, a simplified process, as outlined by the American Society for Quality (ASQ, 2024), typically includes the following steps:

- Define the problem.
- Generate alternative solutions.
- Evaluate and select an alternative.
- Implement and follow up on the solution.

A fundamental requirement for using the waterfall project management approach is that the project outcomes must be defined before the project begins, and the methods to achieve them must be known. The prerequisite is that the outcome must be clearly definable, meaning it is well understood and can be described using a commonly accepted, unambiguous notation. A detailed description of methods may not always be necessary, as many repetitive projects follow established industry standards.

The secondary condition is that the benefits of defining the project outcome in detail must outweigh the associated costs. Most projects with tangible outcomes benefit from detailed planning because, once execution begins, the effort becomes irreversible. It is more cost-effective to carefully design 'on paper,' run simulations of various scenarios, and develop contingency plans than to proceed with a trial-and-error approach, where each mistake leads to irreversible costs. Even more importantly, in many engineering and construction projects errors can be critical, with the potential to cause fatalities. Therefore, for projects with tangible outcomes, the waterfall approach is usually the first choice (Flyvbjerg and Gardner, 2023). In many industries, detailed planning is also a legal requirement.

For projects with intangible outcomes, the level of irreversibility during execution is lower, though not negligible. At the very least, there is no need to demolish incorrectly built structures to start over. However, some projects with intangible outcomes can still benefit from the waterfall approach. One reason is criticality – if failure of the project outcome could have catastrophic consequences, it is crucial to define the outcome in extreme detail. There may also be contractual reasons to apply the waterfall approach to projects with intangible outcomes. For instance, in outcome-based contracts, which shift most or all of the risk to the contractor, a detailed definition of the outcome is required before project initiation, making the waterfall approach a suitable choice.

On the other hand, it's important to remember that waterfall project management incurs the highest costs when it comes to establishing and maintaining project governance mechanisms.

First, the desired outcome must be carefully designed in detail. Then, it must be broken down into work packages so that tasks can be appropriately assigned and scheduled on the timeline. Resources need to be allocated to these tasks, interdependencies between tasks and resources must be identified, and any conflicts must be resolved. All of this requires time and effort, which in turn generates significant costs. If both the project's outcome definition and its internal and external environments remain stable, the design and planning activities are typically performed once, with only minor adjustments needed throughout the project. However, frequent changes in any of these areas can dramatically increase the cost of design and planning.

Additionally, to effectively monitor whether these detailed and complex plans are being implemented as expected, an appropriate governance structure and mechanisms must be established. A reporting system that provides up-to-date information on the current project status is essential. The more complex the design and plan, the more sophisticated the reporting system must be. This system must be supported by a governance structure staffed with appropriately qualified personnel. Correctional mechanisms for addressing any potential deviations must also be designed, implemented, and, if necessary, promptly executed.

While waterfall project management is the most expensive governance framework, it offers the highest level of control and enables the use of 'traditional', operations research-based management approaches, which rely on planning, monitoring, and control.

4.5.1 *Generic Governance Mechanisms*

As outlined in section 2.2.5, the basic non-contractual governance mechanisms in the waterfall approach include:

- Project plan, which consists of, at minimum, the work breakdown structure detailing the desired outcome, a schedule displaying project tasks along a timeline, and a resource plan.
- Project and project management organization and roles, which typically include, at minimum, the Steering Committee, Project Management Team, Delivery Management, and Delivery Teams.
- Project information system, which provides up-to-date information on the project status relative to the plan, as well as identification of any risks or issues.
- Communication mechanisms, which ensure that the plan, detailed down to specific tasks on the timeline, is communicated to the responsible individuals. Additionally, individuals responsible for interdependent tasks must

update each other and collaborate, ensuring that any risks or issues are identified and escalated to project management as needed.
- Control and problem-solving mechanisms, which ensure that deviations from the plan are promptly identified, with corrective actions planned and executed.
- Domain-specific methodology, which describes the structure, roles, processes, and procedures necessary for effectively delivering the project outcome.

Governance mechanisms for the waterfall approach are comprehensively described in project management methodologies such as PMBOK, PRINCE2, and others. There is little more to be added on this specific topic.

4.5.2 *Internal Setup*

Internal contractual setup means that a project owner company is performing a project entirely with the use of their own employees and resources. For a company to successfully execute a project internally, it requires the project capacity: a complete, structured combination of knowledge, skills, and resources tailored to the specific type of project.

Developing this comprehensive and structured combination of knowledge, skills and resources is challenging, time-consuming, and costly. It only makes sense to develop and maintain these resources in-house if the projects of that type occur frequently and regularly so that the resources are fully utilized. For project-based organizations, which deliver their outputs to clients in the form of projects, having this combination is essential to their core operations.

However, this chapter adopts the perspective of a sponsoring organization, where projects are a secondary activity. Still, if projects of a certain type occur frequently, it may be worthwhile to develop and maintain the necessary project capacity internally. Such approach is especially beneficial for projects where the outcome is not fully defined, lacks detail, or when the outcome or other project constraints may change during execution. An internal contractual setup allows the company greater flexibility in reallocating or reconfiguring resources and in adjusting or reassigning tasks among project participants as needed, as compared to other contractual setups.

With project governance and management entirely within the company, it maintains full control over all events and actions occurring within the project.

The capabilities, and structured combination of knowledge, skills and resources necessary to run the project internally include:
- Project capability – the organizational ability to plan, prepare, and execute a project of the given type, i.e. the ability to acquire, integrate, configure, maintain and deploy the required resources in a way that ensures the desired outcome.

- Domain-specific explicit knowledge, including relevant methodology, processes and procedures.
- Individuals with domain-specific knowledge and skills.
- Necessary equipment.
- Domain-specific and domain-agnostic project management knowledge, both explicit and implicit, embedded in individuals aiming at managing the project.

Domain-agnostic knowledge about the governance of waterfall projects is well-documented in project management frameworks such as PMBOK, PRINCE2, and others. Every company undertaking a project should develop its own customized project management methodology, drawing from the guidance of a chosen framework or a blend of several. Equally important is domain-specific project management knowledge: understanding the particular aspects of delivering a specific outcome within a specific environment. This knowledge can only be acquired through years of experience in the field.

The situation becomes even more complex when it comes to project capability: the organizational ability to plan, prepare, and execute a project of a given type. This capability must be embedded within the organization's structure, culture, processes, and procedures. For project-based organizations, project capability is a core intangible asset, central to the business. In contrast, for operations-based companies that aim to execute occasional projects, developing and, more critically, integrating this capability into their existing structure, culture, and processes can be challenging, even if the company hires domain-specific project managers who know what resources are required and how to integrate, configure, and deploy them to achieve the project's goals.

Additionally, the company needs the most crucial element: resources and equipment qualified to perform the project work. Attempting to build and integrate all these elements from scratch is not only costly but filled with uncertainties and risks. Therefore, internal projects are often best handled by specialized, project-based units within operations-focused companies (e.g., an internal Information Systems department tasked with implementing and maintaining information systems within a holding company). Such units operate as a company within a company.

In any case, a project initiation and set-up group must be established or self-constituted to initiate the project and set up all the necessary elements. At a minimum, this group should include:

- Project Sponsor: An individual or group of individuals who propose the project, provide financial resources, and serve as the primary stakeholder interested in the project's success.

- Project Management: An individual or group of individuals appointed by the Project Sponsor, responsible for planning, executing, and controlling the project.
- Project Delivery Management: A domain expert or group of experts tasked with overseeing the physical delivery of the project's outcome.

Additionally, the group may include:

- Major Business Stakeholders: Representatives from the business areas most interested in or affected by the project's outcomes, if they are not already part of the Project Sponsor group.
- Project Management Office (PMO): If present in the organization, the PMO ensures unified standards of project governance and verifies the project's compliance with these standards.

The project initiation and set-up group must:

- Define the project outcome in accordance with industry standards specific to the domain.
- Establish project constraints, including the budget and timeline.
- Secure funding.
- Develop the project plan, including at minimum the work breakdown structure, schedule, and resource plan.
- Acquire resources and assign them to tasks according to the project schedule.
- Establish the project governance framework, including:
  - Project governance,
  - Governance of project contractual relations.

The project governance framework should incorporate the company's standards and regulations for managing project scope and quality, decision-making processes, organizational structure, roles and responsibilities, operational procedures, communication, coordination and cooperation mechanisms, project control, and reporting.

With regards to governance of project contractual relations, since the project is executed entirely with the internal resources of the sponsoring organization, all contractual relationships exist within the company's hierarchy. This hierarchy is reinforced by the principle of forbearance law, meaning that employment contracts are inherently incomplete. Employees, within the limits of their job descriptions, are expected to carry out the instructions of their supervisors. Internal disputes are typically resolved within the organization itself, without the involvement of external legal institutions such as courts. Incentives within this structure are generally weak, as employee compensation is not directly tied to their output. Employees are held accountable for mistakes only if those mistakes are made intentionally or in bad faith.

Applying hierarchy-based contractual relations to projects can have different implications compared to their application in ongoing operations, as these two types of business activities involve distinct dynamics. Due to the temporary nature and, to a certain extent, unique characteristics of projects, work in a project environment is generally less predictable and less structured than in daily operations. On one hand, an incomplete employment contract may offer the flexibility needed to handle unforeseen contingencies more effectively than many contracts between separate legal entities. On the other hand, the uncertainty and temporary nature of a project can demand extraordinary effort, which individuals operating under weak incentives in an employment contract may be unwilling to undertake. Additionally, temporary projects and permanent operations present employees with different motivational factors. For example, an employee in an operations-based company might view an assignment to a temporary project as an obstacle to their career advancement, particularly if it requires stepping down from their current position in the organizational hierarchy.

An internal project requires two fundamental types of contracts:

- Between the Project Sponsor, Project Management, and Delivery Management – outlining the project outcomes and delivery conditions.
- Between Project Management and Project Delivery Teams – defining the responsibilities and participation guidelines for project team members.

Although the Project Sponsor, Project Management, and Delivery Management all represent the same company, an internal agreement should still specify the project's outcomes, budget, schedule, resources, and other constraints and conditions.

The waterfall approach to project management requires a detailed definition of the project's outcome, schedule, budget, and resources. As such, the project initiation and set-up team is responsible for developing these elements, which can then be incorporated into the internal agreement. Additionally, they must define the quality and acceptance criteria for both the final project deliverables and any intermediate products, if applicable.

This leads to the first issue, which is related to the weak incentives typical of employment-based contracts. There is no direct link between the remuneration of Project Management and Delivery Management teams and whether the project meets the established acceptance criteria. In contrast, if the project were executed by an independent contractor under an outcome-based contract, payment would be contingent upon meeting those criteria, thus creating a stronger incentive to deliver according to the agreed-upon terms.

As internal employees, Project Managers and Delivery Teams have less motivation to meet acceptance criteria unless alternative incentives are provided by the Project Sponsor and the company. The most evident one is to integrate project performance measures into employee evaluations. In extreme cases, the continued employment of a Project Manager or Delivery Manager may depend on the project's success. However, this approach could place them in a position similar to that of an external contractor. Given that external contractors often command higher rates, such a situation might lead employees to leave.

Moreover, decisions regarding the termination of an experienced Project Manager or Delivery Manager are more likely to depend on the relevance and indispensability of their knowledge and skills across multiple current and future projects, rather than their performance on a single project.

As mentioned earlier, developing and maintaining a well-organized team of employees with the specific combination of knowledge and skills required to execute certain types of projects is both costly and time-consuming. If a company were to lay off a member of this team, that investment would be lost. Additionally, experienced Project Managers and Delivery Managers are typically involved in multiple projects simultaneously or have future projects planned. This means that the company can spread their costs across several projects, resulting in a lower unit cost per project day compared to hiring an external specialized firm.

Although this approach makes economic sense, it also raises several issues. The first problem, as mentioned earlier, is the reduced motivation to deliver specific projects within the defined constraints due to low-powered incentives, especially compared to inter-company, outcome-based contracts. The second issue is employee lock-in. Over time, internal specialists acquire company-specific project knowledge from previous assignments. They may also become responsible for maintaining the outcomes of past projects, some of which are critical to the company's operations. As a result, they become highly specialized and difficult to replace, which increases their bargaining power while weakening their motivation to deliver future projects on time, on budget, and within the specified scope and quality.

The only viable solution seems to be the separation of project teams from maintenance teams, along with the implementation of a strict evaluation system based on project performance, as is common in project-based organizations. Although an employee cannot be left unpaid for low performance on a specific project, it is possible to design a bonus system that rewards Project Managers and Delivery Managers who deliver projects on time, within scope, and within budget. Those who consistently underperform should, over time, be considered for termination.

The third issue is the overbooking of top talent. In an effort to fully utilize expensive human resources and reduce unit costs by spreading their involvement across multiple projects, the company risks going too far. The best employees may be assigned to so many parallel projects and tasks that they are unable to deliver quality work or meet deadlines for any of them. This problem affects both project-based organizations and project teams within operations-based companies.

Nevertheless, an internal project requires an internal contract that specifies the project outcome, budget, schedule, and resources. Due to the employment-based contractual relationships between the project parties, the internal contract cannot include penalties for the project team if they fail to meet the specified constraints. A partial solution is to incorporate project-related evaluation criteria into the employment contracts of the project team and/or a bonus system rewarding successful project completion.

The second set of contracts involves the internal agreements with members of the Delivery Team(s). In an operations-based organization which recruits project members internally, individuals may find themselves in one of the following situations:

1. They belong to the project-oriented part of the organization, meaning they belong to a specialized project task force dedicated to performing specific types of projects for the company.
2. They are temporarily reassigned from their permanent position within the organizational hierarchy to work on the project full-time.
3. They are required to split their time between their regular duties within the hierarchy and the project, meaning they are assigned to the project part-time.

In any of these scenarios, an employee may also be assigned to more than one project at a time.

The first situation faces issues similar to those described for the internal Project Manager and Delivery Manager. For a delivery specialist who is employed by the project-oriented part of the organization being assigned to a project is a natural situation. Direct incentives are weak in the employment contract, meaning that compensation is not closely tied to project outcomes. However, since an employee's sole responsibility is to deliver projects, their evaluation criteria can and should be based on their performance during these projects. A bonus system could also be implemented to reward employees who consistently meet expectations. The company should avoid assigning employees to both project work and the maintenance of past project outcomes, as well as avoid overburdening them with multiple projects.

The second scenario presents job security concerns when an employee is reassigned from their permanent position within the organizational hierarchy to a project role. While both the 'permanence' of an organization and a role within it are somewhat abstract concepts rather than absolute realities (since employees can be dismissed from 'permanent' jobs, and organizations evolve or even cease to exist), these may still be seen as more stable than project-based work, which, by definition, is temporary. When offered a transition from a permanent role to a project-based one, an individual may face significant dilemmas.

Their position within the permanent organization will likely be filled by someone else during the project. As a result, unless their return to their current (or better) position is contractually guaranteed, they may have no place to return to after the project concludes. One solution I've encountered was to hire replacements through a temporary employment agency, with contractually defined end dates, ensuring that permanent employees assigned to the project could be reassured they would have a role to return to once the project is completed.

Another solution could be to offer the individual subsequent projects or reassign them to the project-based division of the organization. However, not everyone has the mindset required for project-based work. Someone who prefers stability and repetitive tasks may feel uncomfortable in the uncertain, dynamic, and sometimes ambiguous project environment.

In this case, or when an employee cannot be temporarily replaced in their permanent role, the solution is scenario 3: splitting the employee's time between their regular duties and the project. However, this approach also comes with challenges. First, the employee is given new project tasks without being relieved of any permanent responsibilities, which may lead to overtime (requiring additional compensation) and potentially cause personal or mental strain from overwork.

Secondly, most employees are likely to prioritize their permanent tasks over project work, as the project is temporary, while their responsibilities within the permanent organization will continue. Partial solutions to these issues may include offering substantial bonuses for successful completion of project tasks and delegating some permanent duties to temporary staff.

All of these scenarios present challenges related to motivating internal staff to fully engage in temporary project activities. In addition to the previously mentioned tangible incentives, such as bonuses and the inclusion of project success metrics in employee evaluations, intangible incentives also play a significant role. These can be collectively referred to as the 'perception of the project within the organization'. Unlike project-based organizations, where everything revolves around projects, operations-based companies treat projects as a secondary activity. In these companies, projects are not at the core of the organizational culture, processes, or procedures.

In fact, it can be conjectured that, by default, occasional and temporary endeavors like projects would be considered less important than core, operations-based processes and functions. If an initiative intended to deliver a specific outcome within a defined, limited timeframe is regarded as less important than other tasks, it is highly unlikely to succeed.

In order to succeed with an internal project, permanent organization must 'force' its importance through the hierarchy. This involves activities such as:

- Formal inclusion of the project in the company's top priorities.
- Participation of the top management in the project Steering Committee.
- Active involvement of the top management in the project, including high-level decision-making and problem-solving.
- Information campaign regarding the project aims, scope and importance within the organization.
- Formal and informal appreciation of the project participants by the management.

Not without a reason 'top management support' is among the most important success factors in virtually every research regarding Information Systems, for example (Lech, 2016).

Once the project is planned, set up, and initiated, management follows the selected waterfall methodology. This involves comparing the detailed project plan against actual performance over time and implementing corrective actions when deviations are observed.

Despite the potential motivational challenges mentioned above, all project participants are employees of the project owner's company and are contractually obligated to follow the project management's directions. Therefore, the project management team should be able to achieve coordination through generic, non-contractual governance mechanisms embedded in the selected waterfall methodology.

The table 8 below summarizes the governance of a waterfall project using an internal contractual setup.

In summary, all project participants are employees of the project owner company and are therefore required to follow directions from their superiors. Project governance and management rest entirely with the project owner company, which has the capability to configure, reconfigure, and deploy project resources as needed to ensure project success. This arrangement grants the project owner complete control over the project and the flexibility to respond to unforeseen contingencies in a coordinated way. Therefore, project

TABLE 8 Governance of a waterfall project under internal setup

Description	Project is done entirely with the use of the project owner company's internal resources.
Prerequisites	The project owner company must possess: – Project capability – the ability to acquire, integrate, configure, and deploy the required resources in a way that ensures the desired outcome – Domain specific explicit knowledge, – Personnel with domain-specific implicit knowledge and domain-specific skills – Necessary equipment – Domain-specific and domain-agnostic project management knowledge
Contractual governance mechanisms	Forbearance law within the hierarchy. Employees assigned to the project, within the limits of their job descriptions, are expected to carry out the instructions of their supervisors. Internal disputes are resolved within the organization, without the involvement of external legal institutions such as courts. Additional mechanisms may include: – Bonuses for meeting project performance measures – Inclusion of project success metrics in employee evaluations
Type of incentives	Low-powered. The compensation of the employees is not related to the project outcomes.
Coordination mechanisms	Coordination is achieved by directive, as all participants are employees of the project owner company. Under their employment contracts, they are required to follow the instructions of their superiors.
Non-contractual governance mechanisms	Generic waterfall project management mechanisms within the project temporary organization: – Project structure, roles and responsibilities – Assignment of the planned tasks – Control of execution – Corrective actions in case of deviations Assurance of project high importance within the organization.

TABLE 8 Governance of a waterfall project under internal setup (*cont.*)

Pros	In the event of unforeseen contingencies requiring coordinated adaptation, changes can be made without the need for costly and time-consuming contract renegotiations with external providers. Any necessary adjustments can be implemented directly within the project owner organization. This contractual arrangement offers the highest level of flexibility and responsiveness to unexpected situations. The project owner organization maintains full control over all project elements.
Cons	A high level of flexibility and adaptability may lead to the acceptance of unnecessary changes, potentially resulting in scope creep. Additionally, weak incentives could result in low engagement from project participants in their assigned tasks. Unless the project resources and capabilities are fully utilized, internal setup becomes the most expensive option.
When to use	The internal setup requires the company to maintain a full range of resources, knowledge, and capabilities necessary to execute a given type of project. This approach is only practical when projects occur frequently enough to ensure full utilization of the available resources. Maintaining in-house project capabilities becomes more appealing for projects characterized by high levels of volatility, uncertainty, and ambiguity. Reconfiguring internal resources in response to unexpected contingencies may be more cost-effective than renegotiating external contracts. Additionally, handling projects internally may be driven by the need to retain full control and discretion over the project and its outcomes, particularly when strategic importance is involved.

management should be conducted in line with the generic form of the selected waterfall methodology. The project must be planned in sufficient detail to allow the project team(s) to interpret and execute it with minimal ambiguity, while also enabling project management to monitor progress by comparing the actual state of the project against the plan. Non-contractual governance mechanisms from the selected project management methodology take precedence over contractual ones.

A potential problem is the presence of low-powered incentives, which may reduce the motivation of project participants. Another issue could be excessive flexibility, which might lead to accepting unjustified changes to the project, potentially jeopardizing the achievement of project success criteria.

4.5.3 *Multilateral Centralized Setup and Alliance*

A multilateral centralized contractual setup is a scenario in which a project owner intends to fully manage the project but lacks some or all of the necessary resources and, therefore, contracts these needs. To operate effectively in such a setup, the project owner must possess project capability: the organizational ability to plan, prepare, and execute projects of this type, which involves the ability to acquire, integrate, configure, and deploy the required resources to achieve the desired outcomes. Achieving this requires also both domain-specific and general project management knowledge.

The key difference from an internal setup is that some or all of the following are outsourced from other companies:
- domain-specific explicit knowledge, including relevant methodologies, processes, and procedures,
- individuals with domain-specific knowledge and skills,
- necessary equipment.

If the project organization includes a mix of internal and external personnel and resources, the internal team will encounter challenges previously discussed in relation to the internal setup. Therefore, this section will focus solely on issues related to external resources and the interactions between internal and external resources.

In the waterfall approach, the project outcome definition and project plan must be established before the project begins. Since only partial tasks or outcomes will be contracted to various external companies, incorporating all contractors into the initial project definition and planning stages would be complex. Although collaborative planning cannot be completely ruled out, it is generally unlikely. The project owner company should at minimum define the initial project outcomes, divide them into relevant sub-products, and discuss the delivery details with potential contractors.

To manage this effectively, the project owner needs domain-specific knowledge and project capability. If they lack this expertise, they should consider adopting a prime-contractor setup instead.

One can imagine different levels of cooperation between the project owner and contractors during project definition and planning. However, the more contractors involved, the more centralized and less collaborative the process must be, as increased interdependencies would quickly raise planning complexity to an unmanageable level. The degree to which contractors participate in project initiation and planning also depends on the cooperation model and the type of contract involved.

The first model involves cooperation based on a resource-based, time-and-materials contract. In this arrangement, contractors provide resources or organized teams of resources to the project owner for a set period or amount of working time. The project owner has full authority over how these resources are used and directs their work. This enables the project owner to allocate resources as needed and guide tasks to ensure project objectives are met. The contractor's liability is limited to exercising due diligence.

With this type of contract, the project owner relies on general, non-contractual governance mechanisms inherent to the chosen project management methodology to achieve coordination among project participants. The project owner is responsible for all project outcomes and manages the contractors' resources as if they were their own.

When an organized team of resources is contracted, it may be beneficial to assign a contractor team lead who is familiar with the team's internal structure. In this case, the project owner's directives operate at a higher level: they assign broader tasks to the contractor's team, while the team lead determines the specific activities needed to accomplish these tasks.

The second option involves structuring the contractual relationship around outcome-based contracts. Such a contract must specify the contractor's deliverables in detail, along with key aspects like timelines and interdependencies with other contractors' tasks and outcomes. This approach offers the advantage of transferring responsibility, and some risk, associated with delivering specific outcomes to the contractors. However, it comes with a trade-off: reduced flexibility in responding to unforeseen contingencies. Any changes to the original plan must be managed through the contract.

While some contracts include flexible clauses allowing for minor adjustments without full renegotiation, significant changes to the project plan would require contract modifications. The complexity of making these changes increases with project size, particularly as the number of contractors and interdependencies among them grows. Additionally, challenges may arise in establishing responsibility and liability for errors and delays. For example, if multiple contractors rely on the timely and quality completion of another contractor's work, and that contractor fails to deliver, they may not only challenge their contractual obligations related to schedule and quality but also claim compensation for lost profits due to extended resource commitments.

The greater the project complexity, the number of contractors, and the interdependencies among their work and outcomes, the more difficult managing a project through outcome-based contractual governance would be. When creating outcome-based contracts for contractors, it's important that the sub-outcomes within the contract are mostly independent from each other. If they were not, defining clear outcomes for contractual purposes would be impossible, and a resource-based or behavior-based contract would be required instead. However, as previously mentioned, relying solely on contracts is more likely to lead to legal disputes than to the successful completion of the project.

Therefore, each project should incorporate non-contractual governance mechanisms to facilitate ongoing coordination through planning, organizing, directing, controlling, and addressing deviations as they arise. These mechanisms should serve as a platform for communication, cooperation and coordination among all project participants, while also providing the project management team with tools for project planning, controlling and issue resolution.

In the current scenario:

- The project outcome is defined in advance and broken down into sub-outcomes.
- A project plan, which includes scheduled tasks to achieve the project outcome, is prepared before the project begins.
- Some or all sub-outcomes, along with the associated tasks, are outsourced to contractors under outcome-based contracts.
- Interdependencies may exist among the activities and outcomes of contractors, meaning the performance or quality of one contractor's work may rely on the actions or outcome quality of another contractor.
- Project governance and management are conducted by the project owner.

In designing and implementing a blend of contract-based and non-contractual governance mechanisms for such a project, the project owner must balance several potentially conflicting factors:

- Since the contracts are outcome-based, the project manager cannot instruct the contractors' teams on what or even when to perform specific tasks, as long as the final outcome is delivered on time and meets the agreed-upon quality standards.

- As a result, the project manager neither directs nor closely monitors the daily actions of the contractors' team members.
- Nevertheless, some degree of coordination among various sub-teams is necessary, depending on the number and nature of the interdependencies between their tasks and outcomes.

A solution that seems suitable for each possible scenario is to divide the outcomes into smaller parts or stages, allowing for frequent progress checks, early identification of potential issues, and prompt corrective actions. If this approach is linked to partial payments, contractors are likely to support it, as it reduces their risk of non-payment and improves cash flow. The governance mechanisms supporting this solution are primarily contractual, as the partial outcomes or stages should be detailed in the contract, and the control mechanisms can be limited to physical inspections of progress.

This approach may be sufficient for simpler scenarios where contractors' sub-outcomes either depend on each other sequentially or are performed in parallel without significant interdependencies: i.e. when several sub-outcomes are completed independently and then assembled into a final product at the project's end.

Representatives from contractors may be included in the inspection team, allowing them to provide feedback on the quality of sub-outcomes that impact their subsequent stages of work.

For cases where the interdependencies between activities and outcomes of various contractors are more complex, additional non-contractual governance mechanisms should be implemented to ensure ongoing communication, collaboration, and coordination.

To achieve this, mechanisms that facilitate information sharing, alignment, and joint decision-making are essential. The simplest way to ensure these elements is through structured status meetings, supported by an information system for continuous communication, coordination and status tracking.

A representative from each contractor should attend the status meeting. At a minimum, the following items should be discussed:

- The current status of tasks compared to the plan.
- Identification of issues and risks.
- Plans for corrective actions to address identified issues and risks.
- Updates on corrective actions for previously identified issues and risks.
- Task planning for the next reporting period.
- Any coordination points involving two or more contractors related to any of the above items.

The project owner's management team should lead the status meeting and act as arbitrator if disagreements or disputes arise between contractors. If arbitration is unsuccessful, the contracts serve as the final point of reference.

Coordination of plans and ongoing activities, along with the necessary information exchange, must often occur continuously. Therefore, communication and coordination mechanisms between status meetings should be established. The simplest approach is to maintain a contact list with assigned roles, enabling informal communication through any medium. This can be supported by a unified communication platform. Communication outcomes should be recorded as meeting minutes and stored in the project repository.

If formal communication is preferred or a communication history log is required, a project work management and issue-tracking system may be implemented. The need for such systems increases with project complexity. These systems also facilitate activity, risk, and issue reporting and tracking; otherwise, these tasks need to be managed in a RAID log stored in the repository.

In summary, the information system for continuous communication, coordination, and status tracking can be implemented using a range of technical solutions, including:

- **Basic solutions**: a shared project repository, a contact list, communication through various mediums (phone, email, in-person conversations) with follow-up meeting minutes stored in the project repository, and a RAID log maintained in a spreadsheet and saved in the repository.
- **Advanced solutions**: a dedicated project work management and issue-tracking system that integrates a shared workspace, communication platform, and tools for reporting and tracking activities, risks, and issues.

Another non-contractual governance mechanism is the project structure, which includes defined roles and responsibilities. In outcome-based contracts, the project owner does not have authority over the contractors' personnel as long as the agreed-upon outcomes are delivered. Roles and responsibilities within the contractors' teams are assigned by the contractors themselves, with the project owner only able to influence aspects such as health and safety regulations and other general corporate codes of conduct. If the contractors' tasks are either sequentially dependent or executed in parallel without significant interdependencies, a detailed project structure may be unnecessary. In such cases, outcome definitions based on contractual terms, along with inspection and information-sharing mechanisms, can provide sufficient coordination. However, a structured governance mechanism with clearly defined roles and responsibilities becomes essential when continuous coordination is required due to interdependencies between tasks and outcomes or frequent changes to the project environment that impact the outcome or the means of achieving it. In such situations, a resource-based contract may be more appropriate, as discussed. For projects based on outcome-based contracts, a minimal structure should suffice, with each contractor's team functioning as a 'black box'.

The third model is owner alliance contracting, which occupies a middle ground between a resource-based contractual relationship, where the project owner acts as a leader, and a purely outcome-based contractual relationship, where responsibility and risk are transferred to the contractors and the project owner serves as an inspector of outcomes.

In an alliance, the project owner collaborates with non-owner participants (NOPs), who execute the project on the owner's behalf. The contractual relationship is governed by the Project Alliance Agreement, which establishes shared risk and opportunity among all participants, a commitment to 'no disputes,' unanimous best-for-project decision-making, transparency through open-book reporting, a 'no fault – no blame' culture, and cooperation in good faith.

The non-owner participants are compensated based on audited open-book actual costs, covering project costs, project-specific overheads, and a fee for corporate overheads and 'normal' profit. Additionally, they receive an equitable share of the 'pain' or 'gain', depending on how the actual project outcomes align with pre-agreed targets.

Project governance is primarily executed through non-contractual mechanisms, facilitated by a joint management structure that includes all project participants.

The National Alliance Contracting Guidelines – Guide to Alliance Contracting (2015) lists the elements of the project management structure:

- Alliance Leadership Team,
- Alliance Manager,
- Alliance Management Team,
- and Alliance Project Team.

The Alliance Leadership Team serves as the high-level decision-making body for the project. It comprises representatives from all participants and operates on a principle of unanimous decision-making. According to the National Alliance Contracting Guidelines (2015):

"Every Alliance Leadership Team member is entitled to cast a vote in the decision-making process, and the final decision must be unanimous. However, certain important decisions will be reserved for unilateral determination by the Owner, given that the Owner, as the client, will ultimately own and pay for the asset". Such unilateral decisions typically include changes to the project scope, adjustments to the timing and sequence of project components, and decisions regarding project termination.

The Alliance Management Team, responsible for the day-to-day delivery of the project under the leadership of the Alliance Manager, is composed of representatives from all project participants. Similarly, the Alliance Project

Team is described in the National Alliance Contracting Guidelines (2015) as "the integrated, collaborative team of non-owner participants and the owner's professional and support staff that plan, design, and manage the construction and delivery of all aspects of the project". As a result, all levels of the project management and delivery structure consist of mixed teams comprising personnel from both the owner and the contractors.

Although all project members, regardless of their origin, are expected to work collaboratively toward the project goals within a shared project structure, the project owner holds a privileged position. This is because they fund the contractors' efforts and ultimately own the project outcomes. As mentioned previously, non-owner participants cannot alter the project's scope or schedule. The project scope is, in fact, defined by the project owner before the tendering process, typically documented in a Business Case and Value for Money Statement. Contractors submit bids based on price, establishing what is referred to as the Target Outturn Cost.

A portion of the contractors' remuneration is tied to the project's "success," measured as the difference between the Target Outturn Cost and the Actual Outturn Cost. If actual costs exceed the target, contractors forgo any rewards but still have their actual costs and overheads reimbursed. As such, the alliance contract can be categorized as outcome-based non fixed-price contractual relationship.

Project governance is implemented through a mix of contractual and non-contractual mechanisms. This approach reflects the practical application of stewardship theory, as all participants are required to adopt a "best for the project" mindset and act in good faith. The nuances of alliance contracting present a fascinating subject for in-depth empirical study.

In summary, coordination in a multilateral centralized contractual setup is achieved through a combination of contractual and non-contractual governance mechanisms. The specific mix depends on factors such as the definability and stability of the project outcome, the number of interdependencies between sub-outcomes and tasks of various contractors, and the stability of the project environment.

For projects with well-defined, distinct outcomes and a stable environment, outcome-based contracts are typically supported by basic reporting, communication, and coordination mechanisms, such as status meetings and logs. In contrast, alliance contracts involve contractually defined scopes and a joint project structure for execution. Finally, resource-based contracts are a best fit for projects under full responsibility and direction of the project owner.

The summary is presented in Table 9.

TABLE 9 Governance of a waterfall project under multilateral setup

Type of contract	Resource-based	Outcome-based	Alliance
Description	The project owner intends to fully manage a project but lacks some or all of the necessary resources and, therefore, contracts these needs. The contractors provide resources or organized teams of resources to the project owner for the agreed period or amount of working time. The project owner has full authority over how these resources are used and directs their work.	The project owner intends to fully manage a project but lacks some or all of the necessary resources and, therefore, contracts these needs. The contractors agree to deliver specified sub-outcomes for a given price and within the agreed time-frame.	The project owner intends to fully manage a project but lacks some or all of the necessary resources and, therefore, contracts these needs. The contractual relationship assumes risk and opportunity sharing between all the participants, commitment to 'no disputes', best-for-project unanimous decision-making processes; transparency expressed as open book reporting, 'no fault – no blame' culture and cooperation in good faith. The parties are expected to collaborate through a shared project structure to achieve the project goal.
Prerequisites	The project owner must possess project capability: the organizational ability to plan, prepare, and execute projects of a given type, which involves the ability to acquire, integrate, configure, and deploy the required resources to achieve the desired outcomes.	The project owner must possess project capability: the organizational ability to plan, prepare, and execute projects of a given type, which involves the ability to acquire, integrate, configure, and deploy the required resources to achieve the desired outcomes. The sub-outcomes and schedules of each contractor must be defined in detail prior to the project.	The project owner must possess project capability: the organizational ability to plan, prepare, and execute projects of a given type, which involves the ability to acquire, integrate, configure, and deploy the required resources to achieve the desired outcomes. The project outcome must be defined prior to the project.

TABLE 9 Governance of a waterfall project under multilateral setup (*cont.*)

Type of contract	Resource-based	Outcome-based	Alliance
Contractual governance mechanisms	The contractors provide resources or organized teams of resources to the project owner for the agreed period or amount of working time, basing on the resource-based contract. The project owner has full authority over how these resources are used and directs their work. The contractor's liability is limited to exercising due diligence.	Outcome-based contracts specify both the desired outcomes and the conditions and boundaries for achieving them. Contractors are compensated upon successful delivery and assume the risks associated with non-delivery.	Contractual governance is executed via Project Alliance Agreement which assumes risk and opportunity sharing between all the participants, commitment to 'no disputes', best-for-project unanimous decision-making processes; transparency expressed as open book documentation and reporting, 'no fault – no blame' culture and cooperation in good faith. The non-owner participants are paid project costs and project-specific overheads based on audited open-book actual costs, a fee to cover corporate overheads and "normal" profit and an equitable share of the "pain" or "gain" depending on how actual project outcomes compare with the pre-agreed targets.
Type of incentives	Medium-powered. The contractors' remuneration is not tied to the outcome of their work. However, the project owner typically has	High-powered. The contractors' remuneration depends on the delivery of the pre-agreed outcomes according to the contract.	High-powered. The contractors are paid a premium if the final outcome is delivered below the planned cost. However, risk is shared evenly between all the contractors.

TABLE 9 Governance of a waterfall project under multilateral setup (*cont.*)

Type of contract	Resource-based	Outcome-based	Alliance
	the right to cancel the contract on short notice if the contractors' performance is unsatisfactory. Since the project work is central to the contractors' core business, their motivation to perform well in the project may be higher than that of the project owner's internal personnel.		
Coordination mechanisms	Coordination is achieved by directive as all the resources are put at the disposal of the project owner.	Coordination is achieved primarily through formal contracts that align with the project plan. These contracts outline the contractors' responsibilities regarding outcome specifications, timelines, and other conditions. Any significant changes to these terms require contract renegotiation.	Coordination is primarily achieved through non-contractual governance mechanisms within a joint management structure that includes all project participants.
Non-contractual governance mechanisms	Generic waterfall project management mechanisms within the project temporary organization:	A platform for status reporting, issue and risk management, and communication among project participants	A common project management structure, encompassing all project participants, includes:

TABLE 9 Governance of a waterfall project under multilateral setup (*cont.*)

Type of contract	Resource-based	Outcome-based	Alliance
	– Assignment of the planned tasks – Control of execution – Corrective actions in case of deviations	must be established. This should include structured status meetings and a solution for continuous communication, coordination, and status tracking.	– Alliance Leadership Team – Alliance Manager – Alliance Management Team – Alliance Project Team All project participants, regardless of organizational affiliation, are involved in decision-making as well as in planning, designing, managing, and delivering all aspects of the project. However, crucial decisions, such as changes to the project scope, timing and sequence of project components, and project termination, are reserved for the project owner.
Pros	In the event of unforeseen contingencies requiring coordinated adaptation, changes can be made without the need for costly and time-consuming contract renegotiations with external providers. This contractual arrangement offers high level of flexibility and	Outcome-based contracts shift the responsibility and risk for delivering specific project sub-outcomes to the contractors. This approach reduces the management effort required from the project owner, as the contractor's teams manage their work internally.	Alliance contracting seeks to combine two seemingly contradictory governance mechanisms: outcome-based contractual governance and cooperative governance through joint structures and management. Under strict assumptions, such as best-for-project behavior, good faith, cooperative attitudes, and a no-blame culture, this approach

TABLE 9 Governance of a waterfall project under multilateral setup (*cont.*)

Type of contract	Resource-based	Outcome-based	Alliance
	responsiveness to unexpected situations. The project owner organization maintains full control over all project elements.		could serve as an ideal solution for managing projects that require external collaboration.
Cons	All project risks remain with the project owner. In the short term, outsourcing resources from external contractors is likely to be more costly than using internal resources, as profit margins will apply. If project changes extend its duration, contracts will need to be renegotiated. Integrating individuals from different organizations into the project's temporary structure may also pose challenges due to unfamiliarity with the project owner's methodologies, cultural differences, and other factors.	Limited flexibility: In the event of unforeseen contingencies, plan changes, or low performance from other contractors, the contracts may need to be renegotiated. With numerous interdependencies, identifying responsibility and assigning risk can be challenging. Even when responsibilities are clear, smaller contractors may lack the capacity to compensate the project owner or other contractors for potential losses.	The assumptions underlying alliance contracting are challenging to achieve. Contractors must set aside their profit-maximizing mindset and resist the temptation to gain an advantage at the expense of other contractors or the project owner. For some, the prospect of risk-sharing with other project participants may be discouraging, as it involves taking on risks over which they have no control.

TABLE 9 Governance of a waterfall project under multilateral setup (*cont.*)

Type of contract	Resource-based	Outcome-based	Alliance
When to use	A multilateral, centralized setup based on resource-based contracts with contractors is a viable option when the project owner intends and is able to retain full control over all project elements and is prepared to assume all associated risks. This approach is particularly suitable for projects with outcomes that are not fully defined at the outset and/or for projects where critical parameters may be subject to unforeseen changes during the project's course.	A multilateral, centralized setup based on outcome-based contracts with contractors is a suitable approach when the project owner wishes to maintain overall control of the project while transferring responsibility and risk for specific sub-outcomes to the contractors. This approach works well when the project outcome is clearly defined in detail, interdependencies between outcomes are limited, well understood, and clearly described, and when the project is not subject to high volatility, uncertainty, or ambiguity.	This approach is well-suited to environments that are familiar with and accepting of the assumptions underlying alliance contracting. It is most effective in projects where there is a high level of trust between parties, often built through previous collaborations, and in settings where long-term reputation and strong relational capital between the parties hold significant value.

A multilateral centralized setup is suitable when the project owner intends to manage a project but lacks some or all of the necessary resources and must therefore contract them. To effectively manage the project, the owner must possess project capability: the organizational ability to plan, prepare, and execute projects of a specific type, which includes the ability to acquire, integrate, configure, and deploy the required resources to achieve the desired outcomes.

The project owner's approach to coordinating resources from different companies can vary based on their subjective management style, including the level of direction and control they wish to maintain, their attitude toward risk, and their trust in the contractors' competence. However, coordination mechanisms depend predominantly on the objective project parameters such as the level of detail in defining the project outcome, the stability of this definition over time, the stability of the project environment, and the number and complexity of interdependencies among project sub-outcomes, among other factors.

In projects with well-defined and stable outcomes, limited complexity, and few interdependencies, the project owner may choose to govern the project through outcome-based contracts, delegating part of the responsibility and authority to the contractors. However, as project complexity, the number of interdependencies, and volatility increase, and the detail of the project definition decreases, this approach can become costly due to frequent contract renegotiations and disputes.

An alternative solution is to engage contractors through resource-based contracts, integrating their resources into a unified project organization under the project owner's direction. This approach offers advantages such as full control over the project organization, greater flexibility in responding to unforeseen contingencies, and the ability to coordinate responses effectively. However, it also places all responsibility and risk on the project owner.

Alliance contracting represents an attempt to balance these two governance approaches. It establishes a joint organizational structure involving all project participants, shared decision-making, and ongoing collaboration. Agreements with contractors incorporate an outcome-based component and include provisions for risk-sharing in cases of underperformance.

4.5.4 *Prime-Contractor Setup*

A prime-contractor setup addresses situations where a sponsoring organization lacks project capability and project capacity. In such cases, the organization contracts the entire project to a single specialized entity.

The prime-contractor assumes responsibility for ongoing project management, including coordinating activities and resources. The contractor may execute the work using its own resources or subcontract it to other entities. Consequently, the prime-contractor operates within an internal or multilateral centralized governance framework, depending on the arrangement.

This chapter, however, examines the situation from the perspective of the project owner and their role in ensuring project success. Since day-to-day project management is handled by the prime-contractor, the project owner's involvement is primarily limited to defining the desired outcomes and project parameters, and monitoring progress. The extent of involvement depends largely on the nature of the project's objectives.

If the project outcome can be clearly and comprehensively defined in advance, the project owner's role may be restricted to specifying requirements during the design phase, formally approving the design, finalizing an outcome-based contract, and conducting periodic progress reviews based on outcome inspections. However, if project parameters change from those specified in the contract, the project owner must renegotiate the agreement with the prime-contractor. Frequent changes to the project scope or other critical parameters can result in significant costs due to repeated contract renegotiations.

If the project outcome cannot be clearly defined in sufficient detail before the project begins, the project owner's involvement must be adjusted accordingly. This could extend to a continuous co-production model within a shared project structure. In such cases, however, the project would adopt a hybrid governance approach rather than a traditional waterfall model. Hybrid governance will be discussed later in this chapter. A summary is provided in Table 10.

TABLE 10 Governance of a waterfall project under prime-contractor setup

Description	The project owner lacks both domain-specific project management expertise and the resources to execute a project, and contracts the entire project to a single specialized entity.
Prerequisites	None
Contractual governance mechanisms	Outcome-based contract
Type of incentives	High-powered. The contractor is paid if the outcome meets the criteria from the contract.
Coordination mechanisms	Contract-based. The project owner must clearly define their requirements and control the conformance of the actual outcome with those requirements.
Non-contractual governance mechanisms	Not necessary

TABLE 10 Governance of a waterfall project under prime-contractor setup

Pros	The risk is transferred to the contractor, while the project owner's efforts are limited to defining the project outcome and parameters, as well as periodically monitoring progress.
Cons	If changes to the project outcome or parameters are required during the project, contract renegotiation becomes necessary. Additionally, if the project outcome is not accurately defined, identifying issues in time to implement corrective actions may prove challenging.
When to use	For projects with detailed, unambiguous and stable definition of the outcome, performed in predictable environment.

A waterfall project under a prime-contractor setup requires minimal effort from the project owner. While this can be appealing, such an arrangement is effective only when the project outcomes are stable and clearly defined. Applying this setup to other scenarios can lead to frequent and prolonged disputes, contract renegotiations, and, in the worst case, project termination or the delivery of outcomes that fail to meet actual needs. In such cases, the client may receive what they paid for, but not what they truly wanted.

4.6 Governance of an Agile Project

Agile is a family of project management methodologies that emphasize the incremental definition and development of project outcomes within fixed time-boxes. These methodologies rely on constant, synchronous collaboration and direct communication among members of small, cross-functional, and self-organizing agile teams. In agile approaches, the project scope is defined in broad terms rather than detailed specifications before the project begins. The scope remains flexible and can evolve during the project, while the project's duration and resources are fixed. Agile methodologies are particularly well-suited for projects where the outcomes are not fully defined upfront, are ambiguous, or are likely to change over time. Such conditions often arise in some 'soft' projects with intangible outcomes.

4.6.1 *Generic Governance Mechanisms*

Agile methodologies emphasize "individuals and interactions over processes and tools," "customer collaboration over contract negotiation," and "responding to change over following a plan" (Agile Manifesto, 2001). The scope of an agile project is outlined in the product backlog, which includes high-level descriptions of the project's features or deliverables. Each time-boxed iteration, known as a sprint, begins with a sprint planning session where the team selects items from the product backlog to complete during the sprint. Throughout the sprint, the agile team works on items from the sprint backlog. They analyze and refine these items, design solutions, develop and test them, and ensure their approval, aiming to deliver a functional outcome, referred to as an increment, by the sprint's end. Progress during the sprint is monitored through daily stand-up meetings (scrums) and visualized using a Kanban board.

In agile methodologies, coordination and communication primarily rely on interpersonal collaboration. Agile teams are intentionally kept small to enable direct, face-to-face communication among all members. Ideally, these teams work synchronously in the same physical location, facilitating efficient information exchange, decision-making, coordination, and activity synchronization through direct conversations.

At the end of each sprint, progress is evaluated during a sprint review session, where the team presents the sprint's outcomes to stakeholders and collaboratively plans for the next sprint. The scope in the product backlog may be adjusted based on insights gained during the review.

A sprint retrospective is also performed, during which the scrum team discusses the possible improvements in organization of work basing on the experiences from the past sprint

4.6.2 *Internal Setup*

Agile methodologies prioritize "customer collaboration over contract negotiation" and "responding to change over following a plan," making them well-suited for an internal setup where all project participants are employees of a single organization and, thus, are motivated and obligated to perform tasks as outlined in their employment contracts. The project setup and governance should align with the chosen agile project management methodology.

The project owner must have project capability, along with project management knowledge and skills specific to the chosen agile methodology and the project's domain. They should have full access to all resources necessary to complete the project and be responsible for configuring and deploying these resources effectively.

Stakeholders should outline the scope through the product backlog. An agile team, at a minimum consisting of a product owner, a scrum master (or equivalent), and a development team, should be established. The timeframe and the number of time-boxes should be determined, and the team should work on delivering features incrementally within these time-boxes. Each time-box should result in a working solution, which must then be approved by the stakeholders.

Progress should be monitored through daily standups and other relevant practices based on the selected methodology, such as sprint reviews and retrospectives. As the contractual arrangement is based on employment contracts, the incentives are relatively low-powered: employees are compensated for fulfilling their tasks with due diligence, not based on the outcome. However, because agile methodologies do not fix the scope, outcome-based contracts are not feasible under any contractual arrangement. The participants may also face motivation challenges, similar to those found in a waterfall-style internal setup, when dividing responsibilities between the project and the permanent organization.

If the organization is committed to adopting an agile approach, team members should be assigned full-time to the project. This resolves issues related to sharing responsibilities. The remaining challenge is convincing individuals to temporarily leave their permanent roles and join the project. To address this, their return to their previous (or an improved) position should be contractually guaranteed, or they should be employed by the project-based segment of the organization.

The summary is presented in Table 11.

TABLE 11 Governance of an agile project under internal setup

Description	Project is done entirely with the use of the project owner company's internal resources.
Prerequisites	The project owner company must possess: – Project capability – the ability to acquire, integrate, configure, and deploy the required resources in a way that ensures the desired outcome – Domain specific explicit knowledge – Personnel with domain-specific implicit knowledge and domain-specific skills – Necessary equipment – Domain-specific and domain-agnostic project management knowledge regarding the selected agile methodology

TABLE 11 Governance of an agile project under internal setup (*cont.*)

Contractual governance mechanisms	Forbearance law within the hierarchy. Employees assigned to the project, within the limits of their job descriptions, are expected to carry out the instructions of their supervisors. Internal disputes are resolved within the organization, without the involvement of external legal institutions such as courts. Employees should be assigned full-time to the project.
Type of incentives	Low-powered. The compensation of the employees is not related to the project outcomes.
Coordination mechanisms	Interpersonal collaboration and direct communication within the members of the agile team who work closely together on a daily basis.
Non-contractual governance mechanisms	Generic agile project management mechanisms: – high-level outline of the project scope in product backlog – sprint planning and sprint backlog – daily stand-ups – sprint review and sprint retrospective – other mechanisms advised by the selected agile methodology.
Pros	Agile methodologies, by definition, embrace changes at any stage of the project. This adaptability is further enhanced in an internal setup, where modifications to the agile team can be made more easily compared to other contractual arrangements.
Cons	Problems with motivation in case of divided responsibilities.
When to use	In projects with undefined or changing scope.

Agile approaches, which prioritize continuous personal cooperation and flexibility in responding to change, are well-suited for an internal setup where all project participants are employees of a single organization. The project setup and governance should align with the chosen agile project management methodology.

4.6.3 *Multilateral Centralized Setup*

Agile methods emphasize democracy and self-organizing teams, making the term "centralized" somewhat inconsistent with the core principles of agile methodology. In this context, "centralized" refers to a setup where the product owner, scrum master and any type of project lead are part of the project owner's organization, while the realization team is outsourced. Unlike traditional project management methods, agile methodologies inherently exclude outcome-based contracts, as outcomes are not rigidly predefined and changes are welcomed. Consequently, the realization team can be engaged under a resource-based, time-and-materials contract, possibly, with behavior-based parts.

This raises a critical question: to what extent should such a team be self-organizing and autonomous? For instance, during sprint planning, would the project owner permit the realization team to independently select items from the product backlog, or would they prefer to maintain some level of control over the process? In such a scenario, one might anticipate a governance model that is more centralized and directive compared to a setup involving a fully internal team.

Coordination, progress control, and issue-resolution mechanisms should be adapted from the chosen agile methodology and should primarily rely on interpersonal collaboration and direct communication among team members. Key agile practices, such as backlog definition, sprint planning, daily standups, Kanban boards, sprint reviews, and retrospectives, are applicable.

While the outsourced realization team is compensated on a time-and-materials basis, their contract with the external party differs significantly from an employment contract. First, it is typically more temporary, with individuals engaged for a specific project and a defined period. Compensation is often tied to their performance during sprints and the outcomes of those sprints, enabling stronger incentives compared to an employment contract. Additionally, terminating a contract with an external contractor due to unsatisfactory performance or lack of engagement is generally easier than dismissing an employee.

However, arrangements other than full-time engagement for a specified period may introduce complications. Extra efforts may incur additional payments or lead to disputes. Such contractual setups can reduce adaptability to unforeseen contingencies compared to an internal team. Other potential drawbacks include lower team cohesion and the additional time and effort required to achieve high levels of coordination, cooperation, and performance.

The summary is presented in table 12.

TABLE 12 Governance of an agile project under multilateral centralized contractor setup

Description	Product owner, scrum master and any type of project lead are part of the project owner's organization, while the realization team is outsourced.
Prerequisites	Project owner organization must have organizational capabilities and knowledge and personal knowledge and skills to manage an agile project according to a selected methodology.
Contractual governance mechanisms	Resource-based, time-and-materials contract, possibly, with a behavior-based parts.
Type of incentives	Moderate. The contractors cannot be paid basing on the outcome, as outcome is not defined in detail and subject to change. However, they are hired for a specific project, their performance may be evaluated after every time-box, and termination of their engagement in case of mal-performance is fairly easy.
Coordination mechanisms	Interpersonal collaboration and direct communication within the members of the agile team who work closely together on a daily basis
Non-contractual governance mechanisms	Generic agile project management mechanisms: – high-level outline of the project scope in product backlog, – sprint planning and sprint backlog, – daily stand-ups, – sprint review and sprint retrospective other mechanisms advised by the selected agile methodology.
Pros	The project owner retains full control over the project. Due to the relative ease of contract termination, the contractors' motivation may be greater than that of internal employees.
Cons	Achieving team cohesion may be more challenging than with an internal team due to differences in organizational culture among team members. Contractual arrangements that do not involve full-time commitment may lead to disputes if additional work is required.
When to use	When the project owner wants to manage the project and has the ability to do so but lacks the necessary realization resources for its execution.

A multilateral centralized setup, in terms of agile, refers to a situation where the product owner, scrum master, and any type of project lead are part of the project owner's organization, while the realization team is outsourced. This setup imposes a higher level of central management than prescribed in agile frameworks, as the project leadership would likely prefer to maintain some level of control over the outsourced development team. Team members should, if possible, be hired full-time to avoid negotiations and tensions regarding the planned level of involvement.

4.6.4 *Prime-Contractor Setup*

A prime-contractor setup addresses situations where a sponsoring organization lacks project capability, knowledge, and the resources needed to execute a project. In such cases, the organization contracts the entire project to a single specialized entity.

For agile projects, this setup implies that both the project team and the project team lead (if applicable) or scrum master come from the contractor company. Only the product owner and business stakeholders belong to the sponsoring organization. In this arrangement, the primary contractual interface exists between the product owner and the project team lead (if such a role exists within the chosen agile framework) or the scrum master.

While the product owner is always responsible for owning the product backlog, making changes to it, and verifying the completion of its items, the dynamics of interactions in this contractual setup differ from others. In previously discussed setups, the product owner, who understands the business requirements but lacks agile project-related knowledge, and the project lead and/or scrum master, responsible for managing or facilitating daily project work, were part of the same organization. Therefore, their interactions were governed by mechanisms typical of hierarchical structures, ensuring their interests were aligned.

In the scenario under discussion, however, these individuals belong to separate legal entities, potentially leading to conflicting interests. As previously noted, agile inherently excludes the possibility of an outcome-based contract because the outcome is not defined in detail and evolves throughout the project. As a result, the contract would typically be resource-based, using a time-and-materials model, potentially supplemented by behavior-based clauses.

If trust exists between the parties, often established through prior relationships, the dynamics would closely resemble those of the previously discussed scenarios.

In the absence of trust, several challenges may arise:

- Monitoring Challenges: The project owner's representatives often lack expertise needed to effectively monitor the contractor's behavior. They cannot verify whether the contractor's personnel are performing the tasks necessary to achieve the desired outcomes or whether the effort being expended is relevant to those outcomes, even with constant physical observation.
- Extended Task Timelines: Under a non-full-time, time-and-materials contract, the contractor might intentionally prolong task completion to increase revenue for a given task.
- Lower Expertise Staffing: The contractor may assign personnel with lower expertise to the project, resulting in longer task completion times due to the natural inefficiencies of less experienced workers.
- Unrealistic Expectations: The project owner may set unrealistic completion times or demand a suboptimal task sequence, further complicating the project's progress.

Without mutual trust, executing an agile project under a prime-contractor setup presents challenges that cannot be fully addressed through contractual measures. A reasonable approach is to foster close cooperation and maintain open communication, allowing trust to develop gradually over time.

An alternative is a hybrid approach, which partially reduces uncertainty for both parties while incorporating a more structured contractual framework. A summary of governance for an agile project under a prime-contractor setup is presented in Table 13.

TABLE 13 Governance of an agile project under prime-contractor setup

Description	A prime-contractor setup addresses situations where a sponsoring organization lacks project capability, knowledge, and the resources needed to execute a project. In such cases, the organization contracts the entire project to a single specialized entity.
Prerequisites	None
Contractual governance mechanisms	Resource-based, time and material contract with behavior-based clauses
Type of incentives	Weak. The payment is not related to the outcome. The project owner is unable to effectively monitor the contractor due to limited knowledge.
Coordination mechanisms	Interpersonal collaboration and direct communication within the members of the agile team who work closely together on a daily basis

TABLE 13 Governance of an agile project under prime-contractor setup (*cont.*)

Non-contractual governance mechanisms	Generic agile project management mechanisms: – high-level outline of the project scope in product backlog, – sprint planning and sprint backlog, – daily stand-ups, – sprint review and sprint retrospective other mechanisms advised by the selected agile methodology.
Pros	Lower engagement from the project owner compared to other agile setups.
Cons	The project cannot be effectively governed by the project owner, either through contractual or non-contractual mechanisms.
When to use	In situations where the project outcome is poorly defined and subject to significant changes during the project, the project owner lacks the knowledge to manage the project, and there is trust between the parties.

In a prime-contractor setup, a project owner who lacks the capability, knowledge, and resources needed to execute a project contracts the entire project to a single specialized entity. Therefore, the whole agile team, except for the product owner and business stakeholders, originates from the contractor company. As the project owner lacks sufficient knowledge, they must rely on the contractor for virtually every operational aspect of conducting the project. In an agile approach, the project owner does not possess contractual mechanisms to control the contractor. The lack of sufficient knowledge limits their non-contractual options to trust, continuous close cooperation, and open communication.

4.7 Governance of a Hybrid Project

As already discussed, in a broad sense, hybrid project governance can be defined as "any combination of agile and traditional (plan-driven or rich) approaches that an organizational unit adopts and customizes to its own contextual needs" (Kuhrmann et al., 2017). More specifically, the general structure of hybrid methods typically follows the water-scrum-fall model (West, 2011; Schlauderer, 2015). In this model, the initial and final phases of the project are managed using a waterfall approach, while the agile approach is applied during the execution phase. The high-level scope definition is prepared upfront and cannot be freely altered during the project. Instead, any changes are subject to traditional waterfall change management procedures. The detailed analysis of requirements, as well as the design, development, testing, and approval of relevant solutions, is conducted in sprints. However, the final implementation of the solution is executed in a waterfall manner: delivered all at once rather than incrementally, sprint by sprint.

To put it simply, hybrid approaches differ from agile in that hybrid methods plan the project scope upfront and do not permit spontaneous changes to the scope.

4.7.1 *Generic Governance Mechanisms*

In the hybrid approach, non-contractual governance mechanisms constitute a mix of those used in both waterfall and agile methodologies:

- The project plan must be prepared before the project begins and should include a high-level definition of the project outcome, the schedule, and a resource plan. Unlike in the waterfall approach, the project outcome definition does not include a detailed work breakdown structure, as the specifics of the outcome will be determined incrementally during sprints. Similarly, the schedule does not include a detailed allocation of project tasks but instead outlines the placement of individual sprints on a timeline. On the other hand, unlike in the agile approach, the initial allocation of sub-outcomes from the product backlog to sprints should be performed prior to the project. Since the hybrid approach requires the project outcome to be defined and fixed before the project, the project plan must ensure alignment between the scope, schedule, resources, and budget. To achieve this, the planning team must estimate the time and resources needed to accomplish each sub-outcome, ensuring they are sufficient to successfully deliver the final outcome. As a result, the project plan in a hybrid approach should include at minimum:
  - A high- to medium-level definition of the project outcome;
  - A schedule that includes the placement of sprints on the timeline;
  - A breakdown of sub-outcomes assigned to each sprint; and
  - A budget and resource plan for the project.

  While the project scope is fixed and subject to strict, waterfall-like change management procedures, adjustments to the allocation of outcome items between sprints should be allowed, provided they do not impact the overall schedule or budget.

- The project organization and roles would also adopt a hybrid approach, combining elements of both waterfall and agile methodologies. A hybrid project is likely to have high-level organizational structures, such as a Steering Committee and a Project Management Team. These bodies would oversee overall project planning, organization, coordination, control, and, if necessary, provide strategic direction. Delivery teams, however, would function in an agile-like manner. These teams would typically include delivery experts, business stakeholders (e.g., a Product Owner), and potentially a team facilitator (e.g., a Scrum Master) or a team lead, depending on whether the setup is more democratic or centralized. While the plan for each time-box (sprint) would, to some extent, be directed by the Project Management Team, rather than being entirely self-determined by the agile teams, the teams' input may still influence adjustments to the sprint plan. However, the Project Management Team would ensure that such adjustments do not compromise the final project objectives.
- The project information system would operate on two levels:
  - Team Level: Agile routines emphasizing direct and continuous communication and collaboration would be implemented, including practices such as daily stand-ups.
  - Project Level: A centralized information system must be established to provide up-to-date insights on the project's status relative to the plan and to identify any risks or issues. This system would be maintained with input from agile team leads, facilitators, and/or product owners.
- Communication mechanisms within the Development Teams would align with agile principles, emphasizing continuous, personal, and direct communication and collaboration. However, a top-down communication process must also be established to ensure the project plan is effectively conveyed from project management to the teams. Artifacts such as the product backlog and sprint backlog might be used, but the communication mechanisms should be adapted to reflect the centralized nature of waterfall planning. Instead of agile teams autonomously selecting items from the product backlog for their sprint backlogs, the Project Management Team would propose sprint backlog contents and consult with the teams for alignment. At the end of each sprint, the outcomes from sprint reviews must be consolidated into a general status report. This report would support centralized oversight of progress, facilitate risk and issue identification, and aid in the development of mitigation plans.

- Control and problem-solving mechanisms would operate on two levels:
- Delivery Team Level: Agile mechanisms emphasizing continuous communication and real-time collaboration would be employed. Daily stand-ups would serve as the primary control mechanism.
- Project Level: Periodically, waterfall-like control and problem-solving mechanisms would be initiated. These would include:
  - Reporting of status, issues, and risks from the Delivery Teams to the Project Management Team.
  - Joint planning of corrective actions, involving the Project Management Team, the Delivery Team Lead, and, where necessary, some or all Delivery Team members.
  - Implementation of corrective actions by the Delivery Team.
  - Reporting and monitoring of the status of corrective actions.

Although the above list of hybrid governance mechanisms was created deductively, based on the inherent characteristics of the hybrid approach, it resembles the principles of DSDM (DSDM, 2014; AgilePM, 2014). Arguably, DSDM might be better described as a hybrid framework rather than a purely agile one.

4.7.2 *Internal Setup*

An internal contractual setup refers to a project owner company executing a project entirely using its own employees and resources. Contractual relationships in this setup are governed by employment contracts for all project participants.

The advantages and disadvantages of such contractual arrangements align with those of an internal waterfall project, so they will not be reiterated here. Similar to the waterfall approach, a project initiation group must be established to define key project attributes, including scope, budget, and schedule. However, unlike the waterfall method, the scope in this setup is defined more broadly, and the schedule includes an initial allocation of scope sub-items across time-boxes (sprints).

Similar to the waterfall project, there must be two fundamental types of internal contracts:

- Between the Project Sponsor, Project Management, and Delivery Management – outlining the project outcomes and delivery conditions.
- Between Project Management and Project Delivery Teams – defining the responsibilities and participation guidelines for project team members.

The project is then executed according to the selected hybrid project management methodology in its generic form.

The attributes of internal hybrid project setup are presented in table 14.

TABLE 14 Governance of a hybrid project under internal setup

Description	Project is done entirely with the use of the project owner company's internal resources.
Prerequisites	The project owner company must possess: – Domain specific explicit knowledge, – Personnel with domain-specific implicit knowledge and domain-specific skills – Necessary equipment – Project capability – the ability to acquire, integrate, configure, and deploy the required resources in a way that ensures the desired outcome – Domain-specific and domain-agnostic project management knowledge
Contractual governance mechanisms	Forbearance law within the hierarchy. Employees assigned to the project, within the limits of their job descriptions, are expected to carry out the instructions of their supervisors. Internal disputes are resolved within the organization, without the involvement of external legal institutions such as courts. Additional mechanisms may include: – Bonuses for meeting project performance measures – Inclusion of project success metrics in employee evaluations
Type of incentives	Low-powered. The compensation of the employees is not related to the project outcomes.
Coordination mechanisms	Coordination is achieved by directive, as all participants are employees of the project owner company. Under their employment contracts, they are required to follow the instructions of their superiors. High-level coordination is performed by the project management through the project plan. Withing the agile teams, coordination is achieved through continuous cooperation and communication.
Non-contractual governance mechanisms	Generic hybrid project management mechanisms within the project temporary organization.

TABLE 14 Governance of a hybrid project under internal setup (*cont.*)

Pros	In the event of unforeseen contingencies requiring coordinated adaptation, changes can be made without the need for costly and time-consuming contract renegotiations with external providers. Any necessary adjustments can be implemented directly within the project owner organization. This contractual arrangement offers the highest level of flexibility and responsiveness to unexpected situations. The project owner organization maintains full control over all project elements.
Cons	A high level of flexibility and adaptability may lead to the acceptance of unnecessary changes, potentially resulting in scope creep. Additionally, weak incentives could result in low engagement from project participants in their assigned tasks. Unless the project resources and capabilities are fully utilized, internal setup becomes the most expensive option.
When to use	The internal setup requires the company to maintain a full range of resources, knowledge, and capabilities necessary to execute a given type of project. This approach is only practical when projects occur frequently enough to ensure full utilization of the available resources. Maintaining in-house project capabilities becomes more appealing for projects characterized by high levels of volatility, uncertainty, and ambiguity. Reconfiguring internal resources in response to unexpected contingencies may be more cost-effective than renegotiating external contracts. Additionally, handling projects internally may be driven by the need to retain full control and discretion over the project and its outcomes, particularly when strategic importance is involved

An internal hybrid setup requires a project capability and a resulting structured combination of knowledge, skills, and resources tailored to the specific project type. The project is executed according to the selected hybrid methodology in its generic form and faces advantages and disadvantages similar to those in waterfall projects.

4.7.3 *Multilateral Centralized Setup and Alliance*

In a multilateral centralized contractual setup, a project owner aims to fully manage the project but lacks some or all of the required resources, leading to their contracting from external parties. The project owner must possess project capability, general and domain-specific project management knowledge, and sufficient domain understanding to effectively plan, coordinate, and control the project.

In hybrid project governance, the core principle is that the overall project outcome is defined and fixed at a high level, while the detailed attributes of the outcome are developed incrementally in an agile manner throughout the project.

Outcome completion is assessed at two levels:

- Agile Implementation Team Level: The outcome increment is signed off by the product owner, along with other relevant business stakeholders if necessary, at the end of each time-box. This approval is based on requirements that were specified, detailed, and discussed with the implementation team during the same time-box.
- Project Management Level: Progress is tracked based on the completion of outcome items in the product backlog. The evaluation is binary: an item is either completed as planned within the given time-box, or it is not. The specifics of each item are treated as a 'black box,' as they are elaborated, designed, approved, implemented, and signed off by the agile teams during the sprint.

This restricts the possibility of signing outcome-based contracts with contractors to scenarios where each contractor is assigned an exclusive set of atomic outcomes, and the interrelations between the outcomes assigned to different contractors are both limited and manageable.

A single, high-level outcome cannot be contractually assigned to more than one party because it cannot be effectively divided among them, making it impossible to split either the effort required or the responsibility for its delivery. Assigning a specific outcome to a single contractor ensures clear accountability for its completion. Additionally, any opportunistic behaviors within an agile team, such as free-riding by some participants, can be more effectively managed when all team members belong to the same organization, as opposed to dealing with intercompany relationships.

A large number of interrelations between sub-outcomes, even when these sub-outcomes are atomic and assigned to individual contractors, can lead to accountability issues and opportunistic behavior. Since the sub-outcomes are not described in detail, each agile team must elaborate on them during each sprint. This includes detailing the requirements, designing and developing appropriate solutions, testing them, obtaining stakeholder approval, and preparing them for release or integration with other sub-outcomes. The specific approaches to detailing requirements and designing solutions may differ between teams.

If interrelations exist between the sub-outcomes of different teams, these must be resolved before development begins. Teams may engage in debates over whose standards should be followed or may attempt to shift some functionality and workload to other teams.

One potential solution is to establish common procedures and standards for defining outcomes within agile teams, along with centrally managed integration and coordination mechanisms between the teams. However, this approach would likely reduce the project's overall agility.

Another option is to engage contractors through resource-based or behavior-based time-and-materials contracts and monitor their performance through close, ongoing collaboration with in-house product owners, agile team facilitators, and project managers. Given that the primary goal of a centralized setup is to maintain full control over the project, this approach appears to be more practical.

Governance would be carried out using the generic mechanisms of a hybrid approach, which include:

- At the project level: A waterfall-like high-level project plan, project-level progress monitoring, formal project organization and roles, communication mechanisms, and procedures for risk and issue resolution.
- At the team level: Agile-like practices emphasizing direct communication and collaboration routines.

The primary function of the formal contract is to ensure access to individuals with the necessary knowledge and expertise, as well as resources of the required quality.

In fact, hybrid projects are also a good fit for owner alliance contracting, as both promote close collaboration on an open basis between the project participants.

A variation of the centralized setup is the bilateral setup, where all resources are outsourced from a single entity. The governance of contractual relationships in this arrangement can either be resource-based or behavior-based, involving close collaboration with and coordination by the sponsoring organization's product owners and managers, or it can be outcome-based.

In the former case, governance would rely on generic mechanisms. Sourcing all resources from a single company can help minimize cultural adjustment challenges and the associated effort. In the latter case, the contractual setup would typically follow a prime-contractor model, as it would be impractical for the contractor to assume responsibility for the outcome while handing over the authority to manage their own resources in achieving it. The description of the prime-contractor setup follows in the next section.

The summary of governing a hybrid project under centralized setup is presented in Table 15.

TABLE 15 Governance of a hybrid project under centralized setup

Type of contract	Resource-based	Outcome-based
Description	The project owner intends to fully manage a project but lacks some or all of the necessary resources and, therefore, contracts these needs. The contractors provide resources or organized teams of resources to the project owner for the agreed period or amount of working time. The project owner has full authority over how these resources are used and directs their work.	The project owner intends to fully manage a project but lacks some or all of the necessary resources and, therefore, contracts these needs. The contractors agree to deliver specified sub-outcomes for a given price and within the agreed time-frame.
Prerequisites	The project owner must possess project capability: the organizational ability to plan, prepare, and execute projects of a given type, which involves the ability to acquire, integrate, configure, and deploy the required resources to achieve the desired outcomes.	The project owner must possess project capability: the organizational ability to plan, prepare, and execute projects of a given type, which involves the ability to acquire, integrate, configure, and deploy the required resources to achieve the desired outcomes. Each agile team should consist of employees from a single contractor and be assigned a distinct set of sub-outcomes. Clear rules should be established for defining sub-outcomes and managing integration points between them.

TABLE 15 Governance of a hybrid project under centralized setup (*cont.*)

Type of contract	Resource-based	Outcome-based
Contractual governance mechanisms	The contractors provide resources or organized teams of resources to the project owner for the agreed period or amount of working time, basing on the resource-based contract. Project owner has the right to direct the resources at their own discretion.	When the outcome is defined only at a high level, it becomes the responsibility of the agile teams to detail the requirements, design the solution, and implement it. Outcome completion is monitored at two levels: **Agile Implementation Team Level:** Outcome increments are approved by the product owner, along with other relevant business stakeholders if necessary, at the end of each time-box. **Project Management Level:** Progress is tracked based on the completion of outcome items in the product backlog. Evaluation is binary: an item is either completed as planned within the designated time-box or it is not.
Type of incentives	Medium-powered. The contractors' remuneration is not tied to the outcome of their work. However, the project owner typically has the right to cancel the contract on short notice if the contractors' performance is unsatisfactory. Since the project work is central to the contractors' core business, their motivation to perform well in the project may be higher than that of the project owner's internal personnel.	High-powered. The contractors' remuneration depends on the delivery of the pre-agreed outcomes according to the contract.

TABLE 15 Governance of a hybrid project under centralized setup (*cont.*)

Type of contract	**Resource-based**	**Outcome-based**
Coordination mechanisms	Generic hybrid project management mechanisms within the project temporary organization.	High-level coordination is done through assignment of sub-outcomes to the contractors in the formal contracts. Coordination between the teams is achieved via rules for defining the sub-outcomes and managing integration points between sub-outcomes. Project management is responsible for imposing and practical exercising of these rules. Coordination within agile teams is achieved through on-going, synchronous communication and cooperation.
Non-contractual governance mechanisms	Generic mechanisms of a chosen hybrid methodology.	Generic mechanisms of a chosen hybrid methodology with the caveat that high-level arrangement regarding scope, schedule and project conditions arise from the formal contract.
Pros	In the event of unforeseen contingencies requiring coordinated adaptation, changes can be made without the need for costly and time-consuming contract renegotiations with external providers. This contractual arrangement offers high level of flexibility and responsiveness to unexpected situations. The project owner organization maintains full control over all project elements.	Outcome-based contracts transfer some of the responsibility and risk for delivering specific project sub-outcomes to the contractors. However, the high-level definition of outcomes can result in ambiguity and potential disputes.

TABLE 15 Governance of a hybrid project under centralized setup (*cont.*)

Type of contract	**Resource-based**	**Outcome-based**
Cons	All project risks remain with the project owner. In the short term, outsourcing resources from external contractors is likely to be more costly than using internal resources, as profit margins will apply. If project changes extend its duration, contracts will need to be renegotiated. Integrating individuals from different organizations into the project's temporary structure may also pose challenges due to unfamiliarity with the project owner's methodologies, cultural differences, and other factors.	In the event of changes to the plan, the contracts may need to be renegotiated. With numerous interdependencies, determining responsibility and assigning risk can be challenging. A high-level scope definition further exacerbates these issues.
When to use	A multilateral, centralized setup based on resource-based contracts with contractors is a viable option when the project owner intends and is able to retain full control over all project elements and is prepared to assume all associated risks. This approach is particularly suitable for projects with outcomes that are not fully defined at the outset and/or for projects where critical parameters may be subject to unforeseen changes during the project's course.	This approach is applicable only when the sub-outcomes are clearly separated and each can be assigned to a single sub-contractor. The interrelations between the sub-outcomes should be limited and well-defined.

A multilateral centralized hybrid approach requires the project owner to have project capability, general and domain-specific project management knowledge, and sufficient domain understanding to effectively plan, coordinate, and control the project. As the overall project outcome is defined and fixed at a high level, while the detailed attributes of the outcome are developed incrementally in an agile manner throughout the project, it makes sense to either assign a specified sub-outcome to each contractor in an outcome-based contract or to engage external resources based on a resource-based time and materials contract and manage them independently.

4.7.4 *Prime-Contractor Setup*

As previously outlined, a prime-contractor setup is employed when an organization delegates an entire project to a specialized external entity. This approach is typically chosen due to a lack of in-house project capability, knowledge, and resources required for successful project execution.

In the case of hybrid projects, project teams, team leads, and a project manager are provided by the contractor company, while product owners and business stakeholders remain part of the sponsoring organization. To ensure coordinated progress toward the project goal, these individuals must be organized using both contractual and non-contractual governance mechanisms.

In a hybrid approach, the high-level scope definition is prepared upfront and can only be altered after careful evaluation and approval through traditional waterfall change management procedures. However, the detailed analysis of requirements, as well as the design, development, testing, and approval of solutions, is carried out using agile methodologies within time-boxed iterations.

The hybrid prime-contractor setup is, therefore, the ideal approach for projects where the outcomes cannot be fully defined in detail beforehand. It is particularly suited for scenarios where project owners are either unable or unwilling to execute the project using internal resources but wish to establish and maintain a fixed high-level project scope from the outset.

In a hybrid prime-contractor setup, coordination and cooperation are achieved through a combination of contractual and non-contractual governance mechanisms. The high-level project framework is established by the contractual agreement, which should include:

- High-level definition of scope and schedule: This forms the outcome-based component of the agreement.
- Specification of people and resources required for project execution: This constitutes the resource-based element.
- Roles and responsibilities of the parties: This aspect forms the behavior-based component, which ensures close cooperation among project stakeholders in detailing requirements, verifying design and development, and signing off on interim deliverables.

This approach allows the project owner to retain some control over the project scope. However, this control is inherently limited, as the scope items are defined only in general terms and will be refined during the course of the project. As a result, only a high-level assessment of whether a specific item has been completed can be contractually enforced. Additionally, some responsibility for achieving the project outcome is transferred to the contractor. Nevertheless, the contractor cannot deliver the project independently, as they rely on ongoing collaboration with the project owner. This includes detailing requirements, verifying the design and development, approving interim deliverables, and ultimately deploying the final solution.

Since the project requires ongoing co-production, non-contractual governance mechanisms must be implemented to support this collaboration. The core of these mechanisms is a joint temporary project organization that integrates both waterfall and agile elements, ensuring effective cooperation and communication at all organizational levels.

At the highest level, a Steering Committee should be established, comprising senior management from both the client and contractor organizations. The Steering Committee monitors high-level project progress and makes critical decisions on matters not explicitly defined in the contract. These decisions may include, for instance, key design choices when multiple options exist for achieving an outcome outlined only in general terms in the contractual agreement.

The Steering Committee also plays a crucial role in resolving issues and disputes that cannot be settled at lower levels of the project organization, using non-contractual means. In other words, the Steering Committee serves as the highest non-contractual authority for the project. If the Steering Committee is unable to reach an agreement, the matter is escalated to the contractual provisions and, if necessary, to external authorities such as courts.

At the project management level, a dedicated project management team should be appointed to ensure the effective and ongoing oversight of all project aspects. As mentioned earlier, the prime-contractor's teams are managed by their internal project manager. However, the client would likely prefer to stay actively informed about the project's progress. To achieve this, the client may delegate a representative to work alongside the contractor's project manager.

Additionally, due to the high-level nature of the definition of the project outcomes, continuous involvement from the project owner is essential. This includes detailing requirements, verifying design and development, testing, and approving partial results. To coordinate these activities effectively, it is advisable to appoint a project manager or coordinator to lead the project owner's task force. For smaller projects, this role may be fulfilled by the product owner. However, in larger projects, a dedicated project manager is necessary to handle the increased complexity.

The project management team would thus consist of two key roles:

- Prime-contractor's project manager – responsible for managing the contractor's resources.
- Project owner's project manager – responsible for directing and coordinating the activities of the project owner's personnel.

One might imagine a scenario where one of these two individuals takes sole responsibility for managing the entire project. However, this arrangement raises several challenges.

If the project owner's manager is appointed as the sole authority, the responsibility for their actions and the overall responsibility for the project would rest entirely with the client. In this case, the project would follow a multilateral or bilateral centralized setup, as discussed in earlier sections, rather than adhering to the prime-contractor model.

On the other hand, assigning sole authority to the prime-contractor's project manager introduces its own set of issues. The first one is the agency problem: the contractor's project manager may engage in opportunistic behavior to prioritize the contractor's interests, potentially at the client's expense. The second issue is the perceived agency problem: even if the contractor's project manager acts in the best interest of the project, the client's personnel might suspect otherwise, leading them to question the manager's authority and decisions.

Additionally, for client staff, often focused on operations, the project may be an uncommon phenomenon and, in many cases, a secondary responsibility. To ensure proper motivation and alignment, it is crucial for the project manager to possess both formal and informal authority within the team. This authority is more likely to be achieved by someone with an established history and respect within the organization rather than an external hire brought in solely for the project. Assigning the client's project manager to the project fosters cooperation and coordination and enhances the client's control over the project.

The two project managers must mutually coordinate their efforts, which creates an interesting paradox. In most cases, there is a knowledge asymmetry between the prime-contractor's project manager and the project owner's manager, favoring the former. After all, the reason to select a prime-contractor is their expertise and experience in delivering projects of a certain type. Consequently, the project should follow the methodological approach defined by the prime-contractor, with their project manager ensuring adherence to it. This dynamic means the contractor's project manager is effectively directing the client's project manager, determining what tasks the client's personnel should perform and when. In other words, the agent is directing the principal.

Even in cases where no knowledge asymmetry exists between the two project managers, the project is primarily executed by the contractor. Therefore, the contractor's project manager should have the authority to make final decisions regarding the nature and sequence of activities required to achieve the project's objectives. However, the client remains the principal and may wish to exercise authority in certain areas. While the project owner approves both partial and final project outcomes, they may also want to influence the work to some extent or address concerns about the contractor's personnel, such as their behavior or competence. Ultimately, the two project managers must find a balance in their working relationship – an equilibrium that is challenging to formalize in a contract.

The level at which ongoing co-production must take place is within the development teams. These teams should include representatives from the client and contractor companies. The client representatives are, at minimum, responsible for specifying and detailing requirements initially outlined at a high level in the product backlog. They also provide feedback during solution design, test and approve the solutions once developed, and ultimately sign them off for release to production. The representatives from the contractor detail the requirements, design the appropriate solutions, develop, and launch them. As ongoing cooperation is at the heart of agile principles, the fact development teams operate within agile naturally supports this collaboration. This is a key advantage of hybrid project management over the waterfall approach, particularly when the requirements lack sufficient detail at the outset. Another advantage is the gradual process of solution acceptance, which occurs after each sprint. This iterative process allows any differences in understanding of the project outcome to be identified and addressed early. In contrast, the waterfall approach typically delays testing and approval until all developments are completed at the end of the project, which can result in misalignments being discovered much later.

It is important to note that co-production may require from the project owner much more than just elucidating the requirements and supervising, testing and approving the solution. Client representatives may be obliged to perform project tasks equally with the contractor's employees. In any case the team consisting of individuals originating from both organizations must work together in a harmonious and coordinated manner. Although some agile methodologies, such as Scrum, promote self-organizing teams, it appears to be overly optimistic to assume that every group of people who possibly just met for the first time would organically organize itself. At least in some cases, a team leader must be appointed.

As at the project management level, also here the work must be directed by the contractor's representative, as it is the contractor who knows what activities, in what order and when should be taken to achieve a proper result. Clients representative on the other hand, details the requirements regarding the expected outcome, approves the design, tests and signs-off the solution. Therefore, also here the contractor's team lead and the product owner must work-out a cooperative interpersonal relation. The product owner must also have authority to appoint additional people to provide company knowledge to the project team. If the co-production exceeds the provision of information and sign-off of the results, more than only a product owner may be assigned permanently to the project team. A client team lead should then be appointed to coordinate their actions. It may be the product owner or another person, depending on the personal leadership qualifications. A person with biggest knowledge not always is the best candidate for a manager, after all.

Constant, active participation of the client in the project, although imposed by the insufficient level of outcome definition, has additional advantages for the client. It allows for a benign control of the contractor's behavior. By benign control I mean such a way of supervising the contractor that they do not feel controlled. While working together people naturally see each other's behavior, so any unproper activities would be naturally revealed. Also, the fact that people know they are observed (in a noninvasive way) prevent them from behaving unethically. Indeed, control by participation, although costly, may also be introduced in other project contractual setup, beside the currently discussed hybrid prime-contractor one.

The summary of governance of hybrid project under prime-contractor setup is presented in table 16.

TABLE 16 Governance of a hybrid project under prime-contractor setup

Description	Prime-contractor setup is employed when an organization delegates an entire project to a specialized external entity. This approach is typically chosen due to a lack of in-house project capability, knowledge, and resources required for successful project execution.
Prerequisites	None
Contractual governance mechanisms	Combined contract including: – Outcome-based part: Defines the scope at a high to medium level of detail.

TABLE 16 Governance of a hybrid project under prime-contractor setup (*cont.*)

	– Resource-based part: Specifies the people, their knowledge, qualifications, and other resources required from the contractor to execute the project. – Behavior-based part: Determines the roles and responsibilities of the parties, including the necessary involvement of the project owner's personnel.
Type of incentives	High-powered. The contractor is paid if the scope as defined in the contract is delivered.
Coordination mechanisms	Due to the need for co-production by both contractual parties, coordination mechanisms are predominantly non-contractual. These mechanisms rely on a joint, temporary project organization that integrates both waterfall and agile elements, ensuring effective cooperation and communication at all organizational levels. The contract serves as the final point of reference in cases of communication or coordination breakdown. Additionally, it acts as a reference point for determining whether the scope has been completed.

Non-contractual governance mechanisms	A mix of waterfall and agile mechanisms, including:
	– At the project management level:
	  – A high-level plan for the scope and schedule, including a top-down division of scope items across time boxes.
	  – A platform for status reporting, as well as issue and risk management at the project level, supported by structured status meetings.
	– At the team level:
	  – A sprint backlog (partially imposed centrally by project management).
	  – Daily stand-ups.
	  – Sprint review and retrospective sessions (with little to no flexibility to alter the scope).
	  – Interpersonal collaboration and direct communication among agile team members, who work closely together on a daily basis.

Pros	This setup enables the project owner to maintain basic contractual control over a project with poorly defined goals while transferring the majority of responsibility and risk to the contractor.

TABLE 16 Governance of a hybrid project under prime-contractor setup (*cont.*)

Cons	In case of changes in scope, the contract has to be re-negotiated.
When to use	In projects where the following conditions apply: – A detailed definition of the outcome before the project starts is either impossible or economically unjustified. – The high-level scope is known and fixed. – The client lacks the project capability to run the project or does not intend to use it. – The client seeks to minimize their involvement and share of risk.

A hybrid prime-contracting setup is ideal for project owners who lack project management expertise and aim to execute projects with outcomes that are difficult to define in advance.

4.8 Governance of Projects With Undefined Methods

Projects for which the methods of delivering an outcome are unknown are truly unique, as opposed to the majority of projects, which are "routine" and aim to deliver an individual yet standard outcome within a specified timeline.

There are several possible scenarios:

1. The first scenario occurs when a project aims to deliver a unique outcome, never achieved before, using a set of known methods. Such a project would require the development of a new configuration of these methods, which is itself unknown. An example might be a mission to Mars. All individual methods are likely known from previous endeavors, such as Moon exploration, but to reach Mars, they must be configured in a novel way.
2. The second scenario is when a project aims to deliver a unique outcome, never achieved before, and the methods to achieve it also need to be invented. Examples include the Manhattan Project or the first space missions.
3. The third scenario occurs when the aim of a project is to invent new methods to achieve a known goal. Examples include R&D projects in various industries.

In each case, a viable approach is through trial and error. A team, or several parallel teams, works on solving a partial problem or developing several alternative solutions for a partial problem. The solutions are tested, and either the most promising solution is selected, or the teams repeat the process until an acceptable solution is found.

In fact, the process resembles an agile methodology, even when the outcome is tangible. A key difference is that the outcome is lost after every unsuccessful test.

4.9 Biased and Misaligned Drivers of Project Contract Definition and Governance

The governance scenarios presented above were derived deductively, based on the metatheory developed in Chapter 3, which, in turn, integrates existing organizational and management theories used to explain the phenomena of projects, project management, and governance. These scenarios take into account attributes of the project outcome, such as tangibility, definability, and stability, as well as attributes of the project environment, including the knowledge and expertise of the parties, the availability of relevant personnel and resources, the willingness to take responsibility for the project, attitudes toward risk, and the volatility, uncertainty, and ambiguity of the project scope, among other factors.

The resulting governance scenarios also align with common sense. For example:

1. You cannot effectively prepare and sign an outcome-based contract if the outcome is not well-defined.
2. If the outcome changes significantly and frequently during the project, the effort required for constant re-planning would substantially increase the cost of a waterfall, plan-based project.
3. If you outsource the entire project to an external contractor because you believe they possess a unique combination of resources, knowledge, expertise, and skills that your organization lacks, you should not direct the contractor on how to perform their job.
4. If the outcome is not clearly defined, stakeholders must actively participate in the project to specify their requirements, approve the design of the solution, and validate the solution itself.
5. If you choose to implement the project using an agile approach, you must adhere to agile principles.

I have personally experienced the breach of every one of the above in real-life projects. Every project manager on the planet could probably add their own points to this list. The reasons why people tackle projects with the wrong tools could also be much longer, but here are a few:

1. One-size-fits-all approach from purchasing and legal departments. Large corporations rely on rules and procedures. Since purchasing projects is not a daily routine for most operations-based organizations, they may use a single procedure for procuring any kind of project, whether it's the construction of a new plant, a marketing campaign, or the implementation of a new information system. If such a procedure exists, it is likely tailored to "hard" projects with clearly defined scope, firm schedules, and precise assignment of roles and responsibilities between the parties. This approach creates a perception of control and legal protection. However, applying it to projects with poorly defined attributes or VUCA (volatile, uncertain, complex, and ambiguous) projects can lead to constant debates and contract renegotiations, significantly increasing the transactional costs of the project.
2. One-size-fits-all approach from project managers. Some project managers, especially those who have recently completed formal certification through professional project management associations, tend to apply the only solution they know to every situation. As the common proverb says: "To a man with a hammer, everything looks like a nail."
3. Politics (Flyvbjerg, 2021), lack of motivation, and communication problems within and between organizations involved in the project.
4. Opportunistic behaviors between the contractual parties of the project.

These factors sometimes mean that, for a project to be successful, it must be executed not in accordance with, but in spite of, the misaligned governance procedures applied to it. Let's hope such situations remain rare exceptions.

Conclusions

This book explored project governance under various contractual setups, along with the factors influencing their selection and the consequences of these choices.

First, the theories commonly used to explain different aspects of projects were described, drawing on the existing literature. As a result, a definition of a project was developed, as a temporary organization that functions as a nexus of various contracts, established to achieve a specific goal or output within constraints of time, budget, and other resources. Regardless of the types of contractual relationships, a project necessitates the coordinated cooperation of all involved resources. The primary aim of project governance is to provide the project management with the mechanisms and tools securing this coordinated cooperation. Each project also requires a specific, structured combination of knowledge, skills, people, and resources for a designated timeframe – the project capacity. The process of acquiring, configuring, integrating, maintaining, and deploying such a combination of resources incurs significant costs. The ability to carry out this process, referred to as *project capability*, is also expensive to develop and sustain. Given the temporary nature of projects, these costs are justified in-house only if similar projects are executed repeatedly. Otherwise, outsourcing is reasonable due to the lack of reusability. As a result, various forms of hybrid contractual relations play a significant role in governing non-repetitive projects.

Second, the concept of project governance was examined which resulted in the determination of two perspectives:

- Project governance, which depends primarily on the specific attributes of the project, such as the nature and stability of its outcomes, the definability of its methods, and its complexity. It may follow waterfall, agile or hybrid project management methodology.
- Governance of project contractual relations, which depends on the number of legal entities involved in the project and the nature of their interactions.

Every project requires the mix of contractual and non-contractual governance mechanisms.

Based on this analysis, a metatheory of project contractual governance was then developed. The previously identified theories were applied to determine the conditions under which different contractual setups are appropriate, the types of contracts and non-contractual governance mechanisms available, and the implications for all participants involved. What makes this metatheory

© 2026 THE AUTHOR(S) | HTTPS://DOI.ORG/10.1163/9789004758544-007

novel is its comprehensive and deductive use of existing theories across a maximally exhaustive range of project types, contractual arrangements, and contract categories. Firstly, the available options for project contractual governance depend on the accessibility of project capacity, consisting of the structured combination of people with relevant knowledge and skills, physical, financial, organizational, and knowledge resources for the sponsoring company within a desired time frame. To develop project capacity, an organization requires project capability, i.e., the ability to acquire, integrate, configure, maintain and release/deploy people with relevant knowledge and skills, physical, financial, organizational, and knowledge resources in such a way that the project accomplishes its goals in a coordinated manner. Both project capacity and project capability are time-consuming and costly to develop and maintain. Therefore, investing in them is justified only when a company undertakes certain types of projects on a recurring basis.

The attributes of the project, including the definability of the outcome and methods, are the secondary factors determining the particular mechanisms of project contractual governance.

The following governance setups, depending on the number of legal entities involved in a project and the allocation of risk and responsibility among the parties, were identified and elaborated upon regarding the types of contracts, non-contractual governance mechanisms and appropriateness for various types of projects.

- Internal (unilateral) setup, where the project is executed using the knowledge and resources of the sponsoring organization (the project owner).
- Multilateral centralized setup, where the project owner manages the project in cooperation with contractors responsible for specific outcomes or tasks.
- Prime-contractor (bilateral) setup, where the project owner contracts both the execution and management of the project to a specialized external entity.
- Alliance setup, where multiple legal entities share relatively equal roles in managing and executing the project.

The applicability of each setup was initially assessed based on the sponsoring organization's access to project capacity, project capability, and project management knowledge. An internal setup requires the company to possess all three in-house. A multilateral centralized setup demands, at minimum, project capability and project management expertise. An alliance setup requires at least project management knowledge. The prime-contractor setup, meanwhile, is suitable for project owners with limited internal resources and related knowledge.

Subsequently, the potential contract types and associated non-contractual governance mechanisms were examined for each of the aforementioned contractual setups, based on the definability of project outcomes and methods.

Every project requires a combination of contractual and non-contractual governance mechanisms, embodied in a coherent temporary organization, to ensure that project objectives are achieved in a coordinated manner. The balance between these mechanisms, along with their specific characteristics, depends on the contractual setup, the definability of project outcomes and methods, and additional factors such as the sponsoring organization's attitude towards risk, and project involvement orientation.

Projects with well-defined outcomes and methods tend to favor contract-based governance, typically involving outcome-based contracts supported by the waterfall project management methodology. Projects with ill-defined and changing outcomes benefit more from non-contractual governance, relying on agile methods, with contracts specifying only the type and duration of resources. Hybrid approaches are best suited for projects with ill-defined but relatively stable outcomes, providing a balanced mix of contractually secured general scope and agile flexibility in refining the details.

The advantages and disadvantages of each detailed governance scenario were examined from the perspectives of both the sponsoring organization and its contractors, taking into account insights from relevant theories.

Finally, a framework for governing projects with different types of outcomes and various contractual setups was discussed from the perspective of the project owner.

This framework incorporated governance scenarios, grounded in a previously established metatheory, which, in turn, integrated existing organizational and management theories to explain the phenomena of projects, project management, and governance. The scenarios considered both the characteristics of the project outcome, such as its tangibility, definability, and stability, and the attributes of the project environment. These included the parties' knowledge and expertise, the availability of personnel and resources, their willingness to assume responsibility, their attitudes toward risk, and factors like volatility, uncertainty, and ambiguity in the project scope, among others.

References

Abdel-Galil, E., Ibrahim, A. H., & Alborkan, A. (2022). Assessment of transaction costs for construction projects. *International Journal of Construction Management*, 22(9), 1618–1631.

Adler, P. S. (2001). Market, Hierarchy, and Trust: The Knowledge Economy and the Future of Capitalism. *Organization Science*, 12(2), 215–234.

Aghion, P., & Holden, R. (2011). Incomplete Contracts and the Theory of the Firm: What Have We Learned over the Past 25 Years? *Journal of Economic Perspectives*, 25(2), 181–197.

Agile Manifesto (2001). Retrieved from https://agilemanifesto.org/principles.html

Agile Project Management Handbook v2 (AgilePM®, 2014), Agile Business Consortium, Henwood.

Ahola, T., Ruuska, I., Artto, K., & Kujala, J. (2014). What is project governance and what are its origins? International Journal of Project Management, 32(8), 1321–1332.

Akerlof, G. (1970). The Market for "Lemons": Quality Uncertainty and the Market Mechanism. *The Quarterly Journal of Economics, 84*, 488–500.

Al-Ahmad, W., Al-fagih, K., Khanfar, K., Alsamara, K., Abuleil, S., & Abu-Salem, H. (2009). A taxonomy of an IT project failure: Root causes. *International Management Review*, 5(1), 93–104. http://www.mendeley.com/research/taxonomy-it-project-failure-root-causes/.

Aljaber T. (2023). Iron triangle project management and agile. Retrieved from https://www.atlassian.com/agile/agile-at-scale/agile-iron-triangle.

Almeida, F., & Espinheira, E. (2021). Large-Scale Agile Frameworks: A Comparative Review. *Journal of Applied Sciences, Management and Engineering Technology*, 2(1), 16–29.

Al-Najjar, N. I. (1995). Incomplete Contracts and the Governance of Complex Contractual Relationships. *The American Economic Review*, 85(2), 432–436.

Alvesson, M. (1993). Organizations as Rhetoric: Knowledge-Intensive Firms and the Struggle with Ambiguity. *Journal of Management Studies*, 30(6), 997–1015.

Alvesson, M. (2001). Knowledge Work: Ambiguity, Image and Identity. *Human Relations*, 54(7), 863–886.

Ambler, S. W., & Lines, M. (2011). *Disciplined Agile Delivery: An introduction. Disciplined Agile Delivery: An introduction.* Retrieved from http://public.dhe.ibm.com/common/ssi/ecm/en/raw14261usen/RAW14261USEN.PDF.

American Society for Quality (ASQ, 2024). What is Problem Solving? Retrieved from: https://asq.org/quality-resources/problem-solving.

Andersen, E. S. (2006). Toward a Project Management Theory for Renewal Projects. *Project Management Journal*, 37(4), 15–31.

Argyres, N. S., Bercovitz, J., & Mayer, K. J. (2007). Complementarity and evolution of contractual provisions: An empirical study of IT services contracts. *Organization Science*, 18(1), 3–19.

Arrow, K. (1984). The economics of agency.

Arrow, K. (1962). Economic Welfare and the Allocation of Resources for Invention. In *The Rate and Direction of Inventive Activity: Economic and Social Factors* (pp. 609–626). Princeton University Press.

Atkinson, R., Crawford, L., & Ward, S. (2006). Fundamental uncertainties in projects and the scope of project management. *International Journal of Project Management, 24*(8), 687–698.

Aubert, B. a., Rivard, S., & Patry, M. (1996). A transaction cost approach to outsourcing behavior: Some empirical evidence. *Information & Management*, 30(2), 51–64.

Aven, T. (2013). On the meaning of a black swan in a risk context. *Safety Science, 57*, 44–51.

Baccarini, D. (1996). The concept of project complexity – A review. *International Journal of Project Management, 14*(4), 201–204.

Baker, G., Gibbons, R., & Murphy, K. (2002). Relational Contracts and the Theory of the Firm. *The Quarterly Journal of Economics*, 117(1), 39–84.

Barnard Ch. (1938). *The functions of the Executive*, Harvard University Press, Cambridge.

Baumeister, R. M., & Leary, M. R. (1995). The need to belong: Desire for interpersonal attachments as a fundamental human motivation. *Psychological Bulletin*, 117, 497–529.

Beatty R. P. (1989). Auditor reputation and the pricing of initial public offerings. *Accounting Review*, 64(4), 693–709.

Bekker, M. C. (2014). Project governance: "schools of thought." *South African Journal of Economic and Management Sciences, 17*(1), 22–32.

Bernis A. (2022). Where next for management's consiglieri? *The Economist*, October 4th 2022.

Billis, D. (2010). Towards a theory of hybrid organizations. Hybrid Organizations and the Third Sector: Challenges for Practice, Theory and Policy, 46–69.

Biesenthal, C., & Wilden, R. (2014). Multi-level project governance: Trends and opportunities. International Journal of Project Management, 32(8), 1291–1308.

Bransford, J. D., & Stein, B. S. (1984). The ideal problem solver. A guide for improving thinking, learning, and creativity. A Series of Books in Psychology.

Braun, D., & Kramer, J. (2019). *The Corporate Tribe. Organizational Lessons from Antropology*. Routledge.

Cao, Z., & Lumineau, F. (2015). Revisiting the interplay between contractual and relational governance: A qualitative and meta-analytic investigation. *Journal of Operations Management*, 33–34, 15–42.

Cepeda, G., & Vera, D. (2007). Dynamic capabilities and operational capabilities: A knowledge management perspective. *Journal of Business Research*, *60*(5), 426–437.

Cicmil, S., Cooke-Davies, T., Crawford, L., & Richardson, K. (2017). *Exploring the complexity of projects: Implications of complexity theory for project management practice*. Project Management Institute.

Clarkson, G., Jacobsen, T. E., & Batcheller, A. L. (2007). Information asymmetry and information sharing. *Government Information Quarterly*, *24*(4), 827–839.

Coase, R. H. (1937). The nature of the firm. *Economica*, *4*(16), 386–405.

Coase, R. H. (1988). *The Firm, the Market and the Law*. Chicago, IL: University of Chicago Press.

Cole L. (2022). Do McKinsey and other consultants do anything useful? *The Economist*, October 8-th, 2022.

Collyer, S., & Warren, C. M. J. (2009). Project management approaches for dynamic environments. *International Journal of Project Management*, *27*(4), 355–364.

Combs, J., & Ketchen, D. J. (1999). Explaining Interfirm Cooperation and Performance: Toward a Reconciliation of Predictions from the Resource-Based View and Organizational Economics. *Strategic Management Journal*, *20*(9), 867–888.

Conner, K. R., & Prahalad, C. K. (1996). A Resource-based Theory of the Firm: Knowledge Versus Opportunism. *Organization Science*, *7*(5), 477–501.

Connelly, B. L., Certo, S. T., Ireland, R. D., & Reutzel, C. R. (2011). Signaling Theory: A Review and Assessment. *Journal of Management*, *37*(1), 39–67.

Cragg, P., Caldeira, M., & Ward, J. (2011). Organizational information systems competences in small and medium-sized enterprises. *Information & Management*, 48(8), 353–363.

Crawford, L., Cooke-Davies, T. (2009). Project Governance: The Role and Capabilities of the Executive Sponsor. Project Perspectives, vol. XXXI, 66–74.

Crawford, L., & Pollack, J. (2004). Hard and soft projects: A framework for analysis. *International Journal of Project Management*, *22*(8), 645–653.

Curlee, W., & Gordon, R. L. (2010). *Complexity theory and project management*. John Wiley & Sons.

Czakon, W., & Czernek, K. (2016). The role of trust-building mechanisms in entering into network coopetition: The case of tourism networks in Poland. *Industrial Marketing Management*, *57*, 64–74.

Czernek, K., & Czakon, W. (2016). Trust-building processes in tourist coopetition: The case of a Polish region. *Tourism Management*, *52*, 380–394.

Dahlstrom, R., & Ingram, R. (2003). Social networks and the adverse selection problem in agency relationships. *Journal of Business Research*, *56*(9), 767–775.

Darling, E. J., & Whitty, S. J. (2016). The Project Management Office: it's just not what it used to be. *International Journal of Managing Projects in Business*.

Dawson, G. S., Watson, R. T., & Boudreau, M.-C. (2010). Information Asymmetry in Information Systems Consulting: Toward a Theory of Relationship Constraints. *Journal of Management Information Systems, 27*(3), 143–177.

Davis, J. H., Schoorman, F. D., & Donaldson, L. (1997). Toward a stewardship theory of management. *Academy of Management Review*, 22(1), 20–47.

Dellarocas, C. (2003). The digitization of word of mouth: Promise and challenges of online feedback mechanisms. *Management Science, 49*(10), 1407–1424.

Dellarocas, C. (2006). Reputation Mechanisms. In *Handbook on economics and information systems,* (pp. 629–660).

Derakhshan, R., Turner, J. R., & Mancini, M. (2019). Project governance and stakeholders: a literature review. *International Journal of Project Management, 37*(1), 98–116.

Devos, J., Van Landeghem, H., & Deschoolmeester, D. (2008). Outsourced information systems failures in SMEs: a multiple case study. The Electronic Journal Information Systems Evaluation, 11(2), 73–82.

Dibiasi, A., & Iselin, D. (2021). Measuring Knightian uncertainty. *Empirical Economics, 61*(4), 2113–2141.

Disciplined Agile (Disciplined Agile®, 2023), Retrieved from: https://www.pmi.org/disciplined-agile/agility-at-scale

Donaldson, L., & Davis, J. H. (1991). Stewardship Theory or Agency Theory: Australian Journal of Management, 16(June 1991), 49–66. Retrieved from http://aum.sagepub.com/cgi/doi/10.1177/031289629101600103.

Donaldson, T., & Preston, L. E. (1995). The Stakeholder Theory of the Corporation: Concepts, Evidence, and Implications. The Academy of Management Review, 20(1), 65–91.

Doney, P. M., & Cannon, J. P. (1997). An Examination of the Nature of Trust in Buyer–Seller Relationships. *Journal of Marketing, 61*(2), 35–51.

Drees, J. M., & Heugens, P. P. M. A. R. (2013). Synthesizing and Extending Resource Dependence Theory: A Meta-Analysis. *Journal of Management, 39*(6), 1666–1698.

DSDM Agile Project Framework Handbook (DSDM, 2014). Agile Business Consortium, Retrieved from: https://www.agilebusiness.org/dsdm-project-framework.html

Dybek, J., & Glodzinski, E. (2023). Knowledge management challenges: case study of the R&D project-based organization delivering military products. *Procedia Computer Science, 225*, 1486–1494.

Dyduch, W., Chudziński, P., Cyfert, S., & Zastempowski, M. (2021). Dynamic capabilities, value creation and value capture: Evidence from SMEs under Covid-19 lockdown in Poland. *PLoS ONE, 16*(6 June 2021), 1–28. https://doi.org/10.1371/journal.pone.0252423.

Eccles, R. (1981). The Quasifirm in the Construction Industry. *Journal of Economic Behavior and Organization*, December, 335–57.

Eckfeldt, B., Madden, R., & Horowitz, J. (2005). Selling agile: Target-cost contracts. *Agile Development Conference, 2005*, 160–166.

Eisenhardt, K. M. (1989). Agency Theory: An Assessment and Review. *Academy of Management Review*, 14(i), 57–74.

Eisenhardt, K. M., & Martin, J. A. (2000). Dynamic Capabilities: What Are They? *Strategic Management Journal*, 21(10/11), 1105–1121.

Eskerod, P., Huemann, M., & Savage, G. (2015). Project stakeholder management-past and present. *Project Management Journal*, 46(6), 6–14.

Flyvbjerg, B. (2021). Top Ten Behavioral Biases in Project Management: An Overview. *Project Management Journal*, *52*(6), 531–546.

Flyvbjerg B and Gardner D. (2023) How Big Things Get Done, Pan Macmillan, London.

Foss, N. J. (1996). Knowledge-Based Approaches to the Theory of the Firm: Some Critical Comments. *Organization Science*, 7(5), 470–476. https://doi.org/10.1287/orsc.7.5.470.

Foss, K., & Foss, N. J. (2004). The Next Step in the Evolution of the RBV: Integration with Transaction Cost Economics. Management Revue, 15(1), 107–121.

Friedman, M. (1970). The Social Responsibility of Businesses is to Increase Its Profits. *The New York Times Magazine*, September 13.

Freeman, R. E. (1984). Strategic management: A stakeholder approach. Boston: Pitman.

Freeman, R. E. (1994). A Stakeholder Theory of the Modern Corporation. In T. Beauchamp & N. Bowie (Eds.), Ethical Theory and Business (pp. 66–76). Engelwood Cliff: Prentice Hall.

Gallouj, C. (1997). Asymmetry of information and the service relationship: selection and evaluation of the service provider. International Journal of Service Industry Management, 8(1), 42–64.

Gambetta, D. (1988). Trust: Making and Breaking Cooperative Relations. Basil Blackwell, Oxford, U.K.

Gasik, S. (2011). A model of project knowledge management. Project Management Journal, 42(3), 23–44.

Gallouj, C. (1997). Asymmetry of information and the service relationship: selection and evaluation of the service provider. *International Journal of Service Industry Management*, *8*(1), 42–64.

Gemino, A., Horner Reich, B., & Serrador, P. M. (2021). Agile, Traditional, and Hybrid Approaches to Project Success: Is Hybrid a Poor Second Choice? *Project Management Journal*, *52*(2), 161–175.

Goltsman, M., Hörner, J., Pavlov, G., & Squintani, F. (2009). Mediation, arbitration and negotiation. *Journal of Economic Theory*, *144*(4), 1397–1420.

Governance of Portfolios, Programs, and Projects. A Practice Guide (2016). Project Management Institute, Pennsylvania.

Granovetter, M. (1985). Economic Action and Social Structure: The Problem of Embeddedness. *American Journal of Sociology*, 91(3), 481–510.

Grant, Robert, M. (1996). Toward a knowledge-based theory of the firm. *Strategic Management Journal, 17*, 109–122.

Grant, Robert, M., & Baden-Fuller, C. (1995). A Knowledge-Based Theory of Inter-Firm Collaboration. *Academy of Management Proceedings, 1995*(1), 17–21.

Greenwood, R., Li, S. X., Prakash, R., & Deephouse, D. L. (2005). Reputation, Diversification, and Organizational Explanations of Performance in Professional Service Firms. *Organizational Science, 16*(6), 661–673.

Greiner, L., & Ennsfellner, I. (2010). Management Consultants as Professionals, or Are They? *Organizational Dynamics, 39*(1), 72–83.

Gross, C., & Kieser, A. (2006). Are Consultants Moving Towards Professionalization? *Research in the Sociology of Organizations, 24*, 69–100.

Grossman, S., & Hart, O. D. (1986). The Costs and Benefits of Ownership: A Theory of Vertical and Lateral Integration. *Journal of Political Economy, 94*(4), 691–719.

Gulati, R., & Punaram, P. (2009). Renewal Through Reorganization: The Value of Inconsistencies Between Formal and Informal Organization. *Organization Science*, 20(2), 422–440.

Hagen, M., & Park, S. (2013). Ambiguity Acceptance as a Function of Project Management: A New Critical Success Factor. *Project Management Journal, 44*(2), 52–66.

Haigh, N., & Hoffman, A. J. (2012). Hybrid organizations. The next chapter of sustainable business. Organizational Dynamics, 41(2), 126–134.

Haines, M. N., & Goodhue, D. L. (2003). Implementation partner involvement and knowledge transfer in the context of ERP implementations. International Journal of Human-Computer Interaction, 16(1), 23–38.

Hale, D., Shrestha, P., Gibson Jr., E., & Migliaccio, G. (2009). Empirical Comparison of Design/Build and Design/Bid/ Build Project Delivery Methods. *Journal of Construction Engineering and Management, 135*(7), 579–587.

Hasanzadeh, S., & Esmaeili, B. (2022). Influence of best value procurement on design-build projects: a grounded theory study. *International Journal of Construction Education and Research, 18*(3), 270–292.

Hanisch, B., & Wald, A. (2011). A Project Management Research Framework Integrating Multiple Theoretical Perspectives and Influencing Factors. *Project Management Journal, 42*(3), 4–22.

Hanisch, B., & Wald, A. (2012). A Bibliometric View on the Use of Contingency Theory in Project Management Research. Project Management Journal, 43(3), 4–23.

Hart, O., & Moore, J. (1988). Incomplete Contracts and Renegotiation. *Econometrica, 56*(4), 755–785.

Hart, O., & Moore, J. (1999). Foundations of Incomplete Contracts. *Review of Economic Studies, 66*(1), 115–138.

Hillman, A. J., Withers, M. C., & Collins, B. J. (2009). Resource dependence theory: A review. *Journal of Management, 35*(6), 1404–1427.

Howell, D., Windahl, C., & Seidel, R. (2010). A project contingency framework based on uncertainty and its consequences. International Journal of Project Management, 28(3), 256–264.

Hölmstrom, B. (1979). Moral hazard and observability. *Bell Journal of Economics, 10*, (1), 74–91.

Huemann, M. (2024) The project-oriented organization, in: Huemann, M., & Turner, R. (Eds.). (2024). The Handbook of Project Management (6th ed.). Routledge.

Izquierdo, S. S., & Izquierdo, L. R. (2007). The impact of quality uncertainty without asymmetric information on market efficiency. *Journal of Business Research, 60*(8), 858–867.

Jamous, N., Garttan, G., Staegemann, D., & Volk, M. (2021). Hybrid project management methods efficiency in IT projects. *27th Annual Americas Conference on Information Systems, AMCIS 2021*, 0–10.

Jensen, M., & Meckling, W. (1976). Theory of the Firm: Managerial Behavior, Agency Costs, And Ownership Structure. *Joumal of Financial Economics, 3*(4), 305–360.

Jonassen, D. H. (2000). Toward a Design Theory of Problem Solving. *Educational Technology Research and Developmenet, 48*(4), 63–85.

Jones, C., Hesterly, W. S., & Borgatti, S. P. (1997). A general theory of network governance: Exchange conditions and social mechanisms. *Academy of Management Review*, 22(4), 911–945.

Jugdev, K. (2004). Through the Looking Glass: Examining Theory Development in Project Management With the Resource-Based View Lens. Project Management Journal, 35(3), 15–26.

Joskowski, A., & Marcinkowski, B. (2023). Scaling scrum with a customized nexus framework : A report from a joint industry-academia research project. *Softw: Pract Exper*, (January), 1–18.

Kast, F. E., & Rosenzweig, J. E. (1981). General systems theory: Applications for organization and management. *Journal of Nursing Administration*, 11(7), 32–41.

Kappelman, L. a., McKeeman, R., & Zhang, L. (2006). Early Warning Signs of it Project Failure: The Dominant Dozen. *Information Systems Management, 23*(4), 31–36.

Karlsen, J. T. (2002). Project stakeholder management. *EMJ – Engineering Management Journal, 14*(4), 19–24.

Karrbom Gustavsson, T., & Hallin, A. (2014). Rethinking dichotomization: A critical perspective on the use of "hard" and "soft" in project management research. *International Journal of Project Management, 32*(4), 568–577.

Killen, C. P., Jugdev, K., Drouin, N., & Petit, Y. (2012). Advancing project and portfolio management research: Applying strategic management theories. International Journal of Project Management, 30(5), 525–538.

Knight, F. H. (1921) Risk, uncertainty and profit. Hart, Schaffner and Marx, New York.

Kogut, B., & Zander, U. (1992). Knowledge of the Firm, Combinative Capabilities, and the Replication of Technology. *Organization Science*, *3*(3), 383–397.

Koskela, L., & Howell, G. (2002). The underlying theory of project management is obsolete. In *Proceedings of the PMI Research Conference* (pp. 293–302).

Kowalczyk, M., Marcinkowski, B., & Przybyłek, A. (2022). Scaled agile framework. Dealing with software process-related challenges of a financial group with the action research approach. *Journal of Software: Evolution and Process*, *34*(6), 1–21.

Kraaijenbrink, J., Spender, J. C., & Groen, A. J. (2010). The Resource-Based View: A review and assessment of its critiques. Journal of Management, 36(1), 349–372.

Krishnan, J., Sauer, P. C. (2000). The differentiation of quality among auditors: Evidence from the not-for-profit sector. *Auditing: A Journal of Practice & Theory*, 19(2), 9–25.

Krzakiewicz, K., & Cyfert, S. (2014). The Strategic Dimension of the Dynamic Capabilities of Enterprises. *Management*, *18*(2), 7–18.

Kuhrmann, M., Diebold, P., Münch, J., Tell, P., Garousi, V., Felderer, M., … Prause, C. R. (2017). Hybrid software and system development in practice: Waterfall, scrum, and beyond. In *Proceedings of International Conference on Software System Process* (pp. 30–39).

Laplante, P. A., & Kassab, M. (2022). Requirements Engineering for Software and Systems (4th ed.). Auerbach Publications.

Laplume, A. O., Sonpar, K., & Litz, R. a. (2008). Stakeholder Theory: Reviewing a Theory That Moves Us. Journal of Management (Vol. 34).

Lech, P. (2016). Causes and remedies for the dominant risk factors in Enterprise System implementation projects: the consultants' perspective. *SpringerPlus*, *5*(1), 1–12.

Lech, P., & Zamojska, A. (2017). The learning preferences of Enterprise System consultants: towards the preferred learning pattern. *Knowledge Management Research & Practice*, *15*(2), 316–324.

Lech, P. (2021). Ambiguity in information systems projects – The case of enterprise system implementations. *27th Annual Americas Conference on Information Systems, AMCIS 2021*, 1–10.

Lech, P. (2022a). Ambiguity and Knowledge Asymmetry in Knowledge-Intensive Projects – The Case of Enterprise System Implementations. *Pacific Asia Journal of the Association for Information Systems*, *14*(5), 30–50.

Lech, P. (2022b). Knowledge-Intensive Business Service Projects – Characteristics and Implications for Project Management – a Preliminary Study. *Procedia Computer Science*, *207*(C), 176–185.

Lee, Z. P., Rahman, R. A., & Doh, S. I. (2020). Key drivers for adopting design build: A comparative study between project stakeholders. *Physics and Chemistry of the Earth*, *120*(October).

Lehrer, M., Ordanini, A., DeFillippi, R., & Miozzo, M. (2012). Challenging the orthodoxy of value co-creation theory: A contingent view of co-production in design-intensive business services. *European Management Journal*, *30*(6), 499–509.

Leśniak, A., & Plebankiewicz, E. (2015). Modeling the Decision-Making Process Concerning Participation in Construction Bidding. *Journal of Management in Engineering*, *31*(2), 1–9.

Levitt, B. & March, J. G. (1995) Chester I. Barnard and the intelligence of learning. In Organization Theory: from Chester Barnard to the Present and Beyond, ed. O. E. Williamson. Oxford University Press, New York.

Levin, R. C , A. K. Klevorick, R. R. Nelson and S. G. Winter (1987). Appropriating the retums from industrial research and development, *Brookings Papers on Economic Activity*, pp. 783–820.

Li, H., Arditi, D., & Wang, Z. (2015). Determinants of Transaction Costs in Construction Projects. Journal of Civil Engineering and Management, 21(5), 548–558.

Liebeskind, J. (1996). Knowledge, Strategy, and the Theory of the Firm. *Strategic Management Journal*, *17*, 93–107.

Lindkvist, L. (2004). Governing project-based firms: Promoting market-like processes within hierarchies. *Journal of Management and Governance*, 8(1), 3–25.

Littau, P., Jujagiri, N. J., & Adlbrecht, G. (2010). 25 Years of Stakeholder Theory in Project Management Literature (1984–2009). *Project Management Journal*, 41(4), 17–29.

Lockett, A., Thompson, S., & Morgenstern, U. (2009). The development of the Resource-Based View of the firm: A critical appraisal. *International Journal of Management Reviews*, *11*(1), 9–28.

Lundin, R. A. (1995). Editorial: Temporary organizations and project management. *Scandinavian Journal of Management*, 11(4), 315–318.

Lundin, R. a., & Söderholm, A. (1995). A theory of the temporary organization. Scandinavian Journal of Management, 11(4), 437–455.

Lv, L., Chen, C., & Wang, Z. (2023). Resource and cognitive perspectives: Unravelling the influence mechanism of project governance on organizational resilience in infrastructure projects. *Buildings*, 13(11), 2878.

Macaulay, S. (1963). Non-Contractual Relations in Business: A Preliminary Study, *American Sociological Review*, 28 (1), 55–67.

Macbeth, D. (2012). *Contract Lifecycle Management*. bookboon.com.

Mahaney, R. C., & Lederer, A. L. (2003). Information systems project management: An agency theory interpretation. Journal of Systems and Software, 68(1), 1–9.

Mahaney, R. C., & Lederer, A. L. (2010). The role of monitoring and shirking in information systems project management. *International Journal of Project Management*, *28*(1), 14–25.

Makadok, R. (2001). Toward a Synthesis of the Resource-Based View and Dynamic-Capability Views of Rent Creation. *Strategic Management Journal*, 22, (5), pp. 387–401.

Marcinkowski, B, Kuciapski, M (2012). A Business Process Modeling Notation Extension for Risk Handling in: *11th International Conference on Computer Information Systems and Industrial Management* (*CISIM*), Venice, Italy. pp.374–381.

Marnada, P., Raharjo, T., Hardian, B., & Prasetyo, A. (2021). Agile project management challenge in handling scope and change: A systematic literature review. *Procedia Computer Science, 197*(2021), 290–300.

March, J. (1978). Bounded Rationality, Ambiguity, and the Engineering of Choice. *The Bell Journal of Economics, 9*(2), 587–608.

McManus, J., & Wood-Harper, T. (2007). Understanding the sources of information systems project failure.

Ménard, C. (2004). The Economics of Hybrid Organizations. *Journal of Institutional and Theoretical Economics, 160*(3), 345–376.

Ménard, C. (2006). Hybrid Organization of Production and Distribution. *Revista de Análisis Económico, 21*(2), 25–41.

Ménard, C. (2010). Hybrid Organizations. In P. Klein & M. Sykuta (Eds.), The Elgar Companion to Transaction Cost Economics (Vol. 2010, pp. 176–184). Cheltenham: Elgar Publisher.

Ménard, C. (2013). Hybrid modes of organization. In R. Gibbons & J. Roberts (Eds.), *Handbook of Organizational Economics* (pp. 902–941). Princeton: Princeton University Presss.

Ménard, C. (2022). Hybrids : where are we ? *Journal of Institutional Economics, 18*, 297–312.

Midler, C. (1995). "Projectification" of the firm: the Renault case. *Scandinavian Journal of Management, 11*(4), 363–375.

Miles, I., Kastrinos, N., Biderbeed, R., & den Hertog, P. (1995). *Knowledge Intensive Business Services. Knowledge Intensive Business Services. Users, Carriers and Sources of Innovation.* EIMS Publication No 15. Innovation Programme, DGXIII, Luxembourg.

Miles, I. (2005). Knowledge intensive business services: Prospects and policies. *Foresight, 7*(6), 39–63.

Mills, P. K., & Morris, J. (1986). Clients as partial employees of service organizations: role development in client participation. Academy of Management Review, 11, 4, 726–735.

Minchin, R. E., Li, X., Issa, R. R., & Vargas, G. G. (2013). Comparison of Cost and Time Performance of Design-Build and Design-Bid-Build Delivery Systems in Florida. *Journal of Construction Engineering and Management, 139*(10), 1–5.

Miterev, M., Mancini, M., & Turner, R. (2017). Towards a design for the project-based organization. *International Journal of Project Management, 35*(3), 479–491.

Miterev, M., Turner, J. R., & Mancini, M. (2017). The organization design perspective on the project-based organization: a structured review. In *International Journal of Managing Projects in Business* (Vol. 10, Issue 3).

Monteiro, A., Santos, V., & Varajão, J. (2016). Project Management Office Models – a review. Procedia Computer Science, 100, 1085–1094.

Morris, P. W. G., & Geraldi, J. (2011). Managing the institutional context for projects. *Project Management Journal, 42*(6), 20–32.

Mudambi, R. (2008). Location, control and innovation in knowledge-intensive industries. *Journal of Economic Geography, 8*(5), 699–725.

Müller, R. (2009). Project governance. Gower Publishing Limited.

Müller, E., & Doloreux, D. (2009). What we should know about knowledge-intensive business services. *Technology in Society, 31*(1), 64–72.

Müller, R., Andersen, E. S., Kvalnes, Ø., Shao, J., Sankaran, S., Rodney Turner, J., … Gudergan, S. (2013). The interrelationship of governance, trust, and ethics in temporary organizations. *Project Management Journal, 44*(4), 26–44.

Müller, R., & Turner, J. R. (2005). The impact of principal-agent relationship and contract type on communication between project owner and manager. *International Journal of Project Management, 23*(5 SPEC. ISS.), 398–403.

Müller, R. (2017). *Governance and governmentality for projects* (Müller R., Ed.). Routledge.

Müller, R., Alix-Séguin, C., Alonderienė, R., Bourgault, M., Chmieliauskas, A., Drouin, N., … Zhu. (2022). A (meta)governance framework for multi-level governance of inter-organizational project networks. *Production Planning & Control*, 35(10), 1043–1062.

National Alliance Contracting Guidelines (2015). Guide to Alliance Contracting. *Australian Government: Department of Infrastructure and Regional Development.* On-line: https://www.infrastructure.gov.au/sites/default/files/migrated/infrastructure/ngpd/files/National_Guide_to_Alliance_Contracting.pdf.

National Alliance Contracting Guidelines. Guidance Note 4 Reporting Value-for-Money Outcomes (2015). *Australian Government: Department of Infrastructure and Regional Development.* On-line: https://www.infrastructure.gov.au/sites/default/files/migrated/infrastructure/ngpd/files/NACG_GN4.pdf#page=13.05.

Nielsen, B. B., 2010. Strategic fit, contractual, and procedural governance in alliances. *Journal of Business Research*, 63, 682–689.

Nienhüser, W. (2008). Resource Dependence Theory – How Well Does It Explain Behavior of Organizations? *Management Revue, 19*(1/2), 9–32.

Nooteboom, B. (2000). Trust as a Governance Device. In M. Casson & A. Godley (Eds.), *Cultural factors in economic growth.* Springer.

Nwajei, U. O. K. (2021). How relational contract theory influence management strategies and project outcomes: A systematic literature review. *Construction Management and Economics*, 39(5), 432–457.

Ouchi, W. G. (1980). Markets , Bureaucracies , and Clans. *Administrative Science Quarterly, 25*(1), 129–141.

Parasuraman, A., Zeithaml, V., & Berry, L. L. (1985). A Conceptual Model of Service Quality and Its Implications for Future Research. *American Marketing Association, 49*(4), 41–50.

Pfeffer, J., & Salancik, G. R. (1978). The external control of organizations: A resource dependence perspective. New York: Harper & Row.

Pich, M. T., Loch, C. H., & Meyer, A. De. (2002). On Uncertainty, Ambiguity, and Complexity in Project Management. *Management Science*, *48*(8), 1008–1023.

Pitsis, T. S., Sankaran, S., Gudergan, S., & Clegg, S. R. (2014). Governing projects under complexity: Theory and practice in project management. International Journal of Project Management, 32(8).

Penrose, E. (1959). *The Theory of the Growth of the Firm*, Oxford, Oxford University Press.

PM² (2023). PM² – Project Management Methodology Guide 3.1, European Commission, Centre of Excellence in Project Management CoEPM².

PMBOK (2013). *A guide to the project management body of knowledge* (PMBOK® guide) 5th ed., Project Management Institute, Pennsylvania.

PMBOK (2017). *A guide to the project management body of knowledge* (PMBOK® guide) 6th ed., Project Management Institute, Pennsylvania.

PMBOK 7th ed. (2021). *A guide to the project management body of knowledge* (PMBOK® guide) 7th ed., Project Management Institute, Pennsylvania.

Podolny J. M. (1993). A status-based model of market competition. *American Journal of Sociology*, 98(4), 829–872.

Podolny J. M. (1994). Market uncertainty and the social character of economic exchange. *Administrative Science Quarterly*, 39(3), 458–483.

Pollock, R. (2008). The Economics of Knowledge: a Review of the Theoretical Literature (pp. 1–42).

Pollock, R. (2008). The Economics of Knowledge: a Review of the Theoretical Literature.

PRINCE2 (2009) Managing Successful Projects with PRINCE2™ 5th ed., The Stationary Office, Norwich.

Pryke, S. D. (2005). Towards a social network theory of project governance. *Construction Management and Economics*, 23(9), 927–939.

Pryke, S., Badi, S., Almadhoob, H., Soundararaj, B., & Addyman, S. (2018). Self-Organizing Networks in Complex Infrastructure Projects. *Project Management Journal*, 49(2), 18–41.

Ranjan, K. R., & Read, S. (2016). Value co-creation: concept and measurement. *Journal of the Academy of Marketing Science*, *44*(3), 290–315.

Resnick, P., Zeckhauser, R., Friedman, E., & Kuwabara, K. (2000). Reputation systems. *Communications of the ACM*, *43*(12), 45–48.

Riley, J. G. (2001). Silver Signals: Twenty-Five Years of Screening and Signaling. *Journal of Economic Literature*, *39*(2), 432–478.

Roehrich, J. K., Selviaridis, K., Kalra, J., Van der Valk, W., & Fang, F. (2020). Interorganizational governance: a review, conceptualisation and extension. Production Planning and Control, 31(6), 453–469.

Rolland, K. H., Fitzgerald, B., Dingsøyr, T., & Stol, K. J. (2016). Problematizing agile in the large: Alternative assumptions for large-scale agile development. 2016 International Conference on Information Systems, ICIS 2016, (November).

Ross, J. (2003). Introduction to Project Alliancing. *Alliance Contracting Conference, April*, 1–43. https://iccpm.com/sites/default/files/kcfinder/files/Alliancing_30Apr03_D_PCI.pdf.

Ruuska, I., Ahola, T., Artto, K., Locatelli, G., & Mancini, M. (2011). A new governance approach for multi-firm projects: Lessons from Olkiluoto 3 and Flamanville 3 nuclear power plant projects. *International Journal of Project Management*, *29*(6), 647–660.

Sankaran, S., Drouin, N., & Locatelli, G. (2025). Special Issue: Project Governance: Reflections on the Past and Suggestions for the Future. *Project Management Journal*, 56(1), 3–14.

Scaled Agile Framework 6.0 (SAFe, 2023) Retrieved from: https://scaledagileframework.com/safe/.

Scaled Agile Framework – Agile Contracts (SAFe Agile Contracts, 2023) Retrieved from: https://scaledagileframework.com/agile-contracts/.

Schlauderer, S., Overhage, S., & Fehrenbach, B. (2015). Widely used but also highly valued? Acceptance factors and their perceptions in water-scrum-fall projects. In *Thirty Sixth International Conference on Information Systems*, 1–19.

Schmitz, P. W. (2001). The Hold-Up Problem and Incomplete Contracts: A Survey of Recent Topics in Contract Theory. *Bulletin of Economic Research*, *53*(1), 1–17.

Schöttle, A., & Gehbauer, F. (2013). Incentive structure in public design-bid-build tendering and its effects on projects. *21st Annual Conference of the International Group for Lean Construction 2013, IGLC 2013*, *49*(0), 11–20.

Schrader, S., Riggs, M., & Smith, R. (1993). Choice over Uncertainty and Ambiguity in Technical Problem Solving. *Journal of Engineering and Technology Management*, *10*, 73–99.

Schwaber, K., & Sutherland, J. (2020). *The Scrum Guide*. Retrieved from https://scrumguides.org/scrum-guide.html.

Sedera, D. (2009). Knowledge management for enterprise systems: observations from small, medium and large organizations. *PACIS 2009 Proceedings*, 1.

Serrador, P., & Pinto, J. K. (2015). Does Agile work? – A quantitative analysis of agile project success. *International Journal of Project Management*, *33*(5), 1040–1051.

Serrador, P., and J. R. Turner (2013) The impact of the planning phase on project success." *IRNOP (Oslo, Norway)*.

Simon, H. A. (1951). A Formal Theory of the Employment Relationship, Econometrica, 19, 293–305.

Sharma, A. (1997). Professional As Agent: Knowledge Asymmetry in Agency Exchange. *The Academy of Management Review*, *22*(3), 758–798.

Shenhar, A. J. (2001). One Size Does Not Fit All Projects: Exploring Classical Contingency Domains. *Management Science*, *47*(3), 394–414.

Shenhar, A., & Dvir, D. (2007). Project management research – The challenge and opportunity. *Project Management Journal*, *38*(2), 93–99.

Shrestha, P. P., O'Connor, J. T., & Gibson, G. E. (2012). Performance Comparison of Large Design-Build and Design-Bid-Build Highway Projects. *Journal of Construction Engineering and Management, 138*(1), 1–13.

Sliger, M. (2010). Goodbye, scope creep – hello, agile! Paper presented at PMI® Global Congress 2010 – North America, Washington, DC. Newtown Square, PA: Project Management Institute, https://www.pmi.org/learning/library/project-scope-creep-agile-methodologies-6552.

Smith, M., & Erwin, J. (2005). Role & Responsibility Charting (RACI). *Project Management Forum, 5*.

Soda, G., & Zaheer, A. (2012). A Network Perspective on Organizational Architecture: Performance Effects of the Interplay of Formal and Informal Organization. *Strategic Management Journal*, 33(6), 751–771.

Söderlund, J. (2004a). Building theories of project management: Past research, questions for the future. *International Journal of Project Management, 22*(3), 183–191.

Söderlund, J. (2004b). On the broadening scope of the research on projects: A review and a model for analysis. International Journal of Project Management, 22(8), 655–667.

Sommer, S., & Loch, C. (2004). Selectionism and learning in projects with complexity and unforeseeable uncertainty. *Management Science, 50*(10), 1334–1347.

Spałek, S. (2012). The role of project management office in the multi-project environment. *International Journal of Management and Enterprise Development, 12*(2), 172–188.

Spałek, S. (2013). Improving industrial engineering performance through a successful project management office. *Engineering Economics, 24*(2), 88–98.

Spałek, S. (2016). Traditional vs. Modern Project Management Methods. Theory and Practice. *21st International Scientific Conference Economics and Management*, 499–506.

Spence, M. (1973). Job Market Signaling. *The Quarterly Journal of Economics, 87*(3), 355–374.

Špundak, M. (2014). Mixed Agile/Traditional Project Management Methodology – Reality or Illusion? *Procedia – Social and Behavioral Sciences, 119*, 939–948.

Stiglitz, J. E. (1975). The Theory the of "Screening" Education, and the Distribution of Income. *The American Economic Review, 65*(3), 283–300.

Suprapto, M., Bakker, H. L. M., Mooi, H. G., & Hertogh, M. J. C. M. (2016). How do contract types and incentives matter to project performance? *International Journal of Project Management, 34*(6), 1071–1087.

Sutherland, J. (2022). *The* Scrum@Scale® *Guide*. Retrieved from: https://www.scrumatscale.com/scrum-at-scale-guide-online/.

Sydow, J., Lindkvist, L., & Defillippi, R. (2004). Project-Based Organizations, Embeddedness and Repositories of Knowledge: Editorial. *Organization Studies*, 25(9), 1475–1489.

Szpitter, A., & Sadkowska, J. (2016). Using VUCA matrix for the assessment of project environment risk. Zarzadzanie i Finanse, 14(2), 401–413.

Taleb, N. N., 2007. The Black Swan: The Impact of the Highly Improbable. Penguin, London.

Tan, J., & Zhao, J. Z. (2021). Explaining the adoption rate of public-private partnerships in Chinese provinces: A transaction cost perspective. *Public Management Review*, 23(4), 590–609.

Thesing, T., Feldmann, C., & Burchardt, M. (2021). Agile versus Waterfall Project Management: Decision model for selecting the appropriate approach to a project. *Procedia Computer Science*, *181*, 746–756.

Teece, D. J. (1987). Profiting from technological inno- vation: Implications for integration collaboration, licensing and public policy. In D. J. Teece (ed.). The Competitive Challenge. Ballinger, Cambridge, MA, pp. 185–219.

Teece, D. J., & Pisano, G. (1994). The Dynamic Capabilities of Firms: an Introduction. *Industrial and Corporate Change*, *3*(3), 537–556. https://doi.org/10.1093/icc/3.3.537-a.

Teece, D. J., Pisano, G., & Shuen, A. (1997). Dynamic capabilities and strategic management. *Strategic Management Journal*, *18*(7), 509–533.

Teece, D. J. (2003). Expert talent and the design of (professional services) firms. Industrial and Corporate Change, 12(4), 895–916.

Thiry, M. (2002). Combining value and project management into an effective programme management model. *International Journal of Project Management*, *20*(3), 221–227.

Toivonen, A., & Toivonen, P. U. (2014). The transformative effect of top management governance choices on project team identity and relationship with the organization – An agency and stewardship approach. *International Journal of Project Management*, *32*(8), 1358–1370.

Turner, J. R., & Cochrane, R. A. (1993). Goals-and-methods matrix: coping with projects with ill defined goals and/or methods of achieving them. *International Journal of Project Management*, *11*(2), 93–102.

Turner, J. R., & Keegan, A. (2000). The management of operations in the project-based organisation. *Journal of Change Management*, *1*(2), 131–148. https://doi.org/10.1080/714042464.

Turner, J. R., & Simister, S. J. (2001). Project Contract Management and a Theory of Organization. *International Journal of Project Management*, *19*, 457–464.

Turner, J. R. (2004). Farsighted project contract management: Incomplete in its entirety. *Construction Management and Economics*, *22*(1), 75–83.

Turner, J. R., & Müller, R. (2004). Communication and co-operation on projects between the project owner as principal and the project manager as agent. *European Management Journal*, *22*(3), 327–336.

Turner, J. R., & Müller, R. (2003). On the nature of the project as a temporary organization. *International Journal of Project Management*, *21*(1), 1–8.

Turner, J. R. (2006a). Towards a theory of project management: The nature of the project. *International Journal of Project Management, 24*(4), 277–279.

Turner, J. R. (2006b). Towards a theory of project management: The nature of the project governance and project management. *International Journal of Project Management, 24*(2), 93–95.

Turner, J. R. (2006c). Towards a theory of project management: The functions of project management. *International Journal of Project Management, 24*(4), 277–279.

Turner, J. R. (1993). The handbook of project-based Management. McGraw- Hill, London.

Turner, J. R. (1999) The handbook of project based management. 2nd ed. McGraw-Hill, London.

Von Nordenflycht, A. (2010). What Is a Professional Service Firm? Toward a Theory and Taxonomy of Knowledge-Intensive Firms. *Academy of Management Review, 35*(1), 155–174.

Walker, D. H. T., Harley, J., & Mills, A. (2015). Performance of project alliancing in Australasia: A digest of infrastructure development from 2008 to 2013. *Construction Economics and Building, 15*(1), 1–18.

Walker, D. H. T., Davis, P. R., & Stevenson, A. (2017). Coping with uncertainty and ambiguity through team collaboration in infrastructure projects. *International Journal of Project Management, 35*(2), 180–190.

Walker, D. H. T., Vaz Serra, P., & Love, P. E. D. (2022). Improved reliability in planning large-scale infrastructure project delivery through Alliancing. *International Journal of Managing Projects in Business, 15*(5), 721–741.

Wang, L., Wang, X., & Liu, X. (2025). Project Governance and Governance of Interorganizational Project Networks: Toward Understanding Their Relationships and Future Research Agenda. *Project Management Journal*, 56(1), 31–40.

Wernerfelt, B. (1984). A Resource based view of the firm. *Strategic Management Journal, 5*(2), 171–180.

Wernerfelt, B. (2007). The Resource-Based View of the Firm: Ten years later. *Strategic Management Journal, 16*(3), 171–174.

West, D. (2011). Water-Scrum-Fall Is The Reality Of Agile For Most Organizations Today. Forrester: For Application Development & Delivery Professionals.

Wiegers, K. E., & Beatty, J. (2013). Software requirements. Pearson Education.

Williams, T. M. (1999). The need for new paradigms for complex projects. *International Journal of Project Management, 17*(5), 269–273.

Williamson, O. E. (1975). Markets and Hierarchies: Analysis and Anti-Trust Implications, The Free Press, New York.

Williamson, O. E. (1979). Transaction-Cost Economics: The Governance of Contractual Relations. *Journal of Law and Economics, 22*(2), 233–261.

Williamson, O. E. (1981). The Economics of Organization: The Transaction Cost Approach. *American Journal of Sociology*, *87*(3), 548–577.

Williamson, O. E. (1983). Credible commitments: using hostages to support exchange. *American Economic Review*, *73*(4), 519–540.

Williamson, O. E. (1985). The Economic Institutions of Capitalism: Firms, Markets, Relational Contracting. New York, NY: The Free Press.

Williamson, O. E. (1991). Comparative Economic Organization: The Analysis of Discrete Structural Alternatives. *Administrative Science Quarterly*, *36*(2), 269–296.

Williamson, O. E. (1996), The Mechanisms of Governance, Oxford: Oxford University Press.

Williamson, O. E. (2008). Outsourcing: Transaction Cost Economics and Supply Chain Management. *Journal of Supply Chain Management: A Global Review of Purchasing & Supply*, 44(2), 5–16.

Winch, G. (1989). The construction firm and the construction project: a transaction cost approach. *Construction Management and Economics*. 7(4), pp. 331–345).

Wolinsky, A. (1993). Competition in a Market for Informed Experts Competition in a market for informed experts' services. *The RAND Journal of Economics Journal of Economics*, *24*(3), 380–398.

Wrycza, S., and Marcinkowski, B. 2011. "SysML Requirement Diagrams: Banking Transactional Platform Case Study," *Lecture Notes in Business Information Processing* (93 LNBIP), pp. 15–22.

Yan, L., & Zhang, L. (2020). Interplay of Contractual Governance and Trust in Improving Construction Project Performance: Dynamic Perspective. *Journal of Management in Engineering*, *36*(4), 1–12.

Yeo, K. T. 2002. "Critical Failure Factors in Information System Projects," *International Journal of Project Management* (20:3), pp. 241–246.

Zięba, M., & Kończyński, P. (2019). Factors of successful client co-production in knowledge-intensive business services: Case study analysis. *Kybernetes*, *49*(1), 141–164.

Index

www.ingramcontent.com/pod-product-compliance
Ingram Content Group UK Ltd.
Pitfield, Milton Keynes, MK11 3LW, UK
UKHW021031041026
15470UKWH00013B/1313

9 789004 758537